Picture Books for Children

■ FOURTH EDITION ■

PATRICIA J. CIANCIOLO

AMERICAN LIBRARY ASSOCIATION

Chicago and London

1997

Project editor: Louise D. Howe

Text and cover design by Dianne M. Rooney

Indexer: Stuart Hoffman

Cover and title page illustration: Hans Christian Andersen, *Men in a circle holding hearts and hands.* The H. Laage-Petersen Collection, The Royal Library, Copenhagen.

Composed in Melior and Tiffany on Xyvision by the dotted i.

Printed on 50-pound Finch Opaque, a pH-neutral stock, and bound in 10-point coated cover stock by Edwards Brothers

The paper used in this publication meets the minimum requirements of American National Standard for Information Sciences—Permanence of Paper for Printed Library Materials, ANSI Z39.48-1992.♾

Library of Congress Cataloging-in-Publication Data

Cianciolo, Patricia J.
    Picture books for children / Patricia J. Cianciolo. — 4th ed.
        p.   cm.
    Includes index.
    ISBN 0-8389-0701-6
    1. Picture books for children—Bibliography.   2. Illustrated books, Children's–Bibliography.   I. Title.
    Z1037.C565   1997
    [PN1009.A1]
    011.62—dc21   96-51538

Printed in the United States of America.

01 00 99 98 97   5 4 3 2 1

To Polly
and
in fond memory
of my mother
and father.

The gratifying thing about good art is the longer one looks at it the more one sees, the more one sees the deeper one feels, and the deeper one feels the more profoundly one thinks. Looking at art is everything!
                                        P. J. C.

Contents

ɬↄↄↄ

List of
Illustrations

Preface

*I*t is hard to believe twenty-three years have passed between the publication of the first edition and this fourth edition of *Picture Books for Children.* In that span of time many thousands of picture books have been published—some reissues of old favorites, most newly created works. With these publications have occurred some striking changes, resulting in more than a gratuitous parade of fashions in the literary and graphic arts. If anything, the more recently published picture books have become more conceptual, more methodological, and certainly more self-assured and sophisticated. Many are accomplished creations, esoteric and specialized in spirit as well as in the techniques used by the authors and the book artists.

To reflect these changes it was necessary to prepare a major revision for this edition of *Picture Books for Children.* Thus, most of the titles in this fourth edition are new entries. Only a very small percentage of titles from the earlier editions have been carried over. These titles were retained because this author deemed them as appropriate today as they were when originally selected; they seem quite in keeping with the current trends in terms of their content, styles of art, and themes.

The audience and the underlying purpose of this revised and enlarged fourth edition of *Picture Books for Children* remain unchanged. The work is intended to serve as a resource and guide for preservice and in-service teachers of children from nursery school through junior and senior high school, for day-care center personnel, for librarians in school and public libraries, for parents, and for any other adults concerned with the selection of well-written, imaginatively illustrated picture books that are of interest to children of all ages and backgrounds. This publication is also intended to be used as a reference tool for undergraduate and graduate courses in children's and adolescent literature offered by departments of English and by schools of library science and education.

The purpose of *Picture Books for Children* is to identify and describe examples of picture books that will provide children with enjoyable, informative, and discriminating literary experiences, foster the habit of reading, and initiate an appreciation for and an understanding of the beautiful and creative in the graphic arts. I have evaluated at first hand each of the titles listed and I have had occasion to share some of these picture books with individual children and with groups of children in school libraries and classrooms.

Like any other adult whose childhood was lost long ago, I cannot know exactly what goes on in children's minds when they read a picture book or have one read to them. However, numerous recent "response studies" which I and many other professors of literature for children and youth have conducted under controlled situations, and as ethnographic studies, are bringing us a little closer to this knowledge. I have worked frequently and over extended blocks of time in recent years with children and adolescents in school libraries and in classrooms studying their responses to literature in general, but especially to picture books and to book illustrations. Thus, the picture books that are included in this publication were selected on the basis of (a) my personal experiences and knowledge of literature in general and literature for children and adolescents in particular; (b) my experiences and research in young people's response to literature (especially to book illustrations); and (c) the written and oral testimonials of other teachers, librarians, and researchers in which they reported their students' responses to the picture books read to them or read on their own. The best conclusion any adult can arrive at from even the most judicious interviews or observations of children's responses to books is to note that they do indeed respond to certain books (to certain elements of literature and to certain kinds of book art) and that their responses vary in degree, ranging from favorable to unfavorable with varying amounts of intensity.

In all fairness, we have to admit that no adult can select books from a child's point of view. We can and should remember that children are eventually and ultimately the consumers of the books we select. So, with this in mind, I have tried to identify and include in this publication the picture books that I am convinced will be pleasing to children, that will help them perceive picture books (and, by extension, all literature, painting, and the other graphic arts) as something expandable, fulfilling, and pleasurable. It is hoped, indeed it is intended, that among the many titles included in *Picture Books for Children* are some that will help individual children realize that picture books (and again, literature, paintings, and the other graphic arts) offer new ways of "seeing" aspects of the panorama of human experience.

All selections cited in this book are hardbound editions, although many are also available in paperback. The cutoff publication date was August 15, 1996.

Picture Books for Children includes an introductory chapter entitled "The Picture Book: A Distinct Kind of Literary Art." In this chapter literature as art and as a humanity is defined and described, the values and uses of the variety of picture books being produced today are explored, and the current trends in the themes and kinds of picture books being published for young people are examined and described. Criteria for evaluating picture books as a specific literary genre are identified, as are styles of art used in book illustrations. The main body of the work consists of annotated entries, organized into categories that reflect the basic concerns of all people, regardless of age or culture. Each category includes works of fiction, nonfiction, and poetry, arranged alphabetically by author. The title of the book, the illustrator, and the publisher and year of publication follow; the age range of reader appeal or interest is also indicated. The annotations comment on the story or theme and on aspects of the art, as well, for the style of art and the media used in creating the illustrations affect the quality of a picture or book illustration. Some annotations contain suggestions for possible classroom use or point out special reader interest; occasionally titles which one might compare and contrast or supplement with the book under discussion will be identified. New to this edition is a list of Suggested Resources featuring books about creating and responding to visual arts (especially paintings and drawings), book illustrators, famous artists, and books illustrated with reproductions of great art. An index of authors, illustrators, and titles cited is also included.

There is no doubt that another specialist in children's literature would create entirely different bibliographies to meet the same goals. That is as it should be. Although book selection is based on one's knowledge, philosophy of art and literature, accepted principles of child growth and development, and established educational goals and practices, it is also largely influenced by one's affective response to a piece of literature and must, to some extent, involve one's feelings and emotions. Thus, in many respects, this book, while based on extensive professional experience, reflects a consistent set of principles developed from personal judgments.

I am indebted to Sylvia Royt, editor at the American Library Association, for her help in the preparation of the first two editions of *Picture Books for Children.* I also want to thank Helen Cline, who served as my editor in the preparation of the third edition, and last but certainly not least, Patrick Hogan, who served as Acquisitions Editor, and Louise Howe, Project Editor, of this fourth edition of *Picture Books for Children.* I will be forever grateful for their helpful advice, thoroughness, encouragement, and enthusiasm. It has been my privilege and good fortune to have them serve as my editors.

The Picture Book
A Distinct Kind
of Literary Art

Because of its unique blending of illustrations and words, the picture book is considered a genre apart from any other kind of literature. Among the many books published over a period of time are to be found a respectable number of picture books that exemplify high quality writing and illustration. A picture book is a kind of literature that communicates and appeals to children as young as six months of age through adolescence and the young adult years of age eighteen or nineteen. Picture books, like any other literature, can enrich, extend, and expand young readers' background of experiences, their literary and aesthetic interests, tastes, and preferences by providing a variety of sensory images and vicarious experiences, plots, characters, and themes.

The audience for picture books is no longer limited to young children. One can easily find picture books suitable for infants, for children in the primary or upper elementary grades, and others that would be of interest to adolescents and adults. It becomes very obvious, then, that we should no longer classify picture books as "Easy Books." In fact, they are more properly classified as "Everybody's Books" and in many school and public libraries I have visited that is exactly the classification under which they are shelved.

The recognition of things, characters, and actions (in other words, the subject matter of the book) is an important component in the literary and visual experience that occurs with the reading of a picture book. But such an understanding constitutes only one aspect of reading this unique kind of book. There are other factors that affect one's literary experience in response to a picture book and contribute to the particular significance of the picture book. These factors pertain to aspects of the literary and visual arts. The fundamental question is how the literary and visual aspects of a picture book as a complete entity can have meaning. The answer is based in the integration of the subject matter with the artistic aspects of the literary and visual elements that comprise a picture book. It is this integration that establishes the picture book as a distinct work of literary art.

Examination of children's picture books published within the past decade, but especially the last six years, will reveal that they are cosmopolitan and diverse, expansive and varied in scope and direction. One may find a picture book (in English) on almost any topic for readers ranging from toddlers to mature and sophisticated adults. The stories told in picture books may be classified as modern realistic fiction, as here-and-now stories, as historical fiction, and as fanciful fiction. Picture books also may include poetry, biography, and concept or informational books. Among the picture books published in any one year, some are new and some are reissues of old favorites. They are illustrated in diverse styles of art, many written and illustrated by people who not only come from different nations and cultural backgrounds, but who obviously differ in their understanding of and expectations from their target audience.

Some Trends

It seems quite safe to say that at this particular point in time, the state of publishing literature for children and adolescents is very much alive and prospering. There is no dearth of picture books for young people regardless of their age. Among this abundance of picture books, one will find those which provide children as young as six months of age up through age two and one half years or even up to age three years with large, simple pictures, most of which are in bright colors. Children within this age range will find in them easily manageable images of people and objects that are immediately familiar to them. These images are frequently presented in the form of concept books, counting books, or alphabet books, and usually are accompanied by a minimal amount of text. Occasionally one will find some simple nursery rhyme collections for the infant and toddler. The pictures and words may be printed on cloth or stiff board (usually with a glossy finish) which can withstand the destruction children often bring to them and when necessary (which is often the case) can be wiped off with a damp cloth.

In contrast, one will find among this proliferation of picture books those books in which the text and the illustrations play a fairly equal role in the development of the story or the presentation of concepts or information. The appeal of this kind of picture book ranges from the child who is as young as age three years, is unable to read but is quite capable of listening to and understanding the story, to the most mature and sophisticated eighteen-year-old or adult who is an experienced, accomplished, and enthusiastic reader. In these picture books one will often find that the illustrations are superbly accomplished works of visual and graphic art and the texts are written in beautifully expressive language. Of particular significance is that the illustrations are not merely an attractive reiteration or elaboration of what is obvious in the text. Quite the contrary; in addition to bringing out and emphasizing what is in the text, the illustrations convey other meanings and impressions that the readers would not have envisioned from the verbal information alone. With some degree of higher-level thinking and imaginative thinking on their part, readers can and do grasp their meaning and significance and even go well beyond what the illustrator and author suggested. Staying within the children's capacity to understand, these picture books have the potential to take readers well beyond the familiar. More specifically, they can help them view themselves in a different and more informed manner than they did previously and introduce them to more complicated, mature, and remote aspects of their real world (past, present, and future), as well as to the world of make-believe.

Some specific trends I have observed among the picture books published currently are briefly discussed below.

- *An increasing number of picture books are now being published in full (or four) color instead of just black-and-white or pages alternating full (or four) color and black-and-white.*

This trend was in evidence when the third edition of *Picture Books for Children* was being written, and it is very obvious currently. The pastel drawings reproduced in full color in *Wind in the Long Grass: A Collection of Haiku,* edited by William J. Higginson and illustrated by Sandra Speidel (Simon & Schuster, 1991), embellish and heighten the ethereal aura of a special moment or occasion about which each poet speaks in his or her haiku. Each illustration helps the reader sense whatever aspect of nature is commented upon in the accompanying poem in a fresh and new perspective. One will notice the vast range of colors throughout this book. For example, the artist uses a radiant color glowing with light contrasted with those decidedly mellow and muted; there are splotched and mottled grays, glowing peach hues, icy blues mixed with soft white, a clear dark orange yellow, bluish blacks, and brownish blacks. The artist seems to have chosen the "right" colors and hues to evoke the tone and the mood depicted in each poem.

In *Armadillo Rodeo* (Putnam, 1995), a humorous animal fantasy written and illustrated by Jan Brett, one will notice the exquisitely executed realistic line and wash paintings, done in clean, rich colors. The illustrations in this picture book are intricately designed to fill each double-page spread with fascinating visual details which serve to support, extend, and enrich all of the literary elements of this well-written story. Much of the action depicted in this story pertains to the adventures of a curious and nearsighted armadillo named Bo who travels across the Texas hills following what he takes to be a shiny red armadillo who might become his new friend. To his dismay, Bo discovers his "friend" is actually a pair of brand new red leather cowboy boots—"pointy-toed, high-heeled, hand-tooled . . . with fancy cutwork, tall tops, and Curly H brand"—worn by a cowgirl on her way to participate in a rodeo. Worthy of note is the authenticity of Brett's portrayal of the landscapes of the seemingly boundless hilly countryside with its abundance of colorful flora and fauna evocative of Texas plus innumerable events, clothes, and motifs traditionally associated with the Western rodeos.

■ *There are many new authors and illustrators of picture books for children and adolescents, but one still finds the larger percentage to be by established authors and illustrators.*

Among the picture books by the new creators of literature for young children (within the age range of approximately three or four years through six or seven or so) are a growing number of narratives in prose and simplistic verse about characters who look like animals but are given human qualities, express human feelings and human needs, and are coping with human concerns. All too often these stories constitute didactic, far-fetched, trite fantasies illustrated with rather artless cartoon sketches. Years ago this approach to storymaking was called "ourselves in fur," and many examples of picture books in which this approach was implemented most effectively can be cited. It appears, however, that many present-day writers and illustrators of this kind of literature and the editors who accept their work for publication (a) seem to have had little or no experience with young children; (b) hold a "definition" or concept of early childhood that differs drastically from that held by creators of most children's books in past years; and/or (c) do not know what constitutes quality literature for children (or anyone else for that matter).

Among the earlier "ourselves in fur" stories are such classics as Beatrix Potter's books (published by Frederick Warne) *The Tale of Peter Rabbit* (1903) and *The Tale of Jemima Puddle Duck* (1908), Don Freeman's books (published by Viking) *Corduroy* (1968) and *Dandelion* (1964), and Bernard Waber's *An Anteater Named Arthur* (Houghton Mifflin, 1967). These stories are well written in every respect and the illustrations have been artfully executed. As a result most children seem to find them thoroughly believable; consequently, they do indeed tend to see themselves in these stories and identify with the characters in them. It should be emphasized that any number of excellent picture books have been created recently by authors and/or illustrators new to the field of literature for children and these titles are discussed in the chapters that follow. A few recent examples of truly outstanding "ourselves in fur" stories are *Hog-Eye* (Houghton Mifflin, 1995), written by Susan Meddaugh; *Guess How Much I Love You* (Candlewick, 1995), written by Sam McBratney and illustrated by Anita Jeram; and *Papa Gatto: An Italian Fairy Tale* (Little, Brown, 1995), written and illustrated by Ruth Sanderson. (See illustration 1.)

Many other accomplished authors and illustrators new to the field are producing fine literature for children and youth, especially in the picture book genre, including realistic stories, modern fantasy, informational/concept books, retellings of folktales, or poetry. Some of these new authors and illustrators are David Diaz, Ken Robbins, Mary Jane Auch, Deborah Nourse Lattimore, Omar Rayyan, David Shannon, Paul Brett Johnson, Michael Lacapa, Maryanna Cocca-Leffler, Nikki Grimes, Floyd Cooper, and James Ransome. Their works are discussed later in this book.

ILLUSTRATION 1   From *Papa Gatto: An Italian Fairy Tale* by Ruth Sanderson. Copyright © 1995 by Ruth Sanderson. By permission of Little, Brown and Company.

We are also privileged to have so many established authors and illustrators who have continued over the years to create first-rate picture books for children and adolescents. Specific picture books by these authors and illustrators are discussed in the pages that follow; a few of those who have made significant contributions to this aspect of literature over many years are: Eve Bunting, Tom Feelings, Gail Gibbons, Ann Grifalconi, Emily Arnold McCully, Erik Ingraham, Ronald Himler, Leonard Everett Fisher, and Trina Schart Hyman.

■ *While there are many fine books for children from infancy (six months) through age three years, especially concept books and toy books, the proliferation of books for children within this age range seems to have dropped significantly within the last two years.*

Nonetheless, there are still many excellent picture books for children as young as six months of age through ages two and three. In most instances the pictures in these books are of objects or static scenes rather than action scenes, and they are printed on cloth or glossy board. Some parts of the pictures may be textured or have moving or detachable parts. This encourages the children not only to look at the books, but to touch and handle them—to tie and untie, push and pull, fasten and unfasten such things as metal press studs, velcro straps, cords, buttons, and zippers. Thus, they not only find that books are a source from which they can learn about themselves and their world, but that they can get considerable pleasure from them as well. These books can also help in the development of their eye-hand coordination and the large and small muscles in their hands and fingers.

By approximately age six months or one year children are able to get interested in and obviously enjoy pictures in a book; they will sit on one's lap and look at the pictures, often touching them as some older person turns the pages. By age two, they will probably want to turn the pages themselves and will be quite delighted that the picture of a favorite or familiar object is still there. With continued exposure to picture books, they will notice details and point to special features in the pictures that are of particular interest to them; soon they will even make noises that are associated with the animal, machine, or person pictured. *Teddies & Trucks,* written and photographed by Suzanne Haldane (Dutton, 1996), is a board book about various kinds of commonly known trucks attended by teddy bears. The text, printed in bold, heavy primary-sized type, names the type of truck pictured (e.g., garbage truck, livestock truck, car transporter, tow truck). Some of the pictures are full pages or double-page spreads; the photographs of vehicle replicas are reproduced in crisp, bold, and flat full colors; the teddy bears attending the trucks were provided by Wang International.

It is not until they are approximately two years of age that children may be able to listen to and enjoy having a book read through from beginning to end, rather than looking at only a few pictures during one sitting. Around this age they begin to understand and appreciate action-type pictures depicting short here-and-now stories. The four books included in the series A First Lift-the-Flap Book: Hide-and-Seek Surprises! are *Ken's Kitten, Cathy's Cake, Billy's Boots,* and *Meg's Monkey* (Dial, 1996). The infants and toddlers pictured in these delightful board books are of Caucasian, African, Asian, and Hispanic heritage and they are shown playing with or looking for/at/under ordinary toys, a pet kitten (but no puppy!), and household furnishings. The text in each book consists of complete declarative sentences and questions written by Debbie MacKinnon; Anthea Sieveking took the uncluttered photographs which are reproduced in crisp, bright, full colors and printed as full-page illustrations. Children (and adults) are in for some fun, for a surprise greets them each time they lift a flap. Even though children will probably know after the first reading what lies behind each flap, they are certain to ask to have these books reread countless times and most assuredly will continue to be delighted each and every time they lift up the flaps. (Undoubtedly the flaps will eventually have to be reinforced with a sturdy transparent tape.)

- *There is an increasing number of picture books for older readers (ages ten years through young adulthood [eighteen or nineteen years]).*

Except for the fact that the story is developed fairly equally by a combination of pictures and words presented in the picture-book format, one will find that everything about these picture books appeals to the interests of adolescents and challenges them cognitively and affectively: The stories (in prose or verse) challenge the readers to think seriously about important ideas or issues. Both text and pictures offer a complexity of meanings which are obviously for the older and more accomplished readers, but there are also many picture books in which even the most literal readers will be able to find more than a simple story. Such books provide readers with new insights into aspects of themselves and other people. Oftentimes, the authors will make use of literary devices such as satire, irony, cultural allusions, idioms, and dialects and the illustrators will use the most sophisticated forms of expressionism or impressionism, illusionary art, or visual puns. They vary, one from the other, in style, format, and level of sophistication.

The Middle Passage: White Ships/Black Cargo, created by Tom Feelings (Dial, 1995), may be offered as an example of a picture book for mature readers. Except for Feelings' poignant introduction in which he describes his own search for his African heritage and a brief, but very edifying history of the slave trade by John Henrik Clarke, this is a wordless book. As such it provides an intensely moving pictorial account of the incredible and horrifying indignities Africans experienced when they were kidnapped (or sold) from their villages, tortured, and forced to march long distances to the ships where they were yoked or chained and kept confined under cramped and excruciatingly ugly conditions while being transported across the seas to distant countries where they were sold as slaves. I have examined each impressionistic picture in this amazing book numerous times and most certainly will be moved to look at each of them carefully and thoughtfully many more times. Together they constitute an accomplishment too profound for me to describe adequately! I can only imagine how magnificent the original paintings must be. But even when they have been duplicated and published as pictures in a book, which of course is probably the only form in which most of us would be able to see them, one is bound to recognize their artistic merit and realize why it took Feelings almost twenty years to complete them. The journey the readers of *The Middle Passage: White Ships/Black Cargo* experience could never be as intense and life altering as it was for Tom Feelings, but it certainly has the potential to enlighten and impress them with the physical, mental, and spiritual strength and the mettle the African people must have had to live through such heinous ordeals. Tom Feelings was named the recipient of the 1996 Coretta Scott King Award for his illustrations in *The Middle Passage: White Ships/Black Cargo.*

■ *There is a proliferation of books traditionally associated with the "educated" person; i.e., new editions of classics, concept books, informational books, and Bible stories.*

These are types of books teachers and school librarians can use to great advantage in connection with all aspects of the curriculum, thus enabling them to implement the current emphasis on using multiple resources in instructional programs and to use literature across the curriculum. These books also tend to be of interest to the nonprofessional book selector such as the parent, grandparent, relative, or friend who will go into a bookshop to buy a book for that favorite child who is about to celebrate a birthday or special occasion.

Classics

The reissuing of Margaret Wise Brown's classic here-and-now stories and concept books reflects status given to the reading of children's classics, but it also is quite in keeping with the current recognition of the importance of making this kind of literature accessible to preschool children. Thus we have a new edition of Margaret Wise Brown's *The Indoor Noisy Book,* illustrated by Leonard Weisgard (Harper, 1942, 1970, 1994). This story is about the noises a little dog, Muffin, hears inside his house while recovering from a cold. Even though he is housebound and restricted to his bed and his eyes are closed most of the time, his ears are cocked so he can hear innumerable noises including the sweep of a broom, a telephone ringing, someone turning on the bath, a fly buzzing, a pin dropping, someone chewing celery and raw carrots, someone turning on the light in his own room, and the footsteps of everyone in the family coming to see him. One sees the same brightly colored expressionistic style in the four-color illustrations on the cover and endpapers and throughout the 1994 edition of *The Indoor Noisy Book* that appeared in the 1942 and 1970 editions of this classic for three-to six-year-olds. Since new plates had to be made because the original plates were lost, Weisgard created new illustrations for this 1994 edition. Furthermore, the 1994 edition is 7¼″ wide × 9″ long whereas the earlier editions were 7¼″ wide × 10¼″ long. There are six other "Noisy" Books in addition to *The Indoor Noisy Book;* in each picture book, the little dog Muffin hears certain kinds of noises: city noises, country noises, winter noises, seashore noises, quiet noises, and summer noises. Each title in the Noisy Book series alerts the reader to the kind of noises Muffin hears.

In the new edition of Margaret Wise Brown's classic *Sleepy ABC* (Lothrop, Lee & Shepard, 1994), which was originally published more than forty years ago (1953), simple rhymes and plain yet rather sentimental expressionistic paintings reproduced in four colors illustrate bedtime scenes for each letter of the alphabet. This concept book is excellent for reading aloud to toddlers and functions nicely as an introduction to the alphabet. Since the text is printed in large primary-sized type and the rhymes are so easy to read, it also serves as a fine source for a beginning reader in kindergarten or first grade to show off his or her newly acquired literacy skills.

Informational and Concept Books

Informational picture books for children and adolescents abound and many excellent examples are cited in the pages that follow. Two books that demonstrate this important trend are Seymour Simon's *Winter Across America* (Hyperion, 1994) and Isabelle Brent's *An Alphabet of Animals* (Little, Brown, 1995). In *Winter Across America* exquisite colored photographs and Seymour Simon's poetic prose emphasize the wonder and beauty of winter, its harshness, new beginnings, a time of rest and renewal. The reader gets memorable glimpses of winter in many parts of North America, including Alaska, Canada, the bay waters of Baja California, the Sierra Nevada, the Cascades, Death Valley in the Mojave Desert, Minnesota, the Florida Everglades, and so much more. In *An Alphabet of Animals,* Isabelle Brent provides her readers with a brief, well-written statement that presents an array of interesting, sometimes humorous facts about each animal. Full-page, detailed portrait paintings of twenty-six animals are in gold leaf and jewellike colors. They are done in a romanticized and fanciful art style and framed in precise and ornate geometric patterns quite like those found in medieval illuminated manuscripts.

Bible Stories

Diane Wolkstein's *Esther's Story* is a thoroughly polished retelling of the origins of the Jewish Feast of Purim. Esther, the Jewish orphan girl who became queen of Persia, bravely risked her own life to save her people from destruction. Jews throughout the world still celebrate Esther's courageous feat each spring on the holiday called the Feast of Purim. Juan Wijngaard's full-page illustrations in *Esther's Story* were done with jeweled-toned gouache paintings and reproduced in full color. (See illustration 2.) They are exquisitely detailed and not only highlight every aspect of the Persian royalty (circa the fifth century B.C.) and the geography of this southwest Asian country (now known as Iran), but are strongly suggestive of traditional Persian paintings.

ILLUSTRATION 2   From *Esther's Story* by Diane Wolkstein. Illustrations by Juan Wijngaard. Illustration Copyright © 1996 by Juan Wijngaard. By permission of Morrow Junior Books, a division of William Morrow & Company, Inc.

■ *Many series are available; these include picture books about the same story characters, as well as picture books on specific themes or subjects.*

In the main, almost everyone who reads, regardless of age, educational background, or experience with literature, tends to choose books or reject them on the basis of some aspect of their content. A person's interest in a particular topic is a reflection of a desire, conscious or unconscious, to learn more about the human condition. Instinctively people want to know more about themselves and their world. It is the content of the picture book, and the quality of the literary and artistic amalgam resulting from the combination of words and illustrations used to express that content, which facilitates the development of the reader's imaginative, creative, and critical thinking, satisfying his or her basic need to know or fulfilling an innate craving for the beautiful. It is up to book selectors to make accessible to young people the best that is available, so that although children will continue to choose books on the basis of their content, what they select will be of merit—well written and fittingly illustrated. A taste of the best may well whet the appetite of young people for superior reading matter, so that they will, more often than not, select more carefully the books they read. In the case of series it is important that the book selector purchase each book on its individual merits rather than that of the series as a whole. Richard Mühlberger has examined the works of numerous great artists in the series entitled *What Makes a . . . a . . . ?,* copublished by Metropolitan Museum of Art and Viking. Examples of the titles included in this series are *What Makes a Bruegel a Bruegel?* (1993), *What Makes a Cassatt a Cassatt?* (1994), *What Makes a Degas a Degas?* (1993), *What Makes a Leonardo a Leonardo?* (1994). In each book the reader learns what makes one artist's work distinguishable from that of any other by examining that artist's unique use of color, line, shape, composition, subject matter, and brushwork in the full-color reproductions of twelve of his or her masterpieces.

Rosemary Wells has written and illustrated a series of little books about Max, a clever bunny. The books in this series (published by Dial) are much loved by children from ages three through seven. There are probably several reasons for this wide age range of appeal. First and foremost, the children are constantly amazed at and amused by the ludicrous predicaments Max manages to get himself into, yet somehow manages to recover from still intact. Secondly, they are intrigued by the understated humor in the author's play with words as well as the wonderfully expressive pen-and-ink line and full-color watercolor wash cartoon illustrations. Last, but certainly not least, they can see themselves in Max's responses to his family, friends, and the zany predicaments he gets into. Some of the titles in this series are *Max's Dragon Shirt* (1991), *Max and Ruby's First Greek Myth: Pandora's Box* (1993), *Max's Chocolate Chicken* (1989), *Max's Christmas* (1986), and *Max's Birthday* (1985).

A number of series are based on excerpts from classics, award books, and favorite novels. For example, the classic collections of poems and wonderful episodic short stories about Christopher Robin and his toys that come to life (e.g., Winnie-the-Pooh, Tigger, Kanga and Roo, Piglet), written by A. A. (Alan Alexander) Milne and illustrated by Ernest H. Shepard, have lent themselves to the Winnie-the-Pooh's Little Book picture-book series published by Dutton. For example, scenes and memorable moments from Milne's stories and poems collected in *Winnie-the-Pooh's Friendship Book* (1994) celebrate the relationships of the characters mentioned above and others as friends. Other titles in the Winnie-the-Pooh's Little Book series are *Winnie-the-Pooh's Little Book about Food* (1992); *Winnie-the-Pooh's Little Book about Parties* (1992); and *Winnie-the-Pooh's Little Book about Weather* (1992). Each book is 6½″ wide × 5¼″ high and decorated with Shepard's line and watercolor-wash illustrations duplicated in four colors.

■ *There is a noticeable increase in the number of picture books (fiction, poetry, biographies, and informational picture books) for children and adolescents about various aspects of multiculturalism.*

Around 1988 or 1989, concerns regarding multiculturalism began to grow again as the racial-ethnic composition of the populace continued to change. As we are all too well aware, current domestic events show that the tensions between and among members of various racial and ethnic groups, and concerns regarding cultural misunderstandings in general, seem to be increasing. More people now feel freer to vent feelings of hostility and anger whereas in the past they repressed them and, as Andrew Hacker emphasized in *Two Nations: Black and White, Separate, Hostile, Unequal* (Scribner, 1992), race has become a national staple for private conversation and public controversy.

What is expected currently in the multicultural literature is an honest presentation through an approach that values pluralism while not rejecting those traditions that comprise the various segments of the whole. Perhaps the best way to accomplish this is to select literature that depicts two broad categories of the human experiences which all people tend to have sometime during the course of their lifetime. The first category is the *universal experiences,* the kind of experiences we all share in common that result from our very humanness (our needs, feelings, emotions, strengths, weaknesses, etc.), in relations with other people and within ourselves. The second is the *salient shared experiences,* which are the kind of experiences that people identified with a particular cultural or ethnic or racial group tend to have in common *because* of (1) the cultural and ethnic traditions they held on to over many generations and/or (2) the practices, attitudes, structures, etc., that evolved among the members of this group as ways to survive, find solace, or resist negative forces or destructive powers. In contemporary literature for children and adults, persons associated with diverse cultures or ethnic groups (African American, African, Hispanic American, Hispanic, Japanese American, Japanese, Chinese American, Chinese, Vietnamese American, Vietnamese, Pakistani, etc.) are depicted as responding to aspects of the universal experiences as well as to their salient shared experiences. Most of the children's and adolescent literature depicting persons associated with diverse cultural, ethnic, and racial groups focuses on the universal experiences, the experiences these persons share with all persons regardless of their cultural, ethnic, or racial identity. Nonetheless, some of their salient shared experiences are also depicted in literature for children and adolescents.

Interestingly, an increasing number of books published in the 1990s seem to address aspects of salient shared experiences of minority people. I will identify only a few of the many that are worthy of note below, but there are many others described throughout this book. One of the most forthright portrayals of a salient shared experience of African Americans among the picture books published in 1990s is *Uncle Jed's Barbershop,* written by Margaree King Mitchell and illustrated by James Ransome (Simon & Schuster, 1993). Set in the segregated South during the 1920s, where many African Americans were sharecroppers, this is the story of how Uncle Jed, the only barber in the county, managed to open up his own barbershop at the age of seventy-nine despite the delays caused by one financial crisis after another. Ransome's realistic, brightly colored oil paintings skillfully establish the definite sense of time and place and ethnicity that is so crucial to this story.

Amazing Grace is a refreshingly upbeat picture book, written by Mary Hoffman and illustrated with accomplished realistic watercolor paintings by Caroline Binch (Dial, 1991). Grace, the young heroine of this story, is an avid reader and loves to act out stories. On hearing that the class will dramatize the story of *Peter Pan,* Grace announces that she wants to play the part of Peter. Her classmates object, pointing out that she is a girl and Peter Pan is a boy, she is black and Peter is not. Grace's mother and grandmother assure her that she can be anything she wants to be. Confident in herself Grace auditions for the role of Peter Pan and gets it. After the play is performed her classmates agree that she was fantastic as Peter Pan.

The Gift, written by Ailiana Brodmann and illustrated with luminous expressionistic oil paintings by Anthony Carnabuci (Simon & Schuster, 1993), is a first-person account of how a young girl in post–World War II Germany spent the money her father had given her for Hanukkah. After stopping to listen to a street musician who was playing a beautiful tune on his accordion she put her Hanukkah money into his hat. In return, he showed her how to play his accordion, and they were playing tunes together, attracting other donors. Both the young narrator and the readers learn about the true meaning of giving in this touching story.

In *Lights on the River,* written by Jane Resh Thomas and illustrated by Michael Dooling (Hyperion, 1994), one finds a sensitive portrayal of the cultural traditions and values of a Mexican-American family working as seasonal migrant workers. Dooling's full-color impressionistic paintings augment Thomas's competently crafted text to provide a thoroughly convincing and heart-wrenching commentary on the experiences of migrant workers.

As Hazel Rochman said in *Against Borders: Promoting Books for a Multicultural World* (American Library Association, 1993):

The last thing you want to do is overwhelm young people with abstract analysis or with pretentious lectures on the labyrinth as symbol of the unconscious or with feel-good moralistic stuff about following your bliss.

The focus should be on the story, character, and the immediate situation; that's what lures readers into the book. Once inside, they can take it as far as they want to. For many young people, it's an exciting leap of understanding just to discover the universal mythic themes—the hero, the monster, and the perilous journey—in stories of daily experience from all over the world (p. 14).

Bettina Hurlimann said many years ago that "books are bridges." If the literature we make accessible to children and adolescents helps form a bridge that allows them to move easily across cultures and through multiple levels of meaning, then we will be successful in helping young people live comfortably and safely in a multicultural world.

- *There is a noticeable increase in the number of picture books about visual art, artists, and book illustration, as well as books illustrated with works of art.*

Discriminating taste or critical aesthetic response to visual art (or any other kind of art for that matter) is made up of feeling and judgment and is dependent on human nature for the former and education for the latter. In other words, discriminating taste or critical aesthetic response to visual art is acquired; seldom, if ever, is it natural. Samuel F. B. Morse said in a letter to his parents way back in 1814, and the truth in his musings is still valid today:

> Any thoughtful person who will interest himself in art and the study of art may become a person of taste, may be able to discover the different kinds of excellence in art, to separate the real from the false, and justly appreciate the artistic merit of a work of art. On the other hand, the most sensitive feeling about the beautiful is of little avail if it does not receive a proper education. Hence it has been well observed that refined or discriminating taste depends upon sensibility for acuteness and judgment for its correctness. Its progress towards refinement is exactly in proportion to the activity of the mind, the extent of its observation, and the improvement of one's general knowledge about the characteristics of a particular kind of art, and many opportunities to engage in critical thinking about art which one reads and looks at (Morse Papers, U.S. Library of Congress, Washington, D.C.).

The numerous picture books about art, artists, and book illustration, as well as books illustrated with works of art will help parents and educators, children and adolescents to respond more critically aesthetically or be more discriminating in their response to book illustrations and to visual art in general. An extensive bibliography of some of the recent publications that reflect this trend in the publishing of picture books is included in this book, so only a few of them will be cited and briefly discussed here.

Although *The Painter's Eye: Learning to Look at Contemporary American Art* by Jan Greenberg and Sandra Jordan (Delacorte, 1991) focuses on postwar American paintings, what the authors have to say is applicable to what one should notice before passing judgment on the quality of any picture, be it a painting or drawing hanging in a gallery or a home or one that illustrates a story or poem in a book. They ask the viewer of a picture to notice what an artist accomplished or failed to accomplish in terms of: what is included in the picture (content); the composition of the picture in terms of the elements of art (e.g., line, shape, color, and texture); the principles of design (e.g., balance, variety, spatial order, and unity); the feelings expressed in the picture; what feelings were evoked from you as a result of looking at this picture; how adequately or inadequately the illustrations depicted, enhanced, extended, and enriched the text; and the extent to which and the way in which the book illustrator offered unique and unexpected insights or interpretations to the text.

Celebrated Ojibway artist Arthur Shilling provides the readers of *The Ojibway Dream* (Tundra Books, 1986) with an intensely personal and moving autobiographical account of what it was like for him to be an expressionistic painter and to be a native Indian in Canada—probably in all of North America. This picture-book autobiography consists of full-color reproductions of twenty-one full-page paintings, each of which is accompanied by a poetic text. (See illustration 3.) Together the pictures and the text reflect Arthur Shilling's total identification with and responsibility to his cultural and ethnic heritage, his pride in being an artist, and his compulsion for excellence. He used heavy, powerful slashes of solid, bright color in his paintings and implemented the epitome of expressionistic art to convey the suffering, courage, and dignity he and his people experienced. This incredibly powerful picture book demonstrates the potential capability of the visual arts and of a literary biography.

In *Talking with Artists* (Bradbury, 1992) and *Talking with Artists,* Volume 2 (Simon & Schuster, 1995) author/artist Pat Cummings has compiled and edited two important books reporting conversations she had with popular children's book illustrators. Although each book artist responded in her or his own way, Cummings asked each one the same questions, questions we have all heard children and adults ask book artists or ask their teachers about the illustrators of the favorite books: Where do you get ideas? What got you started? Who influenced you? What do you do all day? Do you have any pets? How do you draw those great pictures? In each article about a book illustrator, one will find photographs of him or her as a child and as an adult plus full-color reproductions of examples of his or her book illustrations. These two volumes are certain to be read and used many times over by children and adults.

There are quite a few picture storybooks about an individual artist's approach to painting or drawing. Consider *The Little Painter of Sabana Grande,* written by Patricia Maloney Markun and illustrated by Robert Casilla (Bradbury, 1993), and *The Young Artist,* written and illustrated by Thomas Locker (1989). The story of *The Little Painter of Sabana Grande* is

ILLUSTRATION 3   Taken from *The Ojibway Dream* by Arthur Shilling. Copyright © 1986. Published by Tundra Books.

based on an incident that occurred when the author was living in Panama; she actually traveled to the boy's village in the remote Las Tablas province to see the house he painted. In this story Fernando Espino's teacher taught him how the country people of Panama made their own paints and gave him three paintbrushes. When he was unable to find paper in his home or among his neighbors, he decided, with permission from his parents, to spend his summer vacation painting a mural on the outside of his house. The account of how Fernando made his paints is fascinating and instructive, as is the model he offers the readers of this book of how he used his natural surroundings and the folk-art traditions associated with his own ethnic and cultural background as the basis for his paintings.

Locker's *The Young Artist* is an account of a twelve-year-old boy who was apprenticed to a painter who taught him everything he could within a few years. The boy preferred to paint landscapes, but was also accomplished in painting portraits. Unfortunately, he could only paint the portraits of people as he saw them, not as they wanted to see themselves, a theme Locker emphasizes quite clearly but not didactically in this story. The illustrations were created with oils and reproduced in full color. There is little doubt that Thomas Locker, like the character in his story, favors landscape painting. There are a few close-up pictures of people and one fine portrait of the young apprentice, but by far the majority of the illustrations in this book (as in Locker's other books) are excellent landscape paintings that are suggestive of the Hudson River School, particularly in the way he creates and uses color, shadows, and light.

Some books critically analyze or discuss how people throughout various times in our history, and associated with various ethnic or cultural groups, approached creating visual art. We will highlight two such books here. One of several books on visual arts in the Scholastic Voyages of Discovery series, *Paint and Painting—The Colors, the Techniques, the Surfaces: A History of Artists' Tools* is a superb informational book. Originally published in France in 1993 under the title *L'Invention de la peinture* by Éditions Gallimard Jeunesse, it takes the reader on a voyage of discovery through time from the tools of prehistoric cave artists to the techniques of Picasso and other great masters of the twentieth century. It contains a wealth of short, fairly easy-to-read texts designed to capitalize on what is relevant to today's youth and to extend their knowledge about many historical, social, and cultural aspects of painting. The numerous aspects of paint and painting covered in this truly attractive and interactive book are categorized in a manner that allows one to read only those sections that suit one's immediate interests and attention span. The graphics, overlays, and special effects in this book are absolutely amazing; there are many durable pieces the reader can manipulate, participating actively in the explorations and discovery related to the cultural history and cross-cultural relationships highlighted in this remarkable story of paint and painting. The interactive elements in this book enable the reader do such things as run his or her fingers over the ridges of a cave painting, touch a real piece of papyrus, and see the Sistine Chapel before and after restorations. Noteworthy are the helpful and rather extensive study aids to motivate acquisition of more advanced knowledge, including a Time Line, Bibliography of Titles for Further Reading, Addresses of Museums, and People to Know (including brief biographical sketches).

Animals Observed: A Look at Animals in Art written by Dorcas Mac-Clintock (Scribner, 1993) is a gathering of informed, critical analyses of animal images in art. In addition to her vast knowledge of visual art, Dorcas MacClintock uses the following criteria when critiquing how artists have depicted animals in their works of art: artists must *know* their subject (in this case the animals), must *see* them at close hand, and should depict them in art *from life.* This enlightening picture book is illustrated with full-color and black-and-white reproductions of paintings, drawings, woodcut prints, sculptures, and paper cuttings. MacClintock discusses visual art treasures created by individual artists such as Sweden's Bruno Liljefors, a painter of landscapes with animals in them; Charley Marion Russell, painter of animals of America's Old West; Cecil Aldin, known for his pastel drawings of terriers; Ugo Mochi, famous for his intricate paper cuttings of animals; Rembrandt Bugatti, known for his bronze sculptures of groups of animals of contrasting size and shape; Inuit artist Oshaweetuk, accomplished carver in olivine; and the unnamed but accomplished artists who made prehistoric cave paintings that decorate the rough walls, narrow passages, and low ceilings of the caves in southern France and northern Spain, plus the prehistoric rock engravings of desert areas in Africa.

Literature as an Art

It might be well to pause a bit to define and discuss literature as an art, as well as people's response to both literary and visual art, before identifying the criteria useful in evaluating book illustrations and the picture book as a specific kind of literature.

Webster defines *art* as the conscious use of skill and creative imagination in the production (or creation) of aesthetic objects. So, *literary art* is the use of conscious skill and creative imagination in the creation of a novel, picture book, poem, or drama. The author and book illustrator are both literary artists; the author tells his or her story and creates images with skillful and original use of words; the book illustrator tell his or her part of the story and creates images with skillful and original use of lines and shapes, color and shading. Each kind of literary artist can stimulate the reader to extract new meanings about the aspects of the human condition the author or illustrator chose to represent in the images created through carefully selected words or pictures.

If one agrees that literature is an art, then one must consider that whatever image of reality or aspect of the human condition is depicted in a novel, picture book, poem, or drama is an *illusion* of that reality. The image cannot be a mere mirroring of some aspect of life if it is truly a work of art. Artistic excellence is never identical with photographic accuracy or with mirroring the realities of the human condition. In a work of literary art (be it novel, picture book, poem, or drama), the writer or the book illustrator uses words or lines and shapes to create images that amount to a *selective interpretation* of the reality. The result of this selective interpretation is an *illusion* rather than a miniature of the reality that is depicted in or associated with the story. The illusionary image must be thoroughly identifiable and believable, yet it must not be exactly like life.

There must be some degree of reality inherent in an illusion, otherwise there would be complete abstraction; there certainly would be no story. The literary artist seldom portrays life as it was actually experienced. It is portrayed as the literary artist *chooses* to portray it: perhaps bigger or weaker, or more dramatic or tragic than it would be in real life. And that is as it should be.

The technique of selective interpretation to create an illusion might be likened to an experience I had in China when touring a grand old home that had been owned by a wealthy family before the Communists took over. The windows in the back of this house were of varied shapes and sizes—some circular, others narrow rectangular shapes, some octagonal, some triangular, a few hexagonal; some were small and others rather large. Each of these windows overlooked the same exquisitely landscaped garden. I was fascinated to notice that when I looked out of each of these windows, the view of that garden was limited (selectively determined, if you will) by the shape, size, and placement of the window. Similarly, the content, images, and themes that are depicted in the story, poem, or drama by an author and the pictures each book illustrator creates will be limited and shaped as these artists engage in selective interpretation of aspects of the reality they choose to depict.

What constitutes the "best" in literature for one person by no means coincides with another's idea of the "best." The fact that one's response to literature is personal and subjective has been made quite clear to me repeatedly when my university-level students share their evaluations of the books they have read. I have been reminded of this fact a number of times too when I have served on various committees of professional organizations whose charge is to identify titles that are distinguished or at least notable in one way or another. Members of each of these committees use specific criteria pertaining to the aspects of literary and/or graphic excellence when they evaluate the books. The members of any committee differ from one another in various ways: in personality and disposition, in professional experience and academic preparation, in their concepts of childhood, and in their own familiarity with adult and children's literature. Often each of us has named completely different titles as excellent. It is not unusual, either, to have a title deemed excellent by some committee members and to have one committee member declare it quite ordinary or even mediocre.

Some book selectors consider the 1991 Caldecott Medal–winning picture book *Black and White,* written and illustrated by David Macaulay (Houghton-Mifflin, 1990), one of the most dramatically innovative picture books of the decade, if not the century. In fact, *Black and White* is an *iconoclastic* picture book in every respect: in format, tone, style, structure, and content. It is a sophisticated picture book that will be welcomed with open arms (and open minds!) by some readers and solidly rejected by others. And that is as it should be, for it is important to acknowledge that the tastes and interests of readers will vary and as book selectors we must provide the kinds of variety that will cultivate and satisfy these differences. Furthermore, even if one will not develop a liking for the iconoclastic in literature, it is important that one at least have the opportunity to experience it.

In *Black and White* four stories unfold simultaneously from the beginning of the book to the end in double-page spreads consisting of four fairly equal parts. Although each of these four stories is relatively complete in-and-of itself, they are all connected to each other and ultimately constitute one cause-and-effect story about journeys. These journeys, Macaulay said in his Caledcott acceptance speech, are "specifically about travelers unaware of the effects of their journeys on the journeys of others. Paths that cross by chance. U-turns. Side streets. Dead ends." (Macaulay, "Caledcott Medal Acceptance," *The Horn Book Magazine* 67:420, 1991). The structure of the plot of *Black and White* is definitely not linear. At times it seems confusing, or at best too convoluted to bother about. Persistence is rewarded, for eventually one will notice connections between all the many bits and pieces and will realize that together they all make sense. The graphics are superbly rendered. There is an amazing collection of visual and verbal puns and visual illusions throughout this book and they demand both explicit and implicit interpretations. In other words, the graphics in-and-of themselves are mind stretching and require mental gymnastics that will delight those who are willing and able to meet the challenge they offer. Multiple art styles are used in the illustrations: cartoon art, collage, illusionary art, impressionistic as well as expressionistic art. This multiplicity of styles serves to set the mood and to reinforce the aura of zaniness and confusion that prevails throughout the story. In spite of all the positive qualities one might well point to in this picture book, some children and critics and book selectors simply do not like it. They consider it contrived and self-conscious. Some insist that the most problematic quality about this picture book is that it seems to amount to a clever game between hardcovers instead of an example of quality literature in the picture book genre. They find little in the format that is aesthetically pleasing, particularly because the pictures in each quadrant are so extremely diverse in color, mood, style, and content, resulting in a jarring visual effect.

The subjectivity of what constitutes the "best" in literature may be dramatized further by considering the diverse responses of literary reviewers and critics to *Harriet and the Promised Land,* written and illustrated by Jacob Lawrence (Windmill, 1968). This picture book is a landmark among juvenile books dealing with black history and among picture books in which expressionistic paintings are used to illustrate the text, a narrative poem. Among the reviewers and critics who decided this book was addressed to a "young reading audience" and who were inclined to interpret the art as well as the text of this narrative verse at the literal level, the responses were devastatingly negative. One reviewer found the colors Jacob Lawrence used were "out of harmony" and unsuitable for children; another critic, however, found the contrasting color combinations bold and angry, but completely appropriate for the author's message and for the audience to whom this narrative verse is addressed. Among those who recognized that the intended reading audience included mature and thoughtful juveniles and adults responses were very positive. Their comments indicated that (1) they perceived that Jacob Lawrence expressed ideas and intense emotions and feelings by way of sophisticated expressionistic paintings, (2) the narrative verse and the illustrations pertain to and comment about aspects of black history and the Old Testament in particular and the human condition in general, and (3) the book's symbolism is associated with the intolerable, dehumanizing circumstances many present-day people face daily, as well as with the brutal conditions blacks endured during slavery. Interestingly, when *Harriet and the Promised Land* was reissued in 1994 (Simon & Schuster), reviewers and book selectors welcomed it and said the dynamism and vigor in the illustrations added to the dramatic quality of the book for reading aloud. An example of how concepts and criteria for evaluating literature, and more particularly perhaps picture books, may change over time.

In reviewing current literature, it appears most creators of these selections (no doubt, in some cases, with advice from diligent editors) have avoided using sexist language, nor do their characters epitomize behavior and values that are sexist, unless such images are indicative of the time and place in which the action occurs or around which a conflict develops. What constitutes the "correct" or "proper" image of the female (and thus of the male!) is indeed a timely topic and it is not a question for which one will find a simple answer. The issue of sexism in literature is not one that can be discussed at great length here, but it will be discussed briefly, for it is a perspective about which book selectors must be informed and which they should consider when selecting books for use with children. Sexism is not just a women's issue, it is a human issue. In this context we must be well aware of the implications and the ramifications of our language about and images of girls and boys, women and men created in literature (or elsewhere). Both our language and the images created must enable persons to see themselves and others as free, unique human beings. With the change in the concept of femaleness there has occurred a change in the concept of maleness; these changes affect the extent to which common needs of males and females are polarized, differentiated, or viewed as substantially the same in terms of human (not sexual) needs. The tough, strong, aggressive, macho male has become one who is self-confident, successful, and willing to fight for family and beliefs with warmth and gentleness. Such a man can at times be vulnerable and frightened and capable of using his inner resources to cope and adapt and thus survive. The male does not have to be rugged and domineering to be a hero; he can at times be weak and submissive and at other times independent, self-assertive, compassionate, sensitive, evidencing the gamut of the human emotions, feelings, and needs. A woman, on the other hand, does not need to live and act like a macho male. Nor does she have to be self-obsessed, headstrong, and difficult. She does not have to succeed in areas once thought to be "for men only" to be considered a successful woman.

Two of the hundreds of picture books that avoid sexism are *Meet Danitra Brown,* written by Nikki Grimes and illustrated by Floyd Cooper (Lothrop,

nd *Visions: Stories about Women Artists,* written by
itman, 1993). The reader of *Meet Danitra Brown* is
ale protagonist through thirteen narrative poems
rfully executed, spirited, action-filled portraitlike
. (See illustration 4.) The young protagonist, Danitra
eservedly by her friend Zuri (the narrator) "the most
splendiferous girl in town" and is portrayed in the poems and in the illustrations as a plucky, vivacious, perky, astute individual who seems to know who she is and what she wants to become. In addition to her many attributes Danitra has a few weaknesses, which make her even more believable.

Leslie Sills' *Visions: Stories about Women Artists* focuses on four women artists. A critical biography of each artist is accompanied by full-color and black-and-white reproductions or photographs of her works as well as photographs of her. This combination of informative resources enables the reader to acquire some understanding of how the life experiences of each of these women, the circumstances and expectations of the times in which she lived, her educational opportunities (especially in terms of how her talents were recognized and nurtured), and the nature of her relationships with family and friends tended to inhibit or nurture the development of her artistic talents. The artists focused on in this volume are Mary Cassatt, an American impressionist; Leonora Carrington, an English surrealist; Betye Saar, an African-American sculptor; and Mary Frank, an English-born American sculptor and printmaker. An invaluable bibliography of references for further reading is provided.

Criteria for Evaluating a Picture Book

There is no surefire recipe for looking at and evaluating book illustrations. There is, nonetheless, a fundamental approach one can follow to examine book illustration. First and foremost, one must consider book illustrations works of art. From that point, it might be well to follow the procedure described below by Roger Fry in *Last Lectures,* which calls for confining one's attention to very basic qualities and then comparing a number of different works to see to what extent they possess or lack these qualities (Fry, *Last Lectures,* Beacon Press, 1962). These basic qualities are *sensibility* and *vitality;* they are discussed briefly below.

Sensibility

When considering the quality of sensibility one looks for such characteristics as order and harmony, which are evidenced in the overall design of the picture. Sensibility also includes the characteristics of variety and the uniqueness with which the artist's feelings and sensitivity are expressed in executing the overall design and idea. To get at these aspects of the quality of sensibility, one would ask questions such as the following when examining the illustrations:

ILLUSTRATION 4   From *Meet Danitra Brown* by Nikki Grimes. Illustrations by Floyd Cooper. Illustrations copyright © 1994 by Floyd Cooper. By permission of Lothrop, Lee & Shepard Books, a division of William Morrow & Company, Inc.

How appropriate are the illustrations to the spirit that pervades the story? Do they comply with the mood, pace, or attitude of the human experience that is depicted and commented upon in the story?

Does the treatment of the illustrations vary from page to page? Especially important here is whether or not the illustrations vary in content, size, shape, use of color, and placement from page to page.

Is there a pleasing interplay and balance between pictures and type?

Are the choice and use of color appropriate and interesting?

Is there discernible build-up in the dramatic interest of the pictures? Does it reflect the build-up of tension around the conflict? Does this build-up of tension also reflect the changes in mood or personality of the characters if the story requires it?

Do the illustrations of the characters evidence observable, individual qualities of all people, including minorities, so that stereotyping is avoided?

Vitality

When considering the quality of vitality, one looks for characteristics that focus on the timelessness or the lasting quality of the details of the illustrations, the aura or mood that lingers in one's mind after the illustrations have been viewed. To get to these aspects of the quality of vitality, one would ask questions such as the following when examining the illustrations:

Is there rhythm of line, of movement, of shape and mass in each of the drawings? Are these rhythms in keeping with the tenor and pace of the text?

Do the illustrations not only encourage readers to look at them, but do they add more to the readers' minds and imaginations than the readers would have been able to gain from the text alone? This means that the illustrations should not be too sophisticated or photographically perfect.

Is each picture alive and complete by itself on the page, yet when combined with the other illustrations in the book does it amount to something much more?

A reader who focuses on these questions when looking at picture books, or any illustrated books for that matter, will find that they have the potential to develop the reader's powers of discrimination and enrich his or her literary experiences. Children (even as young as age three!) can be taught how to look at the illustrations in their picture books to find answers to these questions. The questions must be worded, of course, so that the children can understand them and they should be asked after the children have had numerous experiences enjoying stories for the satisfying and pleasant literary experiences they offer.

With these considerations in mind, criteria were formulated to select titles for inclusion in this revised and enlarged edition of *Picture Books for*

Children. The four general criteria guiding the selection of the picture books listed in this edition were excellence in overall literary quality; excellence of execution in the artistic techniques employed; excellence of pictorial interpretation of story elements; and excellence of presentation for the intended audience—children from infancy through age eighteen or nineteen. The more specific criteria applied to the evaluation of the books were: (a) pictures that illustrate a literary selection must convey and enhance the author's meaning, ideas, and moods beyond the merely literal approach to visual communication, stimulating and encouraging the individuality and imagination of the viewers of the book art; and (b) that book art in turn has to exhibit the individuality, the personal style, of the illustrator.

It is important that the result of this union between the author and the book artist should be a oneness (like partners in a marriage), that oneness occurring as a result of wholesome contrasts or compatible similarities. Whatever the combination of individual entities of words and illustrations, the union must result in something that is typified by a unique and beautiful whole. Neither partner in this "marriage" may be more or less important than the other; each must contribute a full share to the literary work, namely the picture book.

Since these criteria, general and specific, seem objective enough, and even readily implementable, one might suppose that anyone using them to evaluate books for inclusion in a collection would identify the same titles. This has not yet happened nor is it likely to happen, for interpretation and implementation of these or any other criteria are ultimately personal and subjective. Frequently, the disagreements book selectors have about the quality of a picture book rest on their response to what the well-known artist and illustrator Ben Shahn referred to as "the shape of the content"; that is to say, the style of art used to create the pictures rather than their content.

Striking contrasts in art styles (to say nothing of the topics dealt with, writing styles, themes, and moods of these books) are immediately apparent when one compares books published in any one period of time, and even more so when comparing books published at different times. Children's books have been and continue to be illustrated in a variety of art styles, ranging from straightforward photographs and the realistic to the surrealistic, from the naive and folk art styles to the highly sophisticated expressionistic and abstract impressionistic art styles. Such variety is fine and should be encouraged. It dramatizes the existence of a wholesome diversity in artistic tastes as well as a wide range of sophistication and appreciation of literary art and fine art, too. This is as it should be, for total conformity in taste may be considered a vice rather than a virtue. To foster conformity suppresses development of independent thinking and inhibits sensitivity to experience and feelings.

Valuing diversity in taste rather than conformity is not to suggest that there are no generalizations, values, precedents, and traditions that one should keep in mind when evaluating picture books or any other kind of children's literature. What I am saying is that there is considerable room for personal and individual response when deciding about the worth and beauty of the visuals and text of picture books. There are many current books which, if they are made available in our schools and libraries, will help foster a wholesome diversity in taste and cultivate positive images of self and of others in the children who read them.

The creation of art for children (and of course this includes the art used in the illustrations in books for children) is not an isolated endeavor; it is part of the whole field of visual and literary art. Nor is there a special way of creating the illustrations for children's picture books. Regardless of what these illustrations portray (people especially), it is important to recognize that much art should not be interpreted on the literal level. Modern expressive art styles present in many picture books simply do not lend themselves to literal interpretation. Indeed, reflective and sophisticated dimensions for interpretation and response frequently must be used in coming to grips with an artist's graphic comments about the people he or she portrays.

Images of Minorities in Book Illustrations

Seldom if ever does one actually see in the real world firmly fixed attributes for all persons of a particular cultural, racial, national, or ethnic group. Therefore, the illustrations in a book about a single cultural or ethnic group should depict all types of people within that group. All black people do not reside in inner-city ghettos, all Mexican Americans are not migrant workers, all Italians do not own or work in shoe repair shops or fruit stands, nor are all Chinese operators of hand laundries or restaurants. Although the features of many ethnic and racial minority groups often are identifiable, nonetheless, within each of these groups, individuals will display a wide variety of facial traits. The illustrator must highlight both common and unique features when depicting ethnic or racial characters. It is important, if one is to view oneself in an adequate and positive manner, that the members of one's particular racial or ethnic group one sees portrayed in books should be depicted in a manner that will permit one to recognize oneself both as a member of that group and as an individual with features, stature, and body build that are definitely unique. For that reason, there should be illustrations that offer each member of each of our diverse cultural groups a fair abundance of models upon which to build a valid and positive self-image.

There are numerous picture books about diverse ethnic and racial groups included in this edition of *Picture Books for Children.* We are indeed fortunate to have such books as *Ragsale,* written by Artie Ann Bates and illustrated by Jeff Chapman-Crane (Houghton Mifflin, 1995), *Clams All Year,* written and illustrated by Maryann Cocca-Leffler (Boyds Mills, 1996), and *Brown Angels: An Album of Pictures and Verse,* written by Walter Dean Myers and illustrated with antique photographs (HarperCollins, 1993). *Ragsale* depicts an Appalachian family's Saturday shopping trip to various ragsales, where they find both items they need and unexpected "treasures." The pictures are so realistic they look quite like photographs, providing a fascinating glimpse of a significant regional culture. *Clams All Year* is an upbeat portrayal of an extended Italian family's response to Grandfather's early-morning call to help gather the "bumper crop" of clams that appeared on their beach after a big thunder-and-lightning storm. The expressionistic illustrations capture the aura of the family's cohesiveness and feeling of well-being during their summer together at their home on the beach. Walter Dean Myers' *Brown Angels: An Album of Pictures and Verse* is a perfect example of a picture book that glorifies and exalts children and childhood. He wrote verses on friendship, prayer, laughter and joy, pride, and the delight of having a boy baby and a girl baby. Each poem dignifies the occasions and attitudes and stances he thought were reflected in the numerous old photographs of African-American children he included in this unique picture book.

It is also vital that the reader's concept of others be positively strengthened by seeing an individual of any race or ethnic group portrayed in a variety of realistic situations, at the same time exhibiting features and qualities unique to that person. Such illustrations permit the reader to react to and identify with each book character as an individual and help one avoid any unconscious preconditioning that could lead to stereotyping and scapegoating. When children learn to understand, respect, and accept diversity, they will less likely fear, or view with disdain, differences in color, status, or life-style.

Research has amply demonstrated the effect illustrations have on their viewer, that book illustrations are an important and effective means by which the reader may learn facts, attitudes, and values—not only about self, but about others. An illustration can show the reader new ways of seeing; it can sharpen (as well as shape) his or her point of view; it can help provide a deeper understanding of the relationships between people who may have backgrounds similar to or different from the reader's. It is important, therefore, for book selectors to keep in mind that the illustrations in the books should portray facts, attitudes, and values that will offer readers acceptable, authentic, positive images of individuals who are members of the many and diverse cultural, ethnic, and racial groups making up our society.

Styles of Art in Book Illustrations

Style is a term that refers to the configuration or gestalt of artistic elements that together constitute a specific and identifiable manner of expression. Style refers to the personal character or form that is recognizable in an artist's work because of his or her particular and consistent treatment of details, composition, and handling of a medium. Also, style refers to the manner that has developed and become standard within a culture or during a particular period of time. It is often difficult to identify a specific artistic character or style used by an individual artist or even by people in a particular era or culture. It is upon these broad characteristics that various styles of art have been labeled as surrealistic, representational, expressionistic, impressionistic or as folk art, cartoon art, or naive art. Whenever the illustrations in a book are strongly suggestive of one of these art styles, mention is made of it in my description of that book. Following are brief descriptions of each of these styles of art, along with titles of one or two picture books in which illustrations exemplifying that art style are found.

Representational or Realistic Art

In representational or realistic art the artist offers direct observations of the reality he or she has observed or experienced. To obtain a realistic visual interpretation, the artist strives for a somewhat photographic exactitude of detail, conveyed in recognizable shapes that are in proper perspective and proportion, though often actually not as detailed as the reality being depicted. Dorcas MacClintock described this kind of art as follows, ". . . even in realism, the eyes and hands of the artist select and modify, with acute perception and, often, with personal sensitivity" (*Animals Observed: A Look at Animals in Art,* Scribner, 1993, p. 1). The watercolor paintings Allen Say created for the 1994 Caledcott Award Medal book *Grandfather's Journey* (Houghton Mifflin, 1993) and the companion picture book *Tree of Cranes* (Houghton Mifflin, 1991) are so precise and realistic in proportion, perspective, and use of line, color, and shading they look like photographs in a family album collected to document a family's intercultural relationships and experiences. David Shannon's realistic illustrations for Martin Rafe's retelling of a Chinook Indian legend entitled *The Boy Who Lived with the Seals* (Putnam, 1993) reaffirm the credibility of this amazing tale. They make aspects of the setting, namely the sea, the habits of seals, and the lifestyle and cultural beliefs of the Chinook Indians very concrete and thus more understandable.

Surrealistic Art

Surreal pictures are composed to suggest the kind of images experienced in dreams, nightmares, or a state of hallucination, yet presented in as graphic a manner as possible. One title that is especially exemplary of surrealism (in the illustrations and in the text) is Michael Garland's *Dinner at Magritte's* (Dutton, 1995). Pierre, a young boy, visits his next-door neighbors, Rene and Georgette Magritte, and is invited to stay and have dinner with them and their guest, Salvador Dali, who is expected to arrive shortly. While waiting for Mr. Dali, Pierre watches Magritte paint and the artist tells him a bit about how he approaches his painting, saying "I like to paint what I think. I paint what I dream. So, when people look at my paintings, they can see what's in my mind." A perfect description of how a surrealist functions! Most of the pictures depicting the activities mentioned in the brief and easy to read text are full-color surrealistic oil paintings suggestive of Magritte and Dali. In some instances, the surrealistic images these famous artists actually included in their paintings are reproduced in this picture book, but Garland created a few of his own pictures "after the fashion" of Magritte and Dali. *Dinner at Magritte's* is a fine book to use for the fun it offers in-and-of itself, but it also serves as an effective way to introduce children to these two great surrealistic artists.

Impressionistic Art

Recognizing that the properties of light and color in the atmosphere permit one a view of nature that constantly changes, the impressionist artist strives to make fixed for all time that which was originally momentary, spontaneous, and transient. In impressionistic art the composition is somewhat informal, the figures frequently appear marginal, colors are broken and juxtaposed and caused to mingle and thus mix in the eye of the viewer. The result is that the contours of the reality (be that reality a person, an object, or even a landscape) are softened and the illusion of mass bulk diminished. One is given the *impression* of a certain aspect of the reality rather than a sharp, detailed description of it. In *Animals Observed: A Look at Animals in Art* (Scribner, 1993), Dorcas MacClintock says the impressionist artist strives "to record an actual moment in time, what the eye saw in a glance. Impressionism . . . is often a sketch. Details are left for the viewer to provide. . . . Yet feeling and sentiment are conveyed in the artist's transient impression. Visual appeal is created and the viewer responds with immediate comprehension" (p. 1). *Hidden in the Sand,* Margaret Hodges' retelling of the tale from the Buddhist classic *The Jataka,* is illustrated by Paul Birling (Scribner, 1994) with impressionistic paintings that offer rich images of the great desert between India and the Middle East. Birling's ability to create visual images that portray the desert as a fierce and harsh place during the day and a wonderfully refreshing place at night through artistic use of splotches of color and light and shadows is quite remarkable. Another example of a book illustrated with impressionistic pictures is *The Tangerine Tree,* written by Regina Hanson and illustrated by Harvey Stevenson (Clarion, 1995). The impressionistic illustrations for this touching story about a Jamaican family's farewell to the father as he prepares to leave for New York, where he has been offered a job which pays far better than any he could possibly get at home, are done in lush, full-color acrylic. Without being maudlin, they reveal convincingly in each of the characters' body posture and facial expressions the loving relationships within the family and their emotional reactions to the impending separation. The aura of the rural and tropical setting, so important to this story, is most aptly conveyed through splotches of color and effects of light to affirm the prevalence of the brilliant colorful flowers and lush greenery of this island world.

Expressionistic Art

Expressionism leans heavily toward abstraction in that it is intended to highlight the form of the reality, the essential or structural quality of the reality. Not only is it counter to academic or realistic art, it is concerned primarily with expressing the artist's subjective, emotional response to the reality that is seen or experienced. Often expressionistic art appears somewhat sophisticated and mature in its subjectivity and abstraction.

Examples of expressionistic illustrations are those created by Ashley Bryan for *What a Wonderful World* by George David Weiss and Bob Thiele (Jean Karl/Atheneum, 1995) and *Zin! Zin! Zin! A Violin,* written by Lloyd Moss and illustrated by Marjorie Priceman (Simon & Schuster, 1995). Ashley Bryan's brilliantly colored tempera and gouache paintings provide a perfect accompaniment for the hand-drawn lyrics of this upbeat, exuberant song celebrating wonderment, love, and hope in the world. (See illustration 5.) Marjorie Priceman's illustrations for *Zin! Zin! Zin! A Violin* are zany expressionistic line and full-color gouache wash paintings. The flow of the

ILLUSTRATION 5   Reprinted with the permission of Atheneum Books for Young Readers, an imprint of Simon & Schuster, from *What a Wonderful World* by George David Weiss and Bob Thiele, illustrated by Ashley Bryan. Illustration copyright © 1995 Ashley Bryan.

lines and placement of the figures (people, animals, and musical instruments) in each picture seem quite compatible and even tend to match the rhythmic verse of the text.

Naive Art

One gets the impression from a painting done in the naive style that the artist is ignorant of the technical aspects of depicting reality in his or her painting. One also may be led to conclude that the artist rejects or is at least removed from artistic traditions, for in the art produced, no particular line of stylistics is developed. Instead, naive artists present the essence and the appearance of objects and scenes out of their own experience. Characteristic of naive art are simplification of what is seen and experienced, vitality and often awkward spontaneity, candidness and intensity. The art of the naive is a pre-perspective art. The viewer notices that there occurs an almost universal adherence to frontal posture or profile and a disregard for anatomy and perspective that suggests either a fairly undeveloped level of consciousness or a lack of skill in expressing a consciousness, if indeed it exists. Exemplary of naive art is that used by Faith Ringgold to illustrate *Aunt Harriet's Underground Railroad in the Sky* (Crown, 1992). In this companion picture book to *Tar Beach* (Crown, 1991), Be Be and Cassie, the characters we all met in that 1992 Caldecott Award Honor Book and Coretta Scott King Award book, travel one of the same routes the runaway slaves took on the Underground Railroad. Faith Ringgold's brief, but informative and significant, text and her emotionally revealing and dramatic naive paintings in rich full color make it possible for young children to understand better and appreciate more fully how amazing and important the accomplishments of Harriet Tubman and others associated with the Underground Railroad actually were. Another example of a picture book illustrated with pictures in the naive art style is *The Legend of the Poinsettia,* retold and illustrated by Tomie de Paola (Putnam, 1994). This picture book retells, first, the Mexican legend of how the poinsettia came to be called *flor de la Nochebuena* (flower of the Holy Night) and, second, how this red and green flowering plant that is traditionally associated with Christmas came to be called *poinsettia* in the United States. The illustrations, done in the naive art style, are perfect for the story of a little girl in rural Mexico who humbly presented a bundle of weeds to the Christ Child figure lying in the manger in the village church during the Christmas Eve Mass. The weeds promptly burst into flaming red star-shaped flowers, and when Mass was over, the people found all of the weeds throughout the town were aflame with the same beautiful red "flowers of the Holy Night." While both of the books discussed above are illustrated in the naive art style, the drawings of the two artists are starkly dissimilar in style, content, and use of medium.

Folk Art

Folk art is a broad designation for the artistic expression of the folk cultures often found in isolated environments or communities in a geographical area inhabited by a dominant ethnic group. Evident in the artwork of any one folk culture will be identifiable traditions, motifs, symbols, treatment of line, modeling, color, volume, and space. There are as many folk-art styles as there are folk cultures. With the proliferation of adaptations of folktales and original tales told in the style of a folktale published each year, one will often find that the artists have included in their pictures many of the characteristics, motifs, and symbols found in the art of the particular folk culture with which the story they are illustrating is associated. Several of the books illustrated by Ed Young include thoroughly authentic graphic interpretations of Persian folk art and Chinese art. For example, one will find exotic Persian miniatures in *The Girl Who Loved the Wind,* an original tale written by Jane Yolen in the style of a folktale. Typical of the Persian miniatures, and of Ed Young's collage pictures, the reader will encounter the perfected draftsmanship that has much in common with children's drawings. They contain a wealth of interesting detail, but the kinds of things that are detailed and the perspective and sense of proportion given to them are reminiscent of the way children portray things: the figures are placed in different planes, that is to say, they are placed in the "high horizon" convention, so that each is seen separately. Human figures, animals, and natural objects are portrayed as idealized symbols; in other words, they are presented in an elaborate but uncomplicated way. The beauty of line, rich, warm tones in the colors used, and, most of all, a perfectionism typical of Persian art are seen in Ed Young's illustrations for this book.

The embroidered figures that make up the exquisite tapestries stitched by You Yang for *The Whispering Cloth: A Refugee's Story,* written by Pegi Deitz Shea (Boyds Mills, 1995), are absolutely true to the traditional Hmong folk style of stitching. It is a common practice for the Hmong women to record significant events in their own lives and those of their people in embroidered tapestries called pa'ndaus. In *The Whispering Cloth: A Refugee's Story* a little girl by the name of Mai is confined in a refugee camp in Thailand with her grandmother and many other Hmong refugees. Actually there are two styles of art used in the illustrations to tell this story. Those depicting aspects of the refugees' life in the camp are poignant, expressive, realistic watercolor paintings created by Anita Riggio. The other style of art is seen in the reproductions of the figures You Yang stitched in the pa'ndaus to tell Mai's life story. (See illustration 6.) You Yang lived in a refugee camp in Thailand for seven years, so she lends a high degree of credibility to her visual telling of Mai's story in the tapestries she stitched for this book. The embroidered figures in Mai's pa'ndau reveal the most memorable aspects of her past, present, and future. Her story is a wrenching one of bombings, escape over land and water, encampment in a crowded refugee camp, making pa'ndaus that tell their life stories to sell to the traders from Chian Khan so they can earn money they need to emigrate to a new country. The figures in the pa'ndau are done in a rather naive style, but because they have been done in this style consistently for generations they are more properly classified as folk art.

ILLUSTRATION 6   Pa'ndau copyright 1995 by Pegi Deitz Shea, stitched by You Yang. From
The Whispering Cloth by Pegi Deitz Shea. Reprinted by permission of Boyds Mills Press.

Cartoon Art

In cartoon sketches the artist resorts to such techniques as slapstick, exaggerations, and absurdities depicting incongruities and incompatible characteristics or situations to the extent that laughter, or at least a smile, is evoked. There is no paucity of illustrations done in the cartoon style. One can count on Steven Kellogg to create detailed, whimsical cartoon-style illustrations for the original, humorous, and thoroughly fantastic adventures he creates. Especially noteworthy are his pencil line and watercolor wash cartoon-style illustrations for the chaotic adventures of a nutty Great Dane named Pinkerton. All are published by Dial; they include *Tally Ho, Pinkerton!* (1982), *Pinkerton, Behave* (1979), *A Rose for Pinkerton* (1981), and most recently, *Prehistoric Pinkerton* (1987). He is also known for the ever-favorite science fantasy picture book *The Mysterious Tadpole* (Dial, 1977). This is a cleverly written story of what happened when Louis received what he thought was a tadpole sent by his uncle from Loch Ness and the tadpole grew and grew and grew and never did turn into a frog, even though Louis's teacher said it would. The detailed, cartoon-style illustrations for which Kellogg is so well known add considerably to the humor of this refreshing whimsy. One examination of these illustrations will definitely not reveal all the wonderfully zany and action-filled details Kellogg has included. In fact, each one warrants careful and repeated examination. Another picture book effectively illustrated with cartoon-style pictures is *I've Got Chicken Pox,* written and illustrated by True Kelley (Dutton, 1994). The cartoon-style line and watercolor wash illustrations masterfully capture a little girl's ups and downs throughout her confinement with the chicken pox. (See illustration 7.) Be certain to notice the designs that frame each full-page picture; they are indicative of the state or phase of the virus in Jess's system and her moods during her ordeal. Worthy of note is that on the bottom of each page in tiny, boldface type, outside of the framed picture, is a "Pox Fact," information about such things as the cause, contagion, and cure of this communicable disease. The cartoon illustrations for each of these facts are also very humorous.

Literature as One of the Humanities

The subject of literature is aspects of the human condition; thus, it may pertain to any human experience, everything that has to do with people—their actions, their needs and desires, their strengths and frailties, their response to the world in which they live. Writing literature, be it fiction, poetry or drama, is not the same as writing a documentary movie, television report, or newspaper article. Those writers who view them as comparable will make little use of their imagination. And imagination is the human faculty that leads the writer (or illustrator) to create a literary work of art: art at its finest and most memorable.

When literature is viewed as one of the humanities, one tends to read a literary selection to find out how the author interprets people's responses to

Oh, *itchy!* I don't even feel like watching Saturday morning cartoons. I just want to scratch.

Dad cuts my fingernails short.

Mom gives me a baking-soda bath.

I hate looking at my own tummy. Gross!

POX FACT: You may get scars, called pockmarks, from chicken pox if you scratch too hard and damage your skin. So cut your fingernails short or wear mittens or gloves.

ILLUSTRATION 7   From *I've Got Chicken Pox* by True Kelley. Copyright © 1994 by True Kelley. Used by permission of Dutton Children's Books, a division of Penguin Books USA, Inc.

certain social issues or to aspects of the human condition. It is used as a source through which one gains an understanding of oneself and one's relationship to other people and things. It is used to find out what an author offers the reader in relation to the perpetual and universal human questions common to people of all ages: Why am I like I am? Who am I? What is life? What is the human experience? This approach to literature is justified if one remembers that literature, as an art form, should not be read on the literal level for actual or even partial answers to these persistent human concerns, nor should it be read as a source for factual information. No attempt should be made to read into these stories or poems or even to judge them in terms of external standards, such as "truth," as though they were factual or informational writing. This view of literature brings us to the four categories around which the annotated bibliographies that appear in this book were developed.

The Organization of This Book

The subject categories in *Picture Books for Children*—"Me and My Family," "Other People," "The World I Live In," and "The Imaginative World"—reflect such basic and universal questions as Who am I? Why am I like I am? and What is the (my) world? What is the world of make-believe? These are fundamental concerns of all children (of all humankind, for that matter) and are reflected in the categories used in this book. Each category mixes realistic fiction and fanciful tales, informative books, and verse, for a child does not necessarily choose a book for its genre. Rather, unwittingly or consciously, a child may choose a book for the mere appeal of its format, but more often because its title or content reflects a particular reading need or interest and suggests that the book might possibly bring her or him closer to an answer to one or another of the basic humanities questions mentioned above.

A gentle reminder is required here. The reader of a picture book must enjoy it in order to identify with and respond to its story line and characters. Furthermore, such emotional identification is likely to occur only when text and illustrations of the book radiate sincere human emotions, warmth, and hope, and when the aspect of the human condition being depicted in the book is comparable to the reader's own experiences or at least within his or her ability to understand. A reader who experiences emotional identification and enjoyment from a literary selection may consciously (or, more likely, subconsciously) continue to read in order to find answers to basic human questions and concerns. A responsive child who is given a picture book that stimulates him or her to think beyond the literal level of the text and illustrations can have reading experiences which open boundless vistas to new thoughts and new worlds.

Literature can inform the young reader about people who are like her or him in many ways, but who look different, who live differently, and who subscribe to different moral, ethical, and religious codes. A picture, being a visual medium, constitutes an obvious and especially powerful means of illustrating the fact that all members of any one group of people are alike in some ways and different in some ways, too; that people are to be viewed as individuals and not lumped together under one faceless anonymity. We are all familiar with the metaphor "every picture is a window." It is this window provided by picture-book illustrations, together with the details in the text, that teaches the reader to respect simultaneously the likenesses as well as the uniqueness and diversities that typify people. Picture books can instill in the reader an appreciation for the challenge and exhilaration of being different from other human beings, and at the same time provide comfort and a feeling of unity with everyone else who is part of our pluralistic society. Books in the section on "Me and My Family" show people as part of one family consisting of (1) individuals who, because they are alike in some ways, share universal experiences; and (2) individuals who, though they are different from most people, still share these differences with some other people (and thus have salient shared experiences). The participants in the Anglo-American Seminar on the Teaching of English, held at Dartmouth in 1966, recommended that literature be used to introduce children to the paradoxes, complexities, and incongruities of life. To a large extent this can be accomplished by making accessible to children picture books that depict individuals engaging in and responding to universal experiences and salient shared experiences.

The concept of cultural pluralism is supported (at least in theory) by a growing number of people in the United States and throughout the world and is fostered by the present trend to publish specific kinds of picture books. Folktales from almost any national, religious, or ethnic group are now being adapted, illustrated, and published as picture books. Effective also in transmitting this concept of cultural pluralism are the many modern literary pieces which are being created as picture books, be these in the genres of historical fiction, modern realistic fiction, modern poetry, fantasy, or informational literature.

Research has demonstrated that people do not become self-actualized and are not likely to come even near to realizing their actual potential, free to be individuals in the best sense, unless their very basic aesthetic and intellectual needs are met. Unfortunately, unless these needs are satisfied early during one's developing years, one's craving for knowledge and the beautiful are too often suppressed. Indeed, the levels of one's thinking powers will not be advanced nor one's aesthetic tastes raised to any significant extent unless one has opportunities to experience the thought-provoking and the beautiful repeatedly in many different ways.

The development of "good taste" and the ability to recognize what is "best" or "beautiful" are acquired and dependent upon exposure to the "best" and the "beautiful." Children, in their search for beautiful and satisfying literature (and picture books are a major genre of literature), will read whatever is at hand. Should they fail to find quality literature among the picture books accessible to them at home or in the school and public library collections, their craving for it will soon wane. It is that easily extinguished. In all probability, the young people in whom this occurs will eventually read little if any literature, except that which is required of them. On the other hand, it is quite likely that children will become avid and discriminating readers if satisfying, exciting, high-quality literary selections are made readily accessible to them. For this reason, the concern that parents, teachers, and librarians have about making available the best literature (including the best picture books) to children is more than justified. It is well worth repeating what was said previously in this chapter: It is up to the book selectors to make accessible to young people the best that is available, so that although children will continue to choose books on the basis of their content, the books they select will be of merit, well written, and fittingly but also beautifully illustrated.

Me and My
Family

The picture books in this section tend to focus on aspects of a child's view of self and his or her relationships with family members and significant others in the child's immediate world, relationships that are comparable to those some children somewhere in today's world could experience, and would be understood by and be of interest to most children in today's world. Some of the selections in this section do not have contemporary settings, nor are they even realistic stories. They are included here because the themes seem to point to some specific aspects of a child's view of self and his or her relationships with family members and significant others.

1   Adler, David A.

ONE YELLOW DAFFODIL: A HANUKKAH STORY   *6–9* YEARS

Illustrated by Lloyd Bloom. San Diego: Gulliver/
Harcourt Brace, 1995

> This story was inspired by the accounts told to Adler by the numerous
> Holocaust survivors he interviewed while doing research for his previous
> books. Morris Kaplan, a Polish Jew who is the lone survivor of a family
> interred in Auschwitz, is invited to share the first night of Hanukkah with
> the family of the children who stopped at his florist shop every Friday
> afternoon to buy flowers and to visit briefly with him. The somber, full-
> page illustrations executed in liquitex acrylic on watercolor paper reflect
> the florist's tragic story. Just as a small daffodil blooming outside Mr. Ka-
> plan's barracks at Auschwitz offered him assurance he would survive, the
> soft glow that appears around each bouquet or vase of flowers in his shop
> suggests that Mr. Kaplan's life will become more cheerful now that he has
> allowed himself to celebrate Hanukkah once again and to accept the Bek-
> kers' overture to make him a part of their family. Compare this story of
> how this lone survivor of the Holocaust celebrated Hanukkah with that
> of another lone Holocaust survivor's celebration of this holiday depicted
> in *The Tie Man's Miracle: A Chanukah Tale,* written by Steven Schnur
> and illustrated by Stephen T. Johnson (Morrow, 1995).

2   Angelou, Maya

NOW SHEBA SINGS THE SONG   *11–18+* YEARS

Illustrated by Tom Feelings. New York: Dutton/Dial, 1987

> Maya Angelou's sensuous poem celebrating the strength and complexi-
> ties of black women the world over was inspired by an incredibly astute
> collection of drawings that Tom Feelings made of black women at ran-
> dom, wherever he happened to travel over the course of twenty-five
> years. The drawings done in black line and in sepia tones accomplish
> most aptly what Feelings said he hoped to accomplish: to show them as
> "different, separate and individual, real women" and to show the fluid
> energy of their rhythmic movements, "and in almost all of them the
> strong presence of a definite dance consciousness in their lives." This is
> a book that will have to be looked at over and over, a little at a time, in
> order to grasp its full significance.

3   Bates, Artie Ann

RAGSALE   *5–9* YEARS

Illustrated by Jeff Chapman-Crane. Boston:
Houghton Mifflin, 1995

The ragsale is a special family event to the people in this Appalachian town. In this beautifully illustrated book, the female members of one family are depicted spending a whole Saturday stopping at one ragsale after the other, looking for clothes and other things they need and things they had not thought about, but once noticed prove to be special treasures. Some of the clothes, books, and other things were obviously used before, but some items still have the original price tags on them. The full-page paintings are so realistic, clear, and crisp they look like colored photographs. (See illustration 8.) Each picture provides a discerning glimpse of an individual's response to searching for or finding the "right" item. Together the pictures and the text provide one with an astute insight into a significant regional cultural event.

ILLUSTRATION 8   Illustration by Jeff Chapman-Crane from *Ragsale* by Artie Ann Bates. Illustration copyright © 1995 by Jeff Chapman-Crane. Reprinted by permission of Houghton Mifflin. All rights reserved.

4   Bauer, Marian Dane
WHEN I GO CAMPING WITH GRANDMA   *5–8 YEARS*
Illustrated by Allen Garns. Mahwah, N.J.:
BridgeWater/Troll, 1995

> A young girl and her grandmother go camping and are enthralled by the
> beauty that surrounds them. The author's sparse lyrical prose describes
> the fondness these two feel for each other, as well as their responses to
> the beauty and harmony in the outdoors: the creatures in the woods and
> water they see and hear around them, the appearance, sounds, smells,
> and taste of the foods they cook over the fire, the stunning sights they see
> when the sun "dips into the edge of the lake" and the moon "floats in the
> bluing sky" as day breaks, and so much more! The illustrator's use of
> color and shading in his beautifully executed impressionistic paintings
> emanates the aura of peacefulness and love along with the sense of ad-
> venture and delight Bauer expressed in the text. Compare the author's
> language, the style of illustrations, the relationships between the camp-
> ers, and the moods depicted in *When I Go Camping With Grandma* with
> those in *Grandfather and Bo,* written and illustrated by Kevin Henkes
> (Greenwillow, 1986), and *Dawn,* written and illustrated by Uri Shulevitz
> (Farrar, Straus, & Giroux, 1974).

5   Bial, Raymond
PORTRAIT OF A FARM FAMILY   *8–11 YEARS*
Illustrated with color photographs by Raymond Bial.
Boston: Houghton Mifflin, 1995

> *Portrait of a Farm Family* offers interesting and inspirational reading fare.
> This is a no-holds-barred delineation of the numerous and many-faceted
> challenges and satisfactions faced by a modern, independent dairy-farm
> family from Illinois. Dennis and Jane Steidinger and their eight children
> confront the uncertainties of weather, luck, and economics, yet they are
> able to profess an abiding faith in their way of life. The bibliography for
> further reading provided at the end of the book should prove helpful for
> those who want clarification or further information about dairy farming.
> The numerous full-color photographs clarify and highlight the indis-
> pensable roles each member of this farm family plays individually and
> as a team.

6   Bonners, Susan
THE WOODEN DOLL   *5–9 YEARS*
Illustrated by Susan Bonners. New York:
Lothrop, Lee & Shepard, 1991

Realistic, yet rather ethereal, line and full-color wash paintings effectively complement a well-written text; together they create a memorable story about a little girl who plays with a wooden nesting doll even though she has been emphatically told by her grandfather that it is not a toy and she is not to touch it. Stephanie discovers that the name "Stephania" is written on the bottom of the doll, the name that only her grandfather calls her. The reason he gives for her name being written on the doll helps her (and the readers!) appreciate why her grandfather, who emigrated from Poland when he was a young man, is so protective of the nesting doll.

7   Brett, Jan

THE TWELVE DAYS OF CHRISTMAS   *ALL AGES*

Musical score arranged by David Wilcocks. Illustrated by
Jan Brett. New York: Metropolitan Museum of
Art/Dodd, Mead, 1986

Crisp, exquisitely detailed realistic watercolor paintings lavishly illustrate the text of this ancient carol and counting game that celebrates the tradition of sharing and gift giving during the twelve days linking Christmas and the Epiphany (December 25 through January 6). A visual feast awaits those who take time to look closely and thoughtfully at the pictures on each page: a love story, a family's preparations for and celebration of Christmas, an array of extravagant gifts given by a suitor to his "true love," the "Merry Christmas" greeting in eleven languages, various folk motifs of Christmas, and an untold variety of wild and domestic animals.

8   Brodmann, Ailiana

THE GIFT   *6–9 YEARS*

Illustrated by Anthony Carnabuci. New York:
Simon & Schuster, 1993

The Gift is a first-person account of how a young girl, who lived in post–World War II Germany, visited various shops before she decided how to spend the money her father had given her for Hanukkah. After stopping to listen to a musician, who was sitting among a pile of blankets in front of the grocery market, play a beautiful tune on his accordion, she put her Hanukkah money into his hat. He asked her to sit down by him and showed her how to play his accordion. Soon he taught her enough so that they could play some tunes together and the people who stopped to watch and listen to the two of them dropped coins into his hat. The young narrator learned about the true meaning of giving and there is little doubt the readers of this touching story will learn that lesson, too. The story is illustrated with luminous expressionistic oil paintings which add considerably to the quality of this picture book and help to make *The Gift* a truly memorable literary experience.

9   Bunting, Eve

FLOWER GARDEN   *4–6* YEARS

Illustrated by Kathryn Hewitt. San Diego: Harcourt Brace, 1994

Rich, crisp, full-color, double-page pictures done in oil paint on paper highlight this easy-to-read, brief, upbeat account of how a little girl, helped by her father, prepares a flower-garden box as a birthday surprise for her mother.

10   Bunting, Eve

I DON'T WANT TO GO TO CAMP   *5–8* YEARS

Illustrated by Maryann Cocca-Leffler. Honesdale, Pa.:
Boyds Mills, 1996

Lin's mother is all excited because she is going to a camp for mothers. Lin insists that neither she nor her favorite stuffed toy, Loppy Lamb, is the least bit interested in going to camp—ever. As Lin goes shopping with her mother to buy her camping gear (a big red flashlight, a blue sleeping bag with a rainbow on it, a yellow duffel bag, and more) the readers (and, of course, Lin's mother) know that Lin's stance about not going to a camp is changing. When Lin, Loppy Lamb, and Dad visit Mom at the camp on Visitors' Day, Lin is thoroughly amazed at what Mom and her friends do at the camp. On their way home from visiting Mom, Lin tells Dad that Loppy Lamb said he might want to go to camp in two years when he is big and that although she really does not want to go to camp, she thinks she will probably have to go with Loppy, for "he's such a baby sometimes." Children are certain to recognize Lin's change of heart and smile smugly to themselves as Dad is shown doing in the book. The colorful and action-filled gouache and colored pencil expressionist illustrations capture the warm, uninhibited relationship between Lin and her parents and they exude Mom's and everyone else's enthusiasm about her stint at camp. This is a refreshingly upbeat story.

11   Bunting, Eve

SMOKY NIGHT   *7–10* YEARS

Illustrated by David Diaz. San Diego: Harcourt Brace, 1994

Full-color expressionistic paintings done in acrylics and mounted on colorful collage backgrounds add considerable depth of understanding and feeling about how the characters respond to the rioting, fires, and looting in the streets in their neighborhood and are forced to go to a shelter in a church nearby. This story makes a grim commentary about what happens when people's pent-up feelings of anger and frustration over racial and ethnic prejudice and poverty reach the point when they cannot be contained and consequently explode; the ultimate message it offers is that these prejudices tend to dissipate as people get to know one another. *Smoky Night* received the 1995 Caldecott Medal Award.

12   Catalanotto, Peter

THE PAINTER   *4–8 YEARS*

Illustrated by Peter Catalanotto. New York:
Richard Jackson/Orchard, 1995

All the members of this wonderfully exuberant family, consisting of a little girl who is the narrator of this here-and-now story, a mother, and a father who is an artist and has his studio in the family's home, obviously enjoy doing things together. Sometimes, when the little girl asks her father to do a puppet show with her or read a book to her he simply replies "Not now," or "Not yet." Her disappointment is apparent, but she knows that he wants to be alone in his studio when he is working on a painting. When she asks him if she may paint and he responds in the affirmative by inviting her into his studio and pointing to her own easel, her delight is unmistakable. Her mother and father as well as the little girl love the picture she paints and there is little doubt that when young readers see it in its full splendor as a double-page spread they will be impressed with it too. The impressionistic watercolor paintings reproduced in rich warm colors are filled with action and vitality and enhance the upbeat mood of this fine family story. (See illustration 9.)

13   Cocca-Leffler, Maryann

CLAMS ALL YEAR   *5–8 YEARS*

Illustrated by Maryann Cocca-Leffler. Honesdale, Pa.:
Boyds Mills, 1996

Every summer a large extended Italian family vacations together at their summer home on the shore in Hull, Massachusetts. Each morning at sunrise Grandfather wakes up eight of his grandchildren to go clam digging. At first all of them are quite enthusiastic about getting up so early and going down to the shore to look for clams. Their enthusiasm diminishes gradually when day after day they return with fewer clams; each day fewer children respond to Grandfather's wake-up call. The morning after a big thunder-and-lightning storm only two of them go down to the shore with Grandfather, but to their amazement and delight the beach is loaded with clams. They go back to the house with their two overflowing pails to share the good news about the "bumper crop." Soon the whole family

ILLUSTRATION 9   From *The Painter* by Peter Catalanotto. Illustration copyright © 1995 by Peter Catalanotto. Reprinted by permission of Orchard Books, New York.

(adults and children), still sleepy-eyed but with pails, shovels, sacks, pans, and a plastic swimming pool in hand, is down at the beach gathering up one clam after another. By seven o'clock in the morning their containers are overflowing. They spend the day cleaning the clams, rinsing the best shells so they can be used to make baked stuffed clams. Not surprisingly, their evening meal consists of clam chowder, baked stuffed clams, and spaghetti with clam sauce. Later that evening they clean and freeze twenty-five more pounds of clam meat. Clams are cooked in various ways each time the family gathers during the rest of the summer, at their Labor Day cookout, Thanksgiving dinner, and on Christmas Eve. The expressionistic illustrations done in gouache and colored pencil and even the grainy-looking sandlike endpapers capture the aura of the family's happy summer on the beach.

14   Cohen, Barbara

MOLLY'S PILGRIM   *6–9* YEARS

Illustrated by Michael J. Deraney. New York:
Lothrop, Lee & Shepard, 1983

Diverse interpretations of the term *pilgrim* are presented in this sensitive story about what happens when a little girl is told to dress a doll as a Pilgrim for the Thanksgiving display at school and her mother dresses the doll as she herself dressed before emigrating from Russia to America to seek religious freedom, stating that she is a Pilgrim, a modern Pilgrim. The realistic black-and-white illustrations reflect aspects of the era and the changing moods that are so important to this story. Compare the way this same theme was developed in the film version, which won the 1985 Academy Award for Best Live Action Short Subject. It is available on video (*Molly's Pilgrim,* Phoenix Films #21285). Also compare the theme developed in the book and film versions of *Molly's Pilgrim* with *Aekyung's Dream,* which Min Paek originally wrote in Korean, translated into English, and illustrated (Children's Book Press, 1988), and *Angel Child, Dragon Child,* written by Michele Maria Surat and illustrated by Vo-Dinh Mai (Raintree, 1983).

15   Day, Nancy Raines

THE LION'S WHISKERS   *6–9* YEARS

Illustrated by Ann Grifalconi. New York: Scholastic, 1995

This Ethiopian folktale portrays the dramatic and courageous effort a woman takes to win love and acceptance from her stepson, who deeply mourns the death of his mother. The collage illustrations are created with pieces of colored and textured papers, materials such as woven mats, straws from a whisk broom, fabric, and photo details. They capture the contrasts of the Ethiopian landscapes and the aura of a remote village in the Ethiopian flatlands where most of the action of this story takes place. These illustrations expertly highlight the strong tension between the woman and the boy and her humility and patience as she waits to win his favor. (See illustration 10.)

ILLUSTRATION 10   Illustration by Ann Grifalconi from *The Lion's Whiskers* by Nancy Raines Day. Illustrations copyright © 1995 by Ann Grifalconi. Reprinted by permission of Scholastic Inc.

16   Demuth, Patricia Brennan

BUSY AT DAY CARE HEAD TO TOE   *3–6 YEARS*

Photographs by Jack Demuth. New York: Dutton, 1996

> Full-color photographs superimposed on children's drawings and paint-
> ings are fused with an easy-to-read text in rhyme, depicting and describ-
> ing in an upbeat, credible, and forthright manner a wide variety of social
> activities that take place in a day-care facility. Children are shown en-
> gaging in an impressive array of actions and movements.

17   Doro, Ann

TWIN PICKLE   *3–7 YEARS*

Illustrated by Clare Mackie. New York:
Bill Martin/Henry Holt, 1996

> Readers will have great fun (as I did) trying to decide if it is Ivory or Jenny
> or both of the twins engaging in the mischievous and energetic activities
> described in verse and depicted in zany, action-filled cartoon-style illus-
> trations done in watercolor and gouache with black ink.

18   Dunrea, Olivier

THE PAINTER WHO LOVED CHICKENS   *6–9 YEARS*

Illustrated by Olivier Dunrea. New York:
Farrar Straus & Giroux, 1995

> All the painter wanted to do was live on a small farm, raise some chick-
> ens, and paint pictures of them. Because most people were not the least
> bit interested in buying paintings of chickens, he also painted pictures of
> people, poodles, penguins. As luck would have it, a woman who came to
> his studio looking for "something different," promptly bought his paint-
> ing of an egg. When he showed her his portfolio of drawings and paint-
> ings of chickens, she wanted to buy all of those pictures, too. He agreed
> to sell all of these except one which he kept for himself. With the money
> she paid him for his pictures, he bought a small farm and a box of newly
> hatched eggs; from that point on he was content to raise chickens and
> paint pictures of them. For many years the woman exhibited his paint-
> ings of chickens and eggs. The painter became famous and the woman
> visited him often; she always left with a portfolio of new paintings and
> a basketful of eggs. Be certain to notice that at the top of each left-hand
> page there is a picture of a different kind of chicken, labeled with its com-
> mon name. On each right-hand page there is a full-page picture depicting
> aspects of this original story; these pictures, which are reproduced in flat,
> bright colors, were done in gouache and are in a naive art style.

19   Fleischman, Paul

SHADOW PLAY   *6–10* YEARS

Illustrated by Eric Beddows. New York:
Charlotte Zolotow/HarperCollins, 1990

> A young brother and sister spend their last twenty cents on admission to
> a shadow puppet show presentation of "Beauty and the Beast." After the
> performance, anyone who is interested is invited to go backstage and "be-
> hold the truth" of this tale. Those who accept this invitation not only see
> how the puppets work, but more importantly they get to meet someone
> who epitomizes the real meaning of this tale, at least as it is perceived by
> the author and thus the puppeteer. Upon meeting the puppeteer, a bulky,
> unattractive man, the children are charmed by the man's smile and warm
> personality; they experience first hand, as did Beauty when she met the
> Beast, that "appearances are as thin and deceptive as shadows." As in
> "Beauty and the Beast," the theme in *Shadow Play* is worth pondering
> over. The two different kinds of illustrations are perfectly suited for this
> story within a story: stylized black-and-white crosshatch sketches con-
> note the characters' real world before, during, and after the performance
> and numerous impeccably detailed silhouette drawings that look exactly
> like paper cuttings denote the shadow puppets in action.

20   Flournoy, Valerie

THE PATCHWORK QUILT   *4–8* YEARS

Illustrated by Jerry Pinkney. New York: Dial, 1985

> A quilt "can tell your life story," said Tanya's grandmother. Indeed the
> quilt this grandmother made with the help of the whole family did just
> that and brought joy to the family as well. The full-color illustrations
> evoke the feeling of love and respect that pervades this African-American
> family; they were rendered in pencil, graphite, and watercolor. See *Tan-
> ya's Reunion,* written and illustrated by Valerie Flournoy (Dial, 1995), for
> another story about Tanya and her family.

21   Ghazi, Suhaib Hamid

RAMADAN   *6–10* YEARS

Illustrated by Omar Rayyan. New York:
Holiday House, 1996

> The author discusses the significance of the month-long celebration of
> Ramadan, which occurs during the ninth and most special month of the
> Muslim lunar year. Numerous things a contemporary Islamic-American
> family does to observe Ramadan are presented in this informational book:
> they do not eat or drink anything from the break of dawn to sunset, but
> they do have two meals together each day. The meal the family has

together before dawn is called Suhur; after sundown, they break their fast by eating a date and then have a big family meal called Iftar. In addition to adhering to stringent fasting to celebrate their faith during Ramadan, Muslims try to clean and purify their bodies and minds by reading the Holy Quran frequently and praying as often as they can. They reflect on their actions, give to charity, and attend the services at their mosque. The detailed ink line and full-color watercolor-wash paintings that illustrate the text are done in two different styles and thereby effect a striking visual contrast. The borders and panels are done in a traditional Islamic style that reflects the rich, ethereal past of Islam; the modern expressionistic drawings are at times cartoonish in appearance and reflect the contemporary American Muslim life portrayed in the story.

22   Gibbons, Faye

NIGHT IN THE BARN   *6–9* YEARS

Illustrated by Erick Ingraham. New York: Morrow, 1995

When their city cousins visit Willie and his younger brother Mike who live on a farm, Willie challenges them all to spend the night in the barn. No one will admit to being afraid, so on this "darker-than-dark" autumn night they not-so-bravely head for the barn. The eerie mood and setting of this well-written, spooky, but very realistic story are enhanced considerably by Ingraham's dark paintings, which were done with varnished watercolors. I had great fun reading this picture book aloud to a third-grade class. The range of emotions the students demonstrated while they listened to this story and looked at the pictures seemed to match those felt by the book characters, especially when the narrator told them he saw two glowing eyes looking straight at him from the darkness and heard the who-oo-oo-oo, who-oo-oo-oo call from outside and when the boys in the story heard something make a rhythmic tapping noise, then a whiffling snort, when it shuffled across the floor below and up the stairs heading directly toward the loft where they boys were gathered, and especially when it appeared as a shadowy shape and pounced on top of them. The anxiety level felt by the students, just like that felt by the book characters, immediately dissipated when they found out who the intruder was and they were quite ready to settle down.

23   Goffstein, M. B.

AN ARTIST   *6–12+* YEARS

Illustrated by M. B. Goffstein. New York:
HarperCollins, 1980

Miniature paintings done in pen and ink and full-color watercolor wash combined with a sparse, precise, poetic prose offer children and adults a message that they can ponder over: an artist, "small, strong, and with limited days . . . tries to make paint sing." For other especially moving picture books that offer equally sophisticated and perceptive statements about other types of creative persons, see Goffstein's *A Writer* (HarperCollins, 1984) and *An Actor* (HarperCollins, 1987).

24   Grifalconi, Ann

THE BRAVEST FLUTE: A STORY OF COURAGE   *5–9 YEARS*
IN THE MAYAN TRADITION

Illustrated by Ann Grifalconi. Boston: Little, Brown, 1994

A message of hope and strength is offered in this story about a spirited young Mayan Native-American boy who led a New Year's Day celebration procession. For his endurance and persistent effort to play his bamboo flute and carry the drum during the long and arduous processional journey, the widow of the town's old master flutist rewarded the boy with her husband's elegant silver and ebony flute and the elders gave him money to buy food and seed for his family. The accomplished poetic text is enhanced by the carefully executed double-page illustrations done in superbly soft and vibrant watercolor paintings; together they authenticate a vast array of the ethnic and cultural traditions of the Mayan people in an unmistakable Central-American setting.

25   Grimes, Nikki

MEET DANITRA BROWN   *5–10 YEARS*

Illustrated by Floyd Cooper. New York:
Lothrop, Lee & Shepard, 1994

"You Oughta Meet Danitra Brown" is title of the first poem in this collection of thirteen short narrative poems about an African-American girl her friend Zuri (who also serves as the narrator) describes as "the most splendiferous girl in town." I agree wholeheartedly with Zuri, Danitra is well worth getting to know. Through each of these short verses plus the wonderfully executed, spirited, action-filled, portraitlike paintings and rubbings we come to appreciate Danitra's many strengths and a few of her weaknesses. She is a plucky, vivacious, perky individual who seems to know who she is and what she wants to become. She gets along well with her mother and some of her peers. She freely offers bits of advice to her friend, some of which is actually quite wise and astute.

26 Hafner, Marilyn

MOMMIES DON'T GET SICK! *4–8* YEARS

Illustrated by Marilyn Hafner. Cambridge, Mass.:
Candlewick, 1995

> Mommy has to stay in bed because she is sick and Daddy has to go to the
> store. Abby, who is absolutely confident that she can make Jell-o for
> lunch, feed her baby brother, and put in the wash, agrees to help while
> her father is away. To her dismay, and no doubt that of the readers as well,
> everything goes dreadfully wrong: the Jell-o will not gel, the baby wails
> hysterically, suds overflow the washing machine, and the dryer will not
> shut off. When her father comes home Abby is quite beside herself. To-
> gether they clear up the mess and ever so confidently invite Mommy to
> come down for lunch. The line and watercolor wash, cartoon-style il-
> lustrations highlight the absolute bedlam that prevails downstairs while
> Mommy is upstairs sleeping (or at least trying to sleep). The side remarks
> the family's dog makes to himself about Abby's disasters add another di-
> mension of humor to this recognizable family situation, however exag-
> gerated it may be.

27 Hanson, Regina

THE TANGERINE TREE *6–9* YEARS

Illustrated by Harvey Stevenson. New York: Clarion, 1995

> This is a very credible, moving account of a Jamaican family's farewell to
> their father as he prepares to leave for New York, where he has been offered
> a job at which he can earn enough money to pay the rent for their house
> and land, buy the children's school clothes and even a cow. Before leaving,
> he gives each of the children a little present. To Ida, the youngest member
> of the family, he gives a book entitled *Stories of the Ancient Greeks,* which
> once belonged to her two older brothers. He tells her he will be back home
> by the time she is big enough to read the book by herself. She is still heart-
> broken that he is going away, but ultimately his time line as to approxi-
> mately when he will come back home provides the concrete assurance she
> needs to be comforted. He asks her if she remembers what she must do to
> help the tangerine tree have the best fruit and, if so, to take charge of it and
> pick the ripe fruit. He also asks her to help Mama sell the fruit in the market
> on Saturdays. Her answers indicate that she is most willing to take charge
> of the tangerine tree and that she knows exactly what she has to do to help
> the tree produce the best fruit. The impressionistic paintings done in lush,
> full-color acrylic reveal convincingly, in each of the characters' body pos-
> ture and facial expressions, their love and respect for each other, their in-
> tense sorrow at having to be separated from their father, and the sense of
> hope they all hold for their future. The rural and tropical setting, so im-
> portant to this story, is made apparent, but not ostentatiously so, through

the bright, colorful flowers, the fruit-laden trees, the lush green leaves, the bright blue sky, and the lightweight, loose-fitting clothing worn by the characters. (See illustration 11.)

28   Hathorn, Libby

WAY HOME   *9–13+ YEARS*

Illustrated by Gregory Rogers. New York: Crown, 1994

> This is a haunting story of homelessness and societal greed and indifference. It is told effectively through the use of narration in approachable poetic prose that is fast paced, is in the present tense, and is juxtaposed with a monologue in a colloquial language spoken by the protagonist, "a boy called Shane," to his newly acquired stray cat. The accomplished double-page illustrations are done in bright colors tempered primarily with charcoal. The manner in which this Australian author and illustrator team portrayed Shane's life as a "street kid" evoked considerable pithy discussion among the many groups of children and adults with whom I shared this literary gem.

29   Hayes, Joe

A SPOON FOR EVERY BITE   *6–10 YEARS*

Illustrated by Rebecca Leer. New York: Orchard, 1996

> Two traditional elements of Hispanic folktales are found in this story. One is the focus on a person who is poor but clever in contrast with a rich person who is vain and ostentatious; the second is the use of the metaphoric phrase "a spoon for every bite" when referring to the tortilla. This second element stems from the southwest Indians' practice of breaking off a piece of tortilla and scooping up some beans; both beans and "spoon" disappear into the mouth never to be seen again. This original fiction tells the tale of a poor husband and wife who trick their rich neighbor who is proud of his fortune and lives extravagantly. The full-color expressionistic paintings done in pastels dramatize the extremes that often exist among the people in Mexico. One easily notices the humble, sparsely furnished home and tattered clothing of the poor couple in contrast to the elegantly furnished big house and nicely tailored clothes belonging to the rich neighbor. The desert landscape rendered by the illustrator portrays the arid and parched terrain and azure blue skies of the Southwest. His skill as a portrait artist is evident in the range of expressions, moods, and personality traits the faces of people in this story convey. Children and adults are certain to enjoy the several levels of humor inherent in this story so well told in the harmonious blending of words and pictures.

ILLUSTRATION 11   Illustration by
Harvey Stevenson from *The
Tangerine Tree* by Regina Hanson.
Illustration by Harvey Stevenson.
Reprinted by permission of Clarion
Books/Houghton Mifflin Company.
All rights reserved.

30 Hayes, Sarah

EAT UP, GEMMA   *3–7* YEARS

Illustrated by Jan Ormerod. New York:
Lothrop, Lee & Shepard, 1988

> A truly credible glimpse of the eating habits of Baby Gemma is offered:
> throwing her breakfast on the floor, squashing grapes, banging her spoon
> on the table, crying to eat the fake fruit off a lady's hat, and so on. Those
> who have younger siblings will be certain to acknowledge the authen-
> ticity of Baby Gemma's antics and those who have no younger siblings
> will no doubt find it enlightening. All will delight in the ingenious way
> Baby Gemma's brother finally got her to eat as she should and what she
> should. See also *Happy Christmas, Gemma,* written by Sarah Hayes and
> illustrated by Jan Ormerod (Lothrop, Lee & Shepard, 1986). Both of these
> picture books were originally published in Australia and all of the char-
> acters are black, but because the experiences of a toddler and her family
> depicted in them are so universal, the characters could easily be inter-
> preted as African American.

31 Henderson, Kathy

THE LITTLE BOAT   *4–8* YEARS

Illustrated by Patrick Benson. Cambridge, Mass.:
Candlewick, 1995

> A little boy makes a boat and plays with it on the beach. Distracted, he
> turns his back momentarily and a wind blows the boat away from him,
> away from the beach, and into the sea. The boat's journey is long and at
> times hazardous, but amazingly (to adults, but probably not to children)
> it survives its journey across the sea. With the help of the breaking waves
> and a white wave it rolls toward land where a little girl is playing on the
> shore of the sea. She picks up the boat when it sails up to her feet and
> plays with it just as the boy did. The author's talented use of lyrical and
> imagery-filled language enables one to envision the moods and ways of
> the ocean on which the boat traveled so far. The very large illustrations
> in-and-of themselves, along with the various perspectives from which
> they depict the boat as it encounters the weather elements, objects, and
> creatures during its travels, serve to dramatize the boat's escapades. Com-
> pare the travels of this boat and the approach the artist used to illustrate
> them with those depicted in the classic picture book and 1942 Caldecott
> Medal Award Honor Book *Paddle to the Sea,* written and illustrated by
> Holling C. Holling (Houghton Mifflin, 1941).

32   Henry, O. (pseud. William Sidney Porter)

THE GIFT OF THE MAGI   *11–16+ YEARS*

Illustrated by Lisbeth Zwerger. Calligraphy by Michael
Neugebauer. Natick, Mass.: Neugebauer Press, 1982.
Distributed by Alphabet Press

> This is an elegant picture book edition of the classic short story about the
> sacrifices a couple made to buy each other a Christmas present: She had
> her beautiful golden brown hair cut and sold it to buy her husband a
> chain for his watch; he sold his watch to buy his wife a set of expensive
> combs for her hair. The full-page expressionistic watercolor paintings re-
> flect the early 1900s setting that is suggested in the text, although the
> theme is timeless. The text in hand calligraphy adds to the elegance and
> romantic aura of the book.

33   Hoffman, Mary

AMAZING GRACE   *5–9 YEARS*

Illustrated by Caroline Binch. New York: Dial, 1991

> *Amazing Grace* is a refreshingly upbeat picture book. Grace, the young
> heroine of this story, loves stories, whether they are read to her, read on
> her own, told to her by her grandmother, or seen in movies. Also, she
> enjoys nothing more than to act out the most exciting parts of all sorts of
> stories. When her teacher announces that the class will dramatize the
> story of *Peter Pan,* Grace announces that she wants to play the part of
> Peter. She is promptly told in no uncertain terms by her classmates that
> she cannot play that role. First, she is a girl and Peter Pan is a boy; second,
> she is black and Peter isn't black. With moral support from her mother
> and grandmother, Grace resolves that she can be anything she wants to
> be. No one is surprised, especially Grace and the readers, that at the au-
> ditions Grace wins the role. Her classmates agree that she does a fantastic
> job as Peter Pan. This fine picture book is illustrated with accomplished
> realistic watercolor paintings. In addition to the content of the pictures,
> it should be pointed out that the artist's use of color and the graceful
> movements in her lines and shapes dramatize what the author tells us
> about Grace's exuberance for life, her wonderful imagination, and her de-
> termination to do her best.

34 Hughes, Monica

A HANDFUL OF SEEDS   *5–9* YEARS

Illustrated by Luis Gray. Toronto: Lester, 1993;
New York: Orchard, 1996

> In a nameless Central-American country, Concepcion lived with her grandmother in a neat and tidy little house on a hill in a rural area. Together they planted and harvested enough corn, chili, and beans to feed themselves, gave some to their landlord, and sold the rest to a neighbor who took it to sell in the city in the valley and brought back fresh buns and fish for them to eat. When her grandmother died, the landlord told her to move. Concepcion bundled up all the homegrown vegetables she could carry as well as the seeds she had saved for the next planting and eventually lived with a gang of homeless children near a dump in the barrio on the edge of the city. How she managed to survive and eventually, with the help of her homeless friends, grow enough corn, chili, and beans to provide food for everyone, to take some to the city to sell, and to save enough seeds for the next planting provides interesting reading. The stylized full-page illustrations look somewhat like mural paintings and convincingly depict the lush growth of vegetation in this part of the world as well as the impoverished conditions under which Concepcion and her homeless friends lived.

35 Hughes, Shirley

ALFIE GETS IN FIRST   *3–7* YEARS

Illustrations by Shirley Hughes. New York:
Lothrop, Lee & Shepard, 1981

> Alfie raced ahead of his mother and sister, Annie Rose, as they returned home from shopping and waited for them smugly on the top step on the porch in front of their house. Then, as soon as his mother unlocked the door, he dashed in ahead of her proudly announcing that he was the winner again. Unfortunately, when his mother goes back outside to get Annie Rose out of her stroller, Alfie accidently locks them out and is unable to reach the latch to let them in or the mail slot to put the key through it. The commotion this crisis causes outside as the neighbors try to help is awesome, but eventually Alfie calms down and solves the problem in his own way—to everyone's relief and satisfaction. The animated realistic full-color illustrations are done with ink and watercolor, and highlight so well the range of emotions Alfie and all the others felt during this not too uncommon predicament. Other Alfie books are: *Alfie's Feet* (1982), *Alfie Gives a Hand* (1983), and *An Evening at Alfie's* (1984).

36   Hughes, Shirley

RHYMES FOR ANNIE ROSE   *2–6 YEARS*

Illustrated by Shirley Hughes. New York:
Lothrop, Lee & Shepard, 1995

> This is a splendid collection of poems about children and their connections with their family, their friends and their immediate world. The twenty-plus original poems have child appeal and show an astute insight into the almost universal physical, social, emotional, and mental needs and interests of children in the nursery and preschool age range. The impressionistic line and watercolor wash highlight the positive feelings and attitudes expressed in the poems, especially those about family relationships and a zest for life. (See illustration 12.)

37   Karim, Roberta

MANDY SUE DAY   *5–9 YEARS*

Illustrated by Karen Ritz. New York: Clarion, 1994

> As a reward for helping to harvest the crops in late autumn, each of the five children in this hard-working family is given a whole day free from chores to spend any way he or she wants. Mandy Sue, who is blind, chooses to spend her day with her horse, Ben. The imagery-filled poetic prose that is at the same time unpretentious, upbeat, and matter-of-fact in tone describes the sounds, smells, tastes, and even the feel of Indian Summer that the two "friends" notice as they wander around the meadow. They return home just in time for Mandy Sue to feed and water the horse quickly and then join her family in a scrumptious dinner in honor of her special day. She ends "Mandy Sue Day" by sleeping in the barn, in the loft directly above Ben's stall. Realistic illustrations executed in watercolor heighten the feeling of completeness about oneself, one's family, and one's world that prevails throughout this happy and secure story.

38   Kelley, True

I'VE GOT CHICKEN POX   *4–8 YEARS*

Illustrated by True Kelley. New York: Dutton, 1994

> For a while Jess is pleased she has the chicken pox and thoroughly delights in all the attention she gets from her family and the mail she receives from her grandmother and classmates. It does not take very long, however, for her to become bored with entertaining herself, and she actually looks forward to going back to school and being with her friends again. The cartoon-style line and watercolor-wash illustrations masterfully capture her ups and downs throughout her ordeal. On the bottom of each page in tiny, bold-face type outside of each framed picture is a "Pox Fact": information about such things as the cause, contagion, and cure for this communicable

ILLUSTRATION 12   Illustration by Shirley Hughes from her *Rhymes for Annie Rose*. Copyright © 1995 by Shirley Hughes. By permission of Lothrop, Lee & Shepard Books, a division of William Morrow & Co., Inc.

64

disease. The designs that frame each full-page picture reflect the state of Jess's disease and her moods during her illness. Read *Betsy and the Chicken Pox,* written and illustrated by Gunilla Wolde (Random House, 1976) to see how another young protagonist and her baby brother responded to getting this communicable disease.

39   Kessler, Christina

ONE NIGHT: A STORY FROM THE DESERT   *7–10 YEARS*

Illustrated by Ian Schoenherr. New York: Philomel, 1995

> This picture book is a handsome tribute to the traditional lifestyle of the Tuarege people (also called the Blue People), a nomadic culture group living in the Sahara. In the style of a storyteller, the author tells her reader the roles of each member of the extended family in carrying out the interrelated traditional ethical, religious, and environmental values of the Tuareges. Mohamad, the young sheep herder and protagonist of this story who seems at peace with his lot in life and with himself, has passed a test of intelligence, a test of strength, and a test of courage—the three "tests of life" his father said he must pass in order to be declared a man and to be declared worthy of wearing a turban made of a fine blue fabric. The full-color impressionistic illustrations, done in rich, warm hues, enrich the aspects of the desert setting, especially the austerity and beauty of the desert at different times of day and night, as well as the Tuareges' cultural traditions described in the text as the people engage in religious rituals, eat meals, and women sing their stories and play their drums around the campfires.

40   Kidd, Richard

ALMOST FAMOUS DAISY!   *6–9 YEARS*

Illustrated by Richard Kidd and with reproductions of
paintings by famous artists. New York: Simon & Schuster, 1996

> Daisy, a determined and ambitious little girl, read an advertisement encouraging artists to enter paintings of their favorite things in the "Famous Painting Competition." Accompanied by her dog Duggie, Daisy traveled to the cities in France, Belarus, Tahiti, Wyoming, and New York where famous artists like Vincent Van Gogh, Claude Monet, Marc Chagall, Paul Gaugin, and Jackson Pollock painted pictures of their "favorite things." Daisy was thrilled at what she saw in each of these faraway places, including the original paintings depicting each of these great artists' "favorite things." She imagined she saw each of these great artists painting these famous pictures, and Kidd's illustrations of Daisy's images of the artists at work are strongly suggestive of the way they really did look. Daisy enjoyed painting pictures of the same sites each of these artists depicted in their paintings and she also tried to use the same techniques

they used. Unfortunately, she never felt that the subjects of these artists' paintings reflected her favorite things and she decided to go back home. Shortly after returning home she realized she was looking at everything differently and her "favorite things" had been in her home all the time. The dawning of this realization motivated her to get busy painting a picture of her favorite things, and her picture was awarded the first prize in the competition.

ILLUSTRATION 13   Illustration copyright © 1990, from *The Flute Player: An Apache Folktale*, written and illustrated by Michael Lacapa, published by Northland Publishing Company.

41   Lacapa, Michael, *Reteller*

THE FLUTE PLAYER: AN APACHE FOLKTALE   *10–14* YEARS

Illustrated by Michael Lacapa. Flagstaff, Ariz.:
Northland, 1990

Told in the style of the Apache storyteller, this fine retelling of the folktale is a charming story about the meeting of a young Indian woman and man and their developing love for one another. Throughout this picture book the imagery in the illustrations by Lacapa, who is a Native American from Arizona, is an absolutely authentic application of the traditions and symbols of the Western Apache culture. (See illustration 13.) Note particularly the traditional zigzag designs and the sunflower pattern, which were and still are used in their basket weavings. The zigzag design in their baskets symbolizes "the river of life," which is eternal—no beginning and no end. Also authentic are Lacapa's allusions to the terrain, the flora and fauna one finds in the southwestern United States, the hairstyles and headgear traditionally worn by the Apache men and women, their musical instruments, and the colors (red symbolizes the male, yellow symbolizes the female). Be certain to compare the colors *and* the content that make up the landscapes in the double-page spreads on the first and last page to see how Lacapa indicated life and death respectively. Without doubt, each picture in this book supports, extends, and enriches the text. Each time one examines the illustrations, there is more to see and think about.

42   Lawrence, Jacob

THE GREAT MIGRATION: AN AMERICAN STORY   *7 YEARS–ADULTHOOD*

Introduction by Jacob Lawrence based on an interview
by Elizabeth Hutton Turner. New York: HarperCollins/
Museum of Modern Art/The Phillips Collection, 1993

This very special book incorporates a narrative series of sixty panels Jacob Lawrence painted in 1940–41 and initially entitled "The Migration of the Negro." The vertical or horizontal paintings were executed in bold, flat planes of color in tempera painted on gesso on 18″ × 12″ panels of composition board. Less than one year after Lawrence finished these pictures, half of them (the odd numbers) were bought by the Phillips Collection in Washington, D.C. and half (the even numbers) were bought by the Museum of Modern Art in New York City, becoming the first paintings by a black artist to be included in that museum's collection. *The Great Migration: An American Story* was published when all sixty paintings in this series were exhibited at the Phillips Collection in November 1993. The exhibition was entitled "Jacob Lawrence: The Migration Series"; after being shown at the Phillips Collection it traveled to several major cities in the United States. As a body of work, this series represents a unique blend of the black American experience, history painting, social commentary, and modern art (expressionism). More specifically, these paintings chronicle what the African Americans experienced when they left their homes and farms in the rural South around World War I and traveled to northern industrial cities hoping to better their lives. Lawrence's pictorial articulation of this historic population shift of the African American in the United States is based in large measure on the experiences of members of his own family and other families he knew as they traveled northward. It is also based on what he learned about the great migration from his teachers, friends, and associates, and the many books he read at the Schomburg Library in Harlem. The text accompanying the pictures in this book is concise, simple, and factual. That is fine, for it includes quite enough to encourage the children to take the time they truly need in order to look at and think about each picture carefully and thoughtfully. I would strongly urge teachers and librarians to read the following references both so they can share some of the important information about Jacob Lawrence's work contained in them with their students, and so they themselves will better understand and appreciate Jacob Lawrence's unique kind of expressionistic art, his allegiance to his cultural heritage so evident in this series and in all of his art, and finally the monumental impact that the form and content of his works create: *Jacob Lawrence: American Painter,* by Ellen Harkins Wheat (University of Washington Press/Seattle Art Museum, 1986); *Jacob Lawrence,* by Milton W. Brown and Louise A. Parks (Dodd, Mead/Whitney Museum of American Art, New York, 1974); and Robert Wernick's critical biographical essay "Jacob Lawrence: Art as Seen through a People's History" (*Smithsonian* 18, no. 3 [June, 1987], pp. 56–67).

43   Lemieux, Margo

PAUL AND THE WOLF   *6–8 YEARS*

Illustrated by Bill Nelson. Parsippany, N.J.:
Silver Press, 1996

Paul's teacher played a recording of *Peter and the Wolf,* by Sergei Prokofiev. The music frightened him then and it frightened him in the dark at night when he was in bed. Paul's father told him the composer intended to have his music make the wolf sound frightening, but also told his son that the Native Americans thought of wolves as their brothers. To demonstrate this last fact, he then told Paul the story of Nesaru, a young Native-American boy, who as part of his initiation rite into manhood, followed a wolf pack for thirteen months. During these many moons Nesaru and a young wolf named Ow-olo developed a very close relationship. When Nesaru returned to his people he was a fine and cunning hunter and a wise man, for he learned about hunting, endurance, and sharing from the wolves and tried to live his life as they did. When he was very elderly and decided he was ready to die he went back to the land of the wolves and settled high on a hilltop where his spirit would be close to the sky. It was there he was reunited once again with Ow-olo, who also was old and frail; it was there the two died together. This story, based on the traditions of the Pawnee, the Crow, and the Blackfoot, seemed to soothe Paul and allay his fears, especially when his father told him that when he was a young boy, he too was frightened by the story of *Peter and the Wolf.* In the very realistic paintings, done in wonderfully rich colors, Nelson made superb use of shadows and the effects of light in the close-up views of animals and people in this story. Consider playing one of the following recordings of Sergei Prokofiev's *Peter and the Wolf:* Peter Ustinov (narrator), Philharmonia orchestra, Herbert von Karajan (conductor) with L. Mozart Cassation (SAX2375) or Leonard Bernstein (narrator) Philharmonic Symphony Orchestra of New York, Leonard Bernstein (conductor) (61057). In addition to playing a recording of this musical tale, one might read aloud one of any number of picture-book adaptations of it. I tend to prefer the following: *Peter and the Wolf* retold and translated by Maria Carlson and illustrated by Charles Mikolaycak (Viking, 1982) and Enra Voight's retelling and illustrated version of *Peter and the*

Wolf, which includes brief selections from the score and pictures of the individual orchestral instruments (Godine, 1980).

44   Lester, Alison
WHEN FRANK WAS FOUR   *3–7* YEARS
Illustrated by Alison Lester. Boston:
Walter Lorraine/Houghton Mifflin, 1996

Each year, seven children experience different events common and not so common to other children of the same age. The action-filled cartoon-style watercolor paintings in this easy-to-read picture book depict the seven children engaging in enjoyable counting and memory games over a span of seven years. *When Frank Was Four* is certain to delight many young readers in the United States as it did those in Australia and New Zealand where it was originally published in 1994 by Hodder Headline Australia Pty., Ltd.

45   Lewin, Ted
SACRED RIVER   *7–9* YEARS
Illustrated by Ted Lewin. New York: Clarion, 1995

This nonfiction picture book was inspired by a trip Lewin and his wife took to Benares, the ancient city in India through which the river Ganges flows. The Hindus believe that participating in a pilgrimage to this venerable city enables them to achieve a feeling of tranquility and a sense of liberation from worldly problems and suffering, that immersing themselves in the sacred water of the Ganges purifies their soul. Lewin's informative text and his splendid impressionistic watercolor paintings capture the religious fervor that typifies the pilgrims as well as the celebratory mood that permeates this huge gathering. The students might find it interesting to examine Lewin's illustrations in Florence Parry Heide and Judith Heide Gilliland's *The Day of Ahmen's Secret* (Lothrop, Lee & Shepard, 1990) to see how he managed to depict, in another crowded ancient city (Cairo, Egypt), the aura of tension resulting from the juxtaposition of the many different smells, sounds, and sights when animals, vehicles, and people of varied ages and ranks or positions crowd the narrow streets, each seemingly quite apart from the others.

46   London, Jonathan
THE VILLAGE BASKET WEAVER   *6–10* YEARS
Illustrated by George Crespo. New York: Dutton, 1996

Elderly and ailing Policarpio, known fondly by his family and fellow villagers as Carpio, is the village basket weaver and is the only person who knows how to weave the secret patterns into his baskets. Each day Carpio's grandson, Tavio, sat under the cashew tree with the old man and watched him weave a new cassava basket, a long cylindrical basket used by the villagers for the making of cassava bread, and listened to stories Carpio told while he worked. Soon Tavio began to make a small basket of his own, using the broken slivers of the long dried river weeds his grandfather had cast aside. When Carpio became very ill and was unable to see anything but the shadows of light, and too weak to work on the cassava basket, Tavio asked him to tell him what to do and thereby help him finish it. Lying in a hammock hung between his cashew tree and a palm tree, the dying man whispered the instructions to the boy. Carpio was pleased when he saw the finished work and predicted that Tavio "would make many more things of value." The story ends with Tavio (and the readers) firmly convinced that, like his grandfather, the boy, who after all is the only one in his village who knows how to make the cassava baskets, will become the village basket weaver. The detailed and expressive illustrations depict the villagers as an industrious and vivacious people. The vibrant colors, typical of the natural beauty prevalent in the small coastal village area in the Carib Territory of Belize which serves as the setting for this moving story and used so extensively in Crespo's baskets, appear throughout each of the full-page illustrations. The design incorporated in the borders around each picture is strongly suggestive of the pattern traditionally used by these island people in the Carib Territory to make the cassava basket.

47   Lyon, George Ella

A DAY AT DAMP CAMP   *6–9 YEARS*

Illustrated by Peter Catalanotto. New York: Orchard, 1996

The technique of creating a montage of pictures illustrating the activities described by several pairs of rhyming words is refreshingly unique. To summarize the consequences of the activities depicted, each series of montages is followed by a double-page impressionistic picture with no accompanying text. For example, the montage illustrating the phrases "damp camp," "green screen," and "hot cot" shows a tired-looking camper resting on a cot on a hot, damp afternoon, with angry flies buzzing at the screen. Another, illustrating "high sky," "back pack," and "snail trail," shows exhausted girls carrying heavy back packs hiking up a steep trail in the wake of a staunchly erect leader. These and other pages of montages and rhyming text are followed by an impressionistic painting showing thoroughly exhausted campers stretched out on the ground while their energetic leader moves ever onward. This sophisticated picture book should help those who have already been to camp to laugh at themselves in retrospect, or at least evoke a few memories, some of which they may or may not enjoy remembering. (It may also serve as fair warning for those who are about to go to camp in the not-too-distant future!)

It certainly calls for accomplished "reading" of illustrations and connecting them with what at first glance is obtuse or unrelated text.

48   Markun, Patricia Maloney

THE LITTLE PAINTER OF SABANA GRANDE   *5–9 YEARS*

Illustrated by Robert Casilla. New York: Bradbury, 1993

> The incident depicted in this picture book tells how a little boy who lived in a village in the remote Las Tablas province in Panama came to paint a mural on the outside of his family's home; the author actually traveled to the village to see the boy's decorated house. In this story Fernando Espino's teacher taught him how the country people of Panama made their own paints and gave him three paintbrushes, varying in size from very small to very large. He decided to spend his "dry-vacation" (when

ILLUSTRATION 14   Reprinted with the permission of Simon & Schuster Books for Young Readers from *The Little Painter of Sabana Grande* by Patricia Maloney Markun, illustrated by Robert Casilla. Illustrations copyright © 1993 Robert Casilla.

the schools are closed) painting, but when he was unable to find paper in his home or among his neighbors, he decided, with permission from his parents, to paint a mural on the outside of his house. Two styles of art are used in the double-spread illustrations in this credible picture story book; both provide an authentic sense of place especially in the content of the pictures, but also in the rich colors commonly found in the flora and fauna of this tropical country in Central America. Most of the pictures in this book are done in the impressionistic art style. However, usually in rather striking contrast to the impressionistic paintings, and sometimes mixed in with them, the pictures that Fernando paints on the outside of the house are suggestive of the style used in traditional Panamanian folk art; e.g., embroideries and decorations on pottery and wooden vessels. (See illustration 14, p. 71.)

49   Mathis, Sharon Bell

THE HUNDRED PENNY BOX   *8–12* YEARS

Illustrated by Leo and Diane Dillon. New York: Viking, 1975

This is a profusely illustrated short story rather than a picture book, but the ten full-page representational watercolor paintings are too exceptional and too much a part of this believable story to omit from this publication. Great-Great-Aunt Dew has a story to go with the year stamped on each of the one hundred pennies in her box, and Michael loves to hear her tell these stories. The conflict that arises because of Aunt Dew's presence in the house and Michael's mother's resolve to dispose of the old box and replace it with a new one make for a warm and touching story.

50   McBratney, Sam

GUESS HOW MUCH I LOVE YOU   *4–8* YEARS

Illustrated by Anita Jeram. Cambridge, Mass.:
Candlewick, 1995

Young readers are certain to enjoy the "guess-how-much-I-love-you" game Little Nutbrown Hare and his father Big Nutbrown Hare play at bedtime. In this game each one tries to top the other with the limitlessness of his affection. Little Nutbrown Hare's expressions of love for his father include as wide as his arms can reach, as high as he can hop, all the way up to his toes. His father says he loves him just the same, but because he is bigger than his son his love for him seems bigger. Big Nutbrown Hare's response to Little Nutbrown Hare's claim that he loves him right up to the moon will delight everyone. The animated pen-and-ink line sketches filled in with watercolor wash in full color highlight the vivacious and loving relationship depicted in this idyllic father-and-son story.

51   Mollel, Tololwa M.

BIG BOY   *5–9 YEARS*

Illustrated by E. B. Lewis. New York: Clarion, 1995

Oli wanted to go bird hunting with his older brother, but his mother told him he was too little and would have to take a nap instead. In response to his question as to when he would be big, she said "Only after many more naps. . . ." Alone in his room, he pulled out his slingshot and sneaked out of the house. As he walked through the woods, he heard the birds "talk" and "a million other sounds." He stopped when he saw an exquisite bird perched on a wild raspberry bush; it had a long twitchy tail and a striking silver wings. As Oli pulled out his slingshot, the bird hopped from one branch to another and finally perched on a branch of a huge baobab tree. Oli sat under the tree and rested and then climbed up the tree to get a closer look at the bird. When Oli got up close to the bird he realized it was Tunukia-zawadi, the bird he learned from his mother's suppertime stories had "bestowed upon wishes untold gifts and powers." When the bird asked him for his wish, Oli told the bird he wanted to be big. His wish was granted. Oli became a gigantic boy and the experiences he had in his new size were awesome; however, he learned in due time that being big has both benefits and disadvantages. Soon he was quite worn out from his escapades. He awoke in his mama's arms at the foot of the baobab tree and realized that his parents and brother had been searching the woods for him. He did not mind in the least when his mother strapped him to her back and carried him back to town. The double-spread watercolor paintings contain numerous details that situate this fantasy in modern rural Tanzania. More specifically, the clothes worn by the adults and children, the architecture, and the flora and fauna are typical of this contemporary rural area of East Africa. It is these details that make the fanciful aspects of this story seem all the more credible.

52   Moon, Nicola

LUCY'S PICTURE   *3–7 YEARS*

Illustrated by Alex Ayliffe. New York: Dial, 1994

In anticipation of her grandfather's visit, Lucy made a collage picture for him. The young readers of this picture book may be surprised to discover that Lucy's grandfather is blind, but they will soon realize that the multi-textured materials she used to make her picture were exactly the right choice, for he could "see" her picture by feeling it. The artwork for this book was created in collage and reproduced in bright, clear flat colors. The endpapers are worth bringing to students' attention, for they consist of many collage pictures created by children.

53   Myers, Walter Dean

BROWN ANGELS: AN ALBUM OF PICTURES AND VERSE   *ALL AGES*

Illustrated with photographs. New York: HarperCollins, 1993

>The turn-of-the-century photographs of African-American children in-cluded in this unique picture book are timeless and universal in their appeal and the statements they make about the beauty and innocence of children and hope for the future. Walter Dean Myers' poems dignify the occasions or the attitudes and stances which seem to be reflected in this wonderful collection of old photographs he collected over many years from antique shops, flea markets, auction houses, and museum collec-tions. For example, there are poems on friendship, prayer, laughter and joy, pride, and the delight of having a boy baby and a girl baby. What a wonderful way to glorify and exalt children and childhood!

54   Nerlove, Miriam

FLOWERS ON THE WALL   *5–9 YEARS*

Illustrated by Miriam Nerlove. New York:
Margaret K. McElderry Books/Simon & Schuster, 1966

>Miriam Nerlove was inspired to write and illustrate this absorbing and sad story after seeing a photograph taken by noted photographer Roman Vishniac on the eve of the Holocaust in Warsaw. A little girl was confined to her bed in a tiny unheated apartment; flowers were painted on the wall behind her bed. Rachel, the young protagonist in Nerlove's picture book, was perpetually hungry; she was weak and ill with a cold and confined to her bed because there was no heat in the one-room basement apartment she and her family occupied in the Jewish section of Warsaw, Poland, during the winter of 1938. Since Rachel wanted to be an artist when she grew up, her father gave her some paints and brushes to alleviate her boredom, but he was not able to get any paper for her. Rachel painted flowers on the walls of the apartment and soon the family's dismal living quarters became a place of beauty and provided some degree of comfort despite their fears when the Germans occupied Warsaw in 1939. Rachel and her family were sent to Treblinka, a concentration camp, and never seen or heard from again. As grim as this story is, the author/illustrator makes it acceptable for young children by emphasizing the family's focus on their dreams and hope for a happier, more secure future as well as their ability to create their own beauty with so little and find joy in that. The full-color and detailed expressionistic illustrations were rendered in watercolor; they add immeasurably to the poignancy and factual aspects of this exquisitely written text. Thus they might well help children, who are likely to be uninformed about the consequences and implications of this tragic historical event, establish a vivid and realistic sense of time, condition, and place germane to how one family, their friends, and neigh-bors were victimized by it. Compare *Flowers on the Wall* with the English

version of the classic *Anne Frank: The Diary of a Young Girl* (Viking, 1952) and *Child of the Warsaw Ghetto,* written by David A. Adler and illustrated by Karen Ritz (Holiday House, 1995).

55   Nunes, Susan Miho
THE LAST DRAGON   *5–8* YEARS
Illustrated by Chris K. Soenptiet. New York: Clarion, 1995

> While shopping for groceries with his great-aunt, who lived in Chinatown and with whom he was spending the summer, Peter noticed a dragon in a store window. The dragon was dusty, faded, ripped; its jaw was broken and it had no eyes, but it had a pearl on its forehead. With the help of talented and resourceful people in the neighborhood and Peter's willingness to repay them for their efforts with his friendship and by running errands for them, the dragon is restored to its original splendor. The careful observer of the detailed watercolor paintings that spill over each double-page spread will discover a wealth of information about aspects of Chinese culture and traditions such as food, clothing, crafts, celebrations, games, and, of course, the Chinese dragons, recognized as a force for good.

56   Oppenheim, Shulamith L.
FIREFLIES FOR NATHAN   *5–8* YEARS
Illustrated by John Ward. New York: Tambourine, 1994

> While six-year-old Nathan is visiting his paternal grandparents during the summer, they help him catch fireflies in a jar just as they did many years before with his father when he was a child. Nathan is delighted to learn that catching fireflies was his father's favorite thing to do when he was six, and that not only is he putting them in the very same jar his father used, but just like Nathan, his father had asked his parents to let the fireflies out of the jar just as soon as he was asleep. Ward's accomplished impressionistic paintings, executed with acrylic on canvas, highlight the love and gentle affection the members of this African-American family feel for each other as well as their uninhibited delight with and appreciation of the natural beauty of their surroundings. The scenes of the countryside at different times of the day and night are also noteworthy. Besides being a wholesome family story, *Fireflies for Nathan* is a fine example of a "mood" book, and that mood is serenity. Compare the family relationships and the overall mood in this book, the author's style and use of language, and the illustrator's techniques and style with those used in *When I Go Camping with Grandma,* written by Marion Dane Bauer and illustrated by Allen Garns (BridgeWater/Troll, 1995); *Dawn,* written and illustrated by Uri Shulevitz (Farrar Straus & Giroux, 1974), and *Ten Flashing Fireflies,* written by Philemon Sturges and illustrated by Ann

Vojtech (North-South Books, 1995). Eric Carle's *The Very Lonely Firefly* (Philomel, 1995) would serve as another delightful supplementary source.

57   Ormerod, Jan

101 THINGS TO DO WITH A BABY   *3–7 YEARS*

Illustrated by Jan Ormerod. New York:
Lothrop, Lee & Shepard, 1986

Brief text (mostly captions) and over one hundred watercolor pictures of assorted sizes and shapes arranged in varied ways on the pages alert a six-year-old girl (and young readers!) to one hundred and one things one can do with a new baby in the family.

58   Oxenbury, Helen

PLAYING   *6 MONTHS–2 YEARS*

Illustrated by Helen Oxenbury. New York:
Simon & Schuster, 1991

On each left-hand page a single, simple word labels a toy or object an infant or toddler is likely to enjoy playing with; on the right-hand page facing each labeled picture, a unisex child is shown playing with that object, be it blocks, a box, ball, wagon, or teddy bear. Typical of Oxenbury's books for the youngest audience, the line-and-wash illustrations are plain, easily recognizable, and lighthearted. Other board books in this series focusing on babies engaging in ordinary activities are *Dressing, Family, Friends,* and *Working.* These same titles are available in boxed sets of four tiny board books, 3⅛″ × 3¼″. Four other books by Oxenbury, namely *All Fall Down, Clap Hands, Say Good Night,* and *Tickle, Tickle* comprise another boxed set of four miniature board books (3⅛″ × 3¼″) about babies' activities (Simon & Schuster, 1995).

59   Paek, Min

AEKYUNG'S DREAM   *5–9 YEARS*

Rev. ed., translated from Korean by Min Paek. Illustrated by
Min Paek. San Francisco: Children's Book Press, 1988

Having lived in America only six months, Korean-born Aekyung was self-conscious about her inability to speak English very well. She was also reluctant to go to school because her classmates teased her about her "Chinese" eyes. Inspired by a dream about the beloved Korean King Syong of the fifteenth-century Yi Dynasty, she grew more determined to learn to speak English better, make friends with her classmates, and make use of her own talents and individuality, especially her cultural heritage. She gradually adjusted to her new country and to her new friends. Illustrated with simple pen-and-ink line and clear brightly colored overlays, the text of this convincing story about a child's adjustment to a new country and new culture is presented in hand-written English lettering and Korean calligraphy. This is a fine story to use with immigrants as well as with native-born Americans. Compare and contrast the immigrant child's experience in *Aekyung's Dream* with *Molly's Pilgrim,* written by Barbara Cohen and illustrated by Michael J. Deraney (Lothrop, Lee & Shepard, 1983).

60   Pilkey, Dav

THE PAPERBOY   *4–8* YEARS

Illustrated by Dav Pilkey. New York: Orchard, 1996

> What a nice tribute to those who deliver the newspaper to our home each day regardless of the weather! The full-color expressionistic pictures, done in acrylics and India ink, create an authentic tone and feeling for what it must be like for this child and his dog to get up out of a nice warm bed very early in the morning while it is still dark outside and deliver the newspapers to his customers, most of whom are still sound asleep. The gradual awakening of the dawn as the paperboy comes to the end of his route is effectively handled by the illustrator. (See illustration 15.) Compare with *Paperboy,* written by Kay Kroeger and Louise Borden and illustrated by Ted Lewin (Clarion, 1996).

61   Plotz, Helen, *Compiler*

A WEEK OF LULLABIES   *3–6* YEARS

Illustrated by Marisabina Russo. New York: Greenwillow, 1988

> Fourteen stylized gouache paintings in bright full color illustrate the same number of poems—lullabies and bedtime poems by such authors as Elizabeth Coatsworth, Nikki Giovanni, Gwendolyn Brooks, and Elizabeth Shub. The poems are grouped by days of the week.

62   Ransome, Candice F.

WHEN THE WHIPPOORWILL CALLS   *6–8* YEARS

Illustrated by Kimberly Bulcken Root. New York:
Tambourine, 1995

> Polly's father told her that, "Sometimes . . . change is good." It took a while before Polly and even her parents realized that her father was quite right. At first no one in this family was happy that an eighty-mile length of woods and streams in the midst of the Blue Ridge Mountains of Virginia was going to be set aside for the Shenandoah National Park. They knew a National Park would attract many people to their beloved

ILLUSTRATION 15 From *The Paperboy* by Dav Pilkey. Illustration copyright © 1996 by Dav Pilkey. Reprinted by permission of Orchard Books, New York.

wilderness. More important, they knew they would have to move to a new home in the valley, for the home they rented and the land they farmed were within the boundaries of the new park. They were soon delighted with the conveniences they now had in their new home. At first the open fields and scattering of trees that were in these flatlands bothered their eyes. Although they could see their beloved mountain from their kitchen window, it looked distant and strange, and they missed hearing the whippoorwill. When Polly and her father walked back up to their mountain, they saw that a new road was being built, briars had taken over the apple orchard, and wisteria was hanging over their cabin doorway. They found some merkles growing in their abandoned orchard and picked a bagful of this tasty brown mushroom that Pap said was "the mountain's secret treasure." When they heard the first whippoorwill Polly turned a perfect somersault as she always did; she did not have to make a wish on it for she knew her wish that the mountain would be theirs again had already come true, if only for a little while. The watercolor paintings, some of them full page and some of them double-page spreads, capture the natural beauty of this region and depict so very well the sereneness, isolation, and hardships the impoverished rural mountain families experienced in the 1930s (and to some extent still do today). The illustrator has captured the effects of the different shades, lights, and shadows that seem to prevail during each season of the year and the array of colors indicative of sunsets and sunrises in the mountains.

63   Rathmann, Peggy

OFFICER BUCKLE AND GLORIA   *4–9* YEARS

Illustrated by Peggy Rathmann. New York: Putnam, 1995

Officer Buckle went to schools to talk to the children about some safety tips they should keep in mind. To his dismay no one listened to him, not even the principal. When he brought his police dog Gloria along with him, the children sat up and listened. When he realized that Gloria was upstaging him, he decided he would no longer do school visits. Instead, another officer took the dog to the school so she could demonstrate the recommended safety tips. The sequence of events that follows is bound to delight the young readers. Be certain to notice that on back and front endpapers there are twenty-eight other safety tips. This amusing but thought-provoking tale, illustrated with action-filled, cartoon-style drawings done with ink line and vibrant full-color wash, was named the 1996 Caldecott Award Medal winner.

64   Ringgold, Faith

DINNER AT AUNT CONNIE'S HOUSE   *8–10+* YEARS

Illustrated by Faith Ringgold. New York: Hyperion, 1993

In this book the readers learn that Aunt Connie has two surprises for her dinner guests: one, she and her husband have adopted a son named Lonnie and two, she has painted twelve portraits of famous African-American women, namely Rosa Parks, Fannie Lou Hamer, Mary McCleod Bethune, Augusta Savage, Dorothy Dandridge, Zora Neale Hurston, Maria W. Stewart, Bessie Smith, Harriet Tubman, Sojourner Truth, Marian Anderson, and Madame C. J. Walker. These women, known for their courage, vision, and creativity, have made great contributions to American history. Each woman talks briefly to Lonnie and his cousin Melody, two young characters in this very special picture book, about her courageous life. The illustrations in this book are done in the naive art style. *Dinner at Aunt Connie's House* was inspired by this award-winning author/artist's painted story quilt entitled "The Dinner Quilt," a piece of art in which she combined storytelling and paintings on quilted canvas.

65   Ringgold, Faith

TAR BEACH   *8–10+ YEARS*

Illustrated by Faith Ringgold. New York: Hyperion, 1991

Part autobiographical and part fictional, the story of this outstanding picture book is about an eight-year-old African-American girl who, with her family and neighborhood friends, cools off on the tar-paper roof and dreams of flying above her tenement home in Harlem, declaring that she and her family are free to go wherever they wish and be employed in jobs for which they qualify regardless of their race. A number of African-American cultural and historical references appear in the precise text and naive-style illustrations. *Tar Beach* received both the 1992 Caldecott Medal Award and the Coretta Scott King Award for Illustrations. The illustrations are full-color reproductions of Ringgold's story quilt of the same name, and which inspired this book.

66   Roche, Hannah

MY MOM IS MAGIC!   *3–7 YEARS*

Illustrated by Chris Fisher. New York: De Agostini, 1996

Jamie watches her mom turn egg whites into fluffy meringues that become a "yummy and sugary" dessert, crisp on the outside and sticky inside. Included at the end of the book are "Notes for Parents" which suggest ways to help children observe and learn more about the ingredients and what happens to them during the process of mixing and baking them. Perhaps best of all is the easy-to-follow recipe which the child with a parent or other responsible older person might prepare. The cartoon-style ink-line and crosshatch sketches colored with clean watercolor wash reflect the fun and togetherness mother, child, and the family's pet dog have as they prepare and then consume this dessert. Also in this series by Roche and Fisher is *My Dad's a Wizard!* (De Agostini, 1996). Dad's dessert (a striped ice cream bombe) involves more steps and takes a bit longer before it is ready to be eaten; fortunately, it is quite easy to prepare. As in *My Mom Is Magic!,* "Notes for Parents" and a recipe are included at the end of this book.

67   Rogers, Jean
RUNAWAY MITTENS   *4–6* YEARS
Illustrated by Rie Munoz. New York: Greenwillow, 1988

A truly believable saga of the varied places a little boy manages to lose (and find!) the new red mittens that his grandmother made especially for him. The brightly colored and simply shaped figures in the paintings that so effectively illustrate this story of people braving the arctic cold are strongly suggestive of the Inuit (Alaskan) felt appliques and drawings.

68   Rounds, Glen
ONCE WE HAD A HORSE   *5–9* YEARS
Illustrated by Glen Rounds. New York: Holiday House,
1971, 1996

Expressive and humorous sketches, done in ink-line and full-color pastel sketches characteristic of this popular author/illustrator, combined with an easy-to-read text (revised), detail several children's attempts to learn how to ride a gentle horse that was left in the yard of their Montana ranch house.

69   Say, Allen
GRANDFATHER'S JOURNEY   *6–10* YEARS
Illustrated by Allen Say. Boston: Houghton Mifflin, 1993

Awarded the 1994 Caldecott Award Medal, the watercolor paintings Say created for *Grandfather's Journey* are so precise and realistic they look like photographs a family collected to document their intercultural experiences as they traveled back and forth from Japan to the United States. Each traveler loves both countries, and each in his own way and for his own reasons wants to be in both places at the same time. I would recommend reading the companion picture book, *Tree of Cranes,* written and illustrated by Allen Say (Houghton Mifflin, 1991), after reading *Grandfather's Journey.* In *Tree of Cranes,* a Japanese boy learns about the Western Christmas tradition of decorating a pine tree as his California-born mother decorates a pine tree with paper cranes and candles. The boy in *Tree of Cranes* represents Allen Say himself and the American-born woman denotes his own mother. Say, who serves as the narrator of *Grand-father's Journey,* also depicted himself as a child visiting his maternal grandfather and again as a young man before moving to California. The female child pictured in this book as an infant, at different stages of childhood years, and finally as a young adult represents Allen Say's mother before she and her parents moved permanently to Japan.

70   Say, Allen

STRANGER IN THE MIRROR   *10–14* YEARS

Illustrated by Allen Say. Boston: Walter Lorraine/
Houghton Mifflin, 1995

> The exquisitely detailed full-page illustrations, so realistic they appear at first glance to be full-color photographs, are a perfect match for this sophisticated, heavily psychological surrealistic story about a boy's response to the sudden disappearance of his very elderly grandfather. (Presumably to a nursing home?) Sam did not want to get old like his grandfather: white hair, deeply wrinkled face, raspy voice, shuffling walk, small and frail. But the morning after his grandfather's unexpected and unexplained departure, the image he saw of himself reflected in the mirror was that of his grandfather. Even though he looked old on the outside, he felt young and full of energy on the inside and Say's picture of the boy on a skateboard and the verbal description of him doing kick-flips, heel-flips, nose-slides, tail-slides, and rail-slides most aptly demonstrate the boy's agility and energy. Implications and innuendoes abound in this unusual picture book and offer mind-jarring topics to think about and discuss; e.g., a family's reaction to placing an elderly relative in a nursing home, how images of self are influenced by how we think significant others see us, society's images and expectations of the elderly, reactions to the visible physical differences among people. (See illustration 16.)

71   Schertle, Alice

DOWN THE ROAD   *5–8* YEARS

Illustrated by E. B. Lewis. San Diego: Browndeer/
Harcourt Brace, 1995

> This story of the very first time Hetty went to the local emporium and dry goods store alone to buy a dozen fresh eggs, but managed to bring home a basket filled with sweet red apples instead, will probably cause many children to wonder if their parents would respond the same way to them as Hetty's mom and dad did to her. The oversized full-color impressionist paintings highlight the love and sense of trust this family seems to have for one another as well as their apparent feeling of being at peace with the beauty and serenity of the countryside that surrounds them.

72   Schwartz, Lynne Sharon
THE FOUR QUESTIONS   *5–10+ YEARS*

Hebrew calligraphy by Lilli Wronker. Illustrations
by Ori Sherman. New York: Dial, 1989

> The four questions that begin the Seder are the focus of this picture-book explanation of the Passover traditions and its celebration of freedom.

Hebrew typography highlights what is told in art and pictures. The animal figures in each of the full-color, split-frame illustrations are suggestive of the techniques used in medieval Haggadahs to avoid the biblical proscription against creating images. The last illustration depicts the Order of the Passover Seder in twelve pictures. Turn the book upside down to get a better view of the Hebrew calligraphy and the split-frame pictures. The gouache paintings are filled with the symbols and rituals of this major Jewish holiday; each picture offers a talented blend of the traditional and the innovative.

73   Shaw-MacKinnon, Margaret

TIKTALA   *6–10* YEARS

Illustrations by László Gál. New York: Holiday House, 1996

The Inuit soapstone carvers are disheartened and alarmed that the new generation of carvers, talented and skilled as they are, seem to be motivated more by the desire to sell their work for high prices than by concern for the animal spirits that enter the stones. The elders of this community in the Far North called a meeting to discuss this problem. When Iguptak, the wisest woman in the village and the leader of the meeting, asked who among the young people present were willing to learn the secrets of the old carvers, Tiktala volunteered. Tiktala aspired to be a famous, admired, and rich soapstone carver and thus gain the attention of her despondent father. What she learned about the spirit of the harp seal (the animal she wanted to make) and how she learned it amount to a fascinating story and provide an insight into the traditions and values of the Inuit soapstone carvers. The beautifully crafted text by a talented Canadian author is enhanced by first-rate paintings by an award-winning Canadian artist. Together the text and the illustrations provide a thoroughly involving story that is marked by a strong sense of place and several timely, thought-provoking themes for children and adults.

74   Shea, Pegi Deitz

THE WHISPERING CLOTH: A REFUGEE'S STORY   *5–10* YEARS

Illustrated by Anita Riggio. Stitched by You Yang.
Honesdale, Pa.: Boyds Mills, 1995

Little Mai, her grandmother, and many other Hmong refugees are confined in a refugee camp in Thailand while they wait to find a country that will accept them. Aspects of the refugees' life in the camp are depicted in expressive, realistic watercolor paintings. Especially poignant, yet without undue sentimentality, are the paintings that portray Mai and her grandmother together. Their fondness and respect for each other are evident in several scenes that show Grandmother teaching Mai how to embroider so she can help make the embroidered tapestries (pa'ndaus) that tell their life stories and which they sell to the Chiang Khan traders, and thereby earn the money they need to emigrate to a new country, Grandmother rubbing Mai's hands when her fingers get cramped after stitching meticulously and too long, and Grandmother comforting Mai by telling her to call her parents' spirits with the words in her fingers when she recalls how they were killed during a bombing. When Mai is ready to make her own pa'ndau, she embroiders the story of her life, narrating the most memorable aspects of her past, present, and future. The embroidered figures that tell Mai's story are absolutely true to the traditional Hmong folk style of stitching. This is a wrenching story for children and adults. Whatever the age of the reader, he or she is bound to hope that Mai and her grandmother will indeed realize the future that Mai has portrayed so convincingly in her pa'ndau.

75   Sisulu, Elinor Batezat

THE DAY GOGO WENT TO VOTE: SOUTH AFRICA,   *5–9* YEARS
APRIL 1994

Illustrated by Sharon Wilson. Boston: Little, Brown, 1996

Everything about this picture book reflects the joyous celebration that resulted from the long-awaited decision to allow black South Africans to vote for the first time in their history. The text clearly describes the determination, delight, and pride a fragile one-hundred-year-old woman, her family, and friends felt when they went to the polling booth, followed the required validating and screening procedures, and finally cast their secret ballots in April 1994. The large, full-color, impressionistic illustrations, done in pastels on sanded board, personalize and humanize this memorable occasion. Several themes are artistically put forth in this beautiful picture book. Worthy of note are the themes focusing on the strength and courage of the South African people and the faith in the future held by its citizens, especially those who are members of the black community. Immediately after a one-hundred-year-old woman voted, a newspaper reporter photographed her and Thembi, her six-year-old great-granddaughter who accompanied the old woman (whom she called Gogo) to the polling booth. The expressions on the old woman's face, revealing her delight in finally being able to vote and the child's obvious pleasure over her great grandmother's happiness, are clearly evident in his photograph of them. Thembi and Gogo are ecstatic when they see their picture in the newspaper and they agree most enthusiastically with the implications of the caption the reporter wrote over the picture: "The past and the future."

76   Smalls, Irene

LOUISE'S GIFT, OR WHAT DID SHE GIVE ME THAT FOR?   *5–9* YEARS

Illustrated by Colin Bootman. Boston: Little, Brown, 1996

It was traditional for Louise's kin to present new babies at a party to the eldest member for formal welcome into the family, so her cousin Kevin was presented to Nana, for she was the eldest. The people in this large extended family believed the eldest to be so wise she could look into a child's eyes and view his or her soul and future. On the day Kevin was welcomed into the family, Nana gave each of the children a special gift and a saying about their future. Louise was devastated and confused and angry with the present Nana gave her—a rumpled and blank piece of paper on which she could put whatever she wished. As the story progresses, Louise responds in a very special way to situations her age-mates and adults find themselves in. If the readers heed Louise's responses to these situations, they will grasp the significance of Nana's gift to Louise before Louise does. The expressive realistic illustrations, done in full color, artfully reinforce and extend the credibility of this fine story.

77   Sneve, Virginia Driving Hawk

THE CHEROKEES   *8–12* YEARS

Illustrated by Ronald Himler. New York: Holiday House, 1996

One of the First Americans Book series, *The Cherokees* provides young readers with a thought-provoking introduction to the a variety of aspects of the Cherokee people's traditional tribal structure, the major stages of their history, and the factors that tended to shape this history, their arts and crafts and ceremonies, and their situation today. The author's technique of initiating her overview of the different stages of the Cherokees' history with a retelling of their creation myth tends to dramatize both the similarity and the differences of the story of their origins compared to those of other races and nationalities. Himler's full-color paintings embellish and clarify quite aptly the historical and cultural aspects touched upon in the text. The map at the beginning of the book showing where the Cherokee tribe lived during the different stages of its history, the index at the back of the book, and the acknowledgments of sources for the poems and quotations used throughout this very well-written informational book should prove helpful. Five other books in this series written by Sneve and illustrated by Himler were published by Holiday House: *The Iroquois* (1995), *The Navajos* (1993), *The Nez Percé* (1994), *The Seminoles* (1994), and *The Sioux* (1993).

78   Sneve, Virginia Driving Hawk, *Selector*

DANCING TEEPEES: POEMS OF AMERICAN   *6–12+* YEARS
INDIAN YOUTH

Translated from Indian languages. Illustrated by
Stephen Gammell, New York: Holiday House, 1989

The songs, stories, chants, lullabies, and prayers in this book were selected from the oral tradition of numerous North American Indians as well as from anthologies by contemporary tribal poets. The collections reflect the theme of youth and their rites of passage from birth through adolescence. The illustrations are suggestive of the designs found in work by such tribes as the Navaho, Sioux, Crow, Wintu, Apache, and Osage.

79   Stolz, Mary
STORM IN THE NIGHT   *4–7* YEARS
Illustrated by Pat Cummings. New York: HarperCollins, 1988

In the darkness during a power outage caused by a thunder-and-lightning storm a black grandfather tells his young grandson about his experiences during a frightening storm when he was a child. The realistic gouache paintings in luminous full color highlight the mood of this intimate story and help one see the often unappreciated beauty offered by the flashes and slashes of lightning, the sounds of the wind and rain, or the scents of the rain-soaked garden soil. Compare and contrast the language, illustrations, and mood of this book with those in *Tornado* by Arnold Adoff (Delacorte, 1977) and *Thunderstorm* by Mary Szilagyi (Bradbury, 1985).

80   Thomas, Jane Resh
LIGHTS ON THE RIVER   *5–10* YEARS
Illustrated by Michael Dooling. New York: Hyperion, 1994

This book offers a sensitive portrayal of the cultural traditions and values held by a Mexican-American family working as seasonal migrant workers. The competently crafted text coupled with the insightful pictorial images found in the accomplished full-color impressionistic paintings results in thoroughly convincing and wrenching comments about the hardships and maltreatment migrant workers often experienced in the past and, to a large extent, continue to experience to this day.

81   Turner, Robyn Montana
FAITH RINGGOLD   *8–12+* YEARS
Illustrated with photographs in full color and
black-and-white. Boston: Little, Brown, 1993

This is a picture book biography of Faith Ringgold, the accomplished author and artist. Like all of the others in the Portraits of Women Artists for Children series, this biography is short, but fairly comprehensive. Many of Ringgold's story quilts are commented upon quite aptly and are reproduced in full color. Unfortunately, Faith Ringgold's artistic accomplishments discussed in this biography do not include the picture books inspired by her story quilts, namely, *Tar Beach* (Crown, 1991), *Aunt Harriet's Underground Railroad* (Crown, 1992), and *Dinner at Aunt Connie's House* (Hyperion, 1993). What Turner did emphasize about Ringgold's approach to story quilts [which I think applies equally to the picture books inspired by them], is that the stories on Ringgold's quilts are dilemma tales; that is to say, they present problems without solutions. In this way, she follows an African tradition in which the storyteller does not make judgments; instead, she leaves the audience with questions that might have many answers (p. 20). The illustrations in this picture book are full-color reproductions of Ringgold's story quilts. Another good source for biographical information about Faith Ringgold and her artistic accomplishments is *Talking with Faith Ringgold* by Faith Ringgold, Linda Freeman, and Nancy Roucher (Crown, 1996). This book is also illustrated with photographs in full color and black-and-white. Unlike the biography by Turner, the tone of this book is more informal and it is more child-oriented in that it offers directly to the child readers (7–12+ years) some suggestions for thought-provoking and educationally sound art activities. Included in *Talking with Faith Ringgold* are an index and separate bibliographies of her children's books, videos about Faith Ringgold, works by her housed in museums and public collections, and art works by her discussed in this book. Compare Faith Ringgold's approach to making story quilts with those created by Harriet Powers, discussed by Mary E. Lyons in *Stitching Stars: The Story Quilts of Harriet Powers* (Scribner, 1993).

82   Uchida, Yoshiko, *Reteller*

THE WISE OLD WOMAN   *5–9 YEARS*

Illustrated by Martin Springett. New York:
Margaret K. McElderry/Macmillan, 1994

> The expressive, richly hued airbrush-and-ink paintings are strongly suggestive of traditional Japanese woodcut prints and effectively capture the mood and setting of this forthright tale of how an elderly woman, whom the cruel young lord of the village considered no longer useful because of her advanced age, completed three tasks the six wisest men of village were unable to figure out. The woman demonstrated how one could make a coil of rope out of ashes, run a single thread through the length of a crooked log, and make a drum that sounds without being beaten, and she saved her small village from being conquered by the overlord of the region. She also convinced the young lord that old people should be treated with respect and honor and be allowed to share the wisdom of their years with those younger than themselves instead of being sent into the mountains and left to die.

83   Weidt, Maryann

DADDY PLAYED MUSIC FOR THE COWS   *4–8* YEARS

Illustrated by Henri Sorensen. New York:
Lothrop, Lee & Shepard, 1995

>This book is quite like a picture album documenting a little girl's growth from early infancy through preteen years and her relationships with her father as he attends to his farm chores, usually with a radio nearby playing the country music he loves to listen to, hum or sing along, or dance to. The easy-to-read text printed in large type and the double-spread realistic paintings in bright clean colors add to the upbeat mood that pervades this story about a wholesome and congenial rural American family.

84   Wells, Rosemary

EDWARD'S OVERWHELMING NIGHT   *3–6* YEARS

Illustrated by Rosemary Wells. New York: Dial, 1995

>Edward is a timid little bear who, in every way, acts and thinks like a human being. When he is invited to go to his friend Anthony's house and play, Edward's mother accepts the invitation for him. Assured twice by his parents that they will come for him soon, he goes over to Anthony's house quite willingly. When it starts to snow, he enjoys making a snowman with Anthony, but when his mother phones to tell him that he will have to spend the night at his friend's home because the snow is too deep for his parents to drive over to pick him up, Edward is utterly disconcerted and inconsolable. Children are bound to understand, even perhaps empathize with him, and most assuredly they, like Edward, will be delighted at the end of the story, when his parents figure out a way to get him back home. Edward and his parents agree that no one in this close-knit family is quite ready for Edward to spend the night away from home. Rosemary Wells' ink drawing with watercolor paintings express so cleverly Edward's vast variety and range of emotions, be they apprehension, dismay, fear, devastation, contentment, self-satisfaction, or pleasure. Other titles in Wells' Edward, the Unready series are *Edward in Deep Water* and *Edward Unready for School* (Dial, 1995).

85   Wells, Rosemary

MAX'S DRAGON SHIRT   *5–7* YEARS

Illustrated by Rosemary Wells. New York: Dial, 1991

>Max, a clever little rabbit, and his sister Ruby go shopping for a new pair of pants for Max. How he manages to convince her to buy him a green dragon shirt instead will intrigue and humor young readers as will the wonderfully expressive line and full-color watercolor-wash cartoon illustrations. (See illustration 17.) There are many other stories about Max,

ILLUSTRATION 17   From *Max's Dragon Shirt* by Rosemary Wells. Copyright © 1991 by Rosemary Wells. Used by permission of Dial Books for Young Readers, a division of Penguin Books. USA.

including *Max and Ruby's First Greek Myth: Pandora's Box* (Dial, 1993); *Max's Chocolate Chicken* (Dial, 1989); and *Max's Christmas* (Dial, 1986).

86   Williams, Vera B.

MUSIC, MUSIC FOR EVERYONE   *4–8 YEARS*

Illustrated by Vera B. Williams. New York: Greenwillow, 1983

At first Rosa played her accordion to entertain her grandmother who was sick and had to stay upstairs in bed, but soon her friends Leora, Moe, and Jenny joined her in making music for grandmother. The four girls decided to form a combo which they called the "Oak Street Band," and Rosa saved her share of the money the band earned to help her mother pay for the expenses incurred in caring for her grandmother. Each of the expressionistic watercolor illustrations is framed and each frame is fashioned from the story elements contained in the illustrations. The details in the illustrations provide a superb sense of place as well as a definite personality and sociology to Rosa, her family, friends, and community. *Music, Music for Everyone* follows two other books about these same people written and illustrated by Vera B. Williams; they are *A Chair for My Mother* (Greenwillow, 1982), winner of both the 1983 Caldecott Honor Award and the 1983 Boston Globe-Horn Book Award for Illustration, and *Something Special for Me* (Greenwillow, 1983).

87 Wyeth, Sharon Dennis

ALWAYS MY DAD   *5–8* YEARS

Illustrated by Raúl Colón. New York: Apple Soup/Knopf, 1995

Feelings of any kind are hard for children (and adults) to understand and almost impossible to verbalize, especially feelings of separation. Through the use of narration and dialogue the author of *Always My Dad* informs the reader about the children's father; e.g., he has worked at a variety of jobs over the years, he is having a problem getting his life together, he does indeed love them, he is and always will be their dad. Illustrations in this book depict much more concretely than the text does the range of feelings the children and their father have for each other. The full-color expressionistic illustrations are done in watercolor, charcoal, colored pencils, and lithograph pencils, and are etched with crosshatchings to give added dimensions to the figures and depict the effects of light and shadows on them. They enhance the range of emotions the little girl and her three brothers feel when their father is away and when they are together during his all-too-brief visits.

88 Yolen, Jane

THE GIRL WHO LOVED THE WIND   *5–9* YEARS

Illustrated by Ed Young. New York: Crowell, 1972

A stunning array of refined Persian miniatures skillfully reflect and extend the content, mood, and writing style in this thought-provoking Oriental tale of a king who wished to protect his beautiful daughter from the harsh realities of life. A literary gem in every respect.

Other People

*T*he picture books in this section are about accomplishments and experiences of individuals who actually lived or might have lived in times past, who actually experienced or might have experienced significant historical events or conditions.

89   Adler, David A.

CHILD OF THE WARSAW GHETTO   *8–11* YEARS

Illustrated by Karen Ritz. New York: Holiday House, 1995

> The text and the illustrations are printed on gray paper, emphasizing the
> grimness of this true story about Froim (Erwin) Baum, a Polish Jew born
> in Warsaw on April 15, 1926, an amazing survivor! Froim survived both
> the Great Depression of Poland, which began in 1929, and the Nazi oc-
> cupation of Poland during World War II. Around March 1938 Froim en-
> tered the famous Janusz Korczak Orphan's House, which was located on
> Krochmalna Street and later moved to a school within the Warsaw
> Ghetto. On the morning of August 6, 1942, Dr. Korczak and the children
> were taken from the orphanage and sent to Treblinka, a Nazi death camp;
> Froim was not among them, for he had spent the previous night with his
> mother. In November 1942, Froim and his family were captured and
> taken to Auschwitz. He was sent to several other death camps; when the
> war ended, Froim was in Dachau and was liberated by the American sol-
> diers. He lived for a while in Munich where his name was changed to
> Erwin, was reunited with two of his brothers in 1947, and after living in
> Belgium, Luxembourg, Israel, and Canada, he settled in the United States
> in the early 1950s. The illustrations appear to be done in black grease
> pencil and pastels, but whatever media the artist did use to create them,
> she made excellent use of crosshatching and soft tones of blue, yellow
> red, olive green, and brown in her illustrations to emphasize the horrors
> experienced by Froim, his family, and other Polish Jews during the Nazi
> occupation of Poland.

90   Anderson, Joan

JOSHUA'S WESTWARD JOURNEY   *5–10* YEARS

Illustrated with photographs by George Ancona. New York:
Morrow, 1987

> In 1836, young Joshua Carpenter and his family traveled westward on the
> National Road in their horse-drawn Conestoga wagon, leaving their home
> in Indianapolis to make a new home. The black-and-white photographs
> add more vivid details to Joshusa's fact-filled journal, and thus foster a
> greater degree of appreciation and understanding of this family's coura-
> geous, challenging, and sometimes frightening trip to their new home, a
> small town in Illinois.

91   Brent, Isabelle

NOAH'S ARK   *4–9* YEARS

Illustrated by Isabelle Brent. Boston: Little, Brown, 1992

> This well-known story of Noah, who was chosen by God to build an ark so that he, his family, and the innocent creatures of the world could escape the Great Flood, is a brief and simple retelling of the text of the Revised English Bible. Full-page, romanticized and fanciful paintings of Noah and his wife, his sons and their wives, and all the animals, insects, and birds are in gold leaf and jewel-like colors. Each picture is framed in precise and ornate geometrical patterns suggestive of those found in medieval illuminated manuscripts.

92   Brodsky, Beverly, *Reteller*

THE STORY OF JOB   *7–11+* YEARS

Illustrated by Beverly Brodsky. New York: George Braziller, 1986

> This retelling of the Old Testament story of how God tests Job's faith by letting terrible misfortunes happen to him is a very special picture book! The text for this accomplished piece of writing is illustrated with dramatic and absolutely remarkable expressionistic pictures done in ink and vivid full-color wash. Another *fait accompli* by this award-winning author/artist!

93   Bruchac, Joseph

A BOY CALLED SLOW: THE TRUE STORY   *7–9* YEARS
OF SITTING BULL

Illustrated by Rocco Baviera. New York: Philomel, 1994

> In this partial biography of Sitting Bull, Bruchac focuses on what the great hero from the Hunkpapapa band Lakota Sioux did to warrant having his childhood name *Slon-he,* which in English means "Slow," changed to *Tatan'ka Iyota'ke,* which in English means "Sitting Bull." As a toddler he was named Slow because his every action was slow; by the time he was about seven the name Slow alluded to the fact he was careful and deliberate, and by age ten Slow connoted his determination and courage. When he was fourteen and old enough to join his father and some other men in a battle against the Crow, Slow mounted his horse, raced past all of the men in his war party, and charged down the hill toward the Crow warriors. One of the Crow warriors who was in the lead drew an arrow to his bowstring, but Slow struck the warrior's arm with his coup stick, causing him to lose his aim. The Crow fighters turned back when they saw Slow and the other Lakota warriors. Because of the youth's quick and

brave action the raid was a success, no one was injured, and the Lakota Sioux warriors brought back many of the Crow's fine horses and weapons. In recognition of his bravery and determination, his father declared that he was no longer to be called Slon-he, he was to be called by his father's name Tatan'ka Iyota'ke, or Sitting Bull, the name by which most of us have come to know him. The full-color paintings are done on a coarse canvas and many of the animals are drawn in the traditional style that the Sioux and other Plains Indians drew on their lodges (teepees). Individually each picture is quite striking, but because so many of the scenes take place at twilight or around sunset or late at night, the overall effect is somber. Unfortunately, most of these pictures of the nighttime activities of the Lakota Sioux suggest that they were continually on their way to fight a battle, engaging in one, or returning from one. Admittedly, wars are mentioned often in this short biographical sketch and the narrator does indicate they took place at night, but there were also a number of situations in which Slow or the other members of his band were involved which occurred or could have occurred during daylight hours.

94   Coerr, Eleanor

SADAKO   *7–10* YEARS

Illustrated by Ed Young. New York: Putnam, 1993

Ed Young's impressionistic pastel paintings add an immeasurable depth of feeling in response to this true story of the courage and strength twelve-year-old Sadako Sasaki (1943–1955) demonstrated in her struggle against "the atom-bomb disease" (leukemia), which she developed ten years after she was exposed to the radiation rays during the bombing of Hiroshima. Eleanor Coerr wrote the classic transitional novel *Sadako and a Thousand Paper Cranes,* originally illustrated by Ronald Himler (Putnam, 1977). She also wrote a new text about Sadako's story for this picture-book version which is illustrated by Ed Young with pastel paintings selected from nearly three hundred paintings he created for the thirty-minute award-winning video (also a 16 mm film) version entitled *Sadako and the Thousand Paper Cranes.* The reading of this picture book, paired with the video that inspired it, provides an unforgettable and quality literary experience for children. Without undue sensationalism, but with controlled honest realism, children and adults are helped to understand more fully the tragic consequences of exposure to radiation and to appreciate the significance of the Japanese legend which holds that if a person who is ill makes a thousand paper cranes, the gods will grant that person's wish to be well again. (In addition to being illustrated with Ed Young's striking paintings, this video is narrated by Liv Ullmann, accompanied with solo guitar music by George Winston, directed and produced by George Levenson; it is distributed by Informed Democracy of Santa Cruz, Calif.) Teachers and librarians may want to read the biography *Children of the Paper Crane: The Story of Sadako Sasaki and Her*

Struggle with the A-Bomb Disease, written by Masamoto Nasu and translated by Elizabeth W. Baldwin, Steven L. Leeper, and Kyoko Yoshida (Armonk, N.Y.: Sharpe, 1991) and share with their students some of its substantive information about Sadako, the members of her family, her classmates, and how through her courageous battle against the disease, she turned paper cranes into an international symbol of peace and became the inspiration for the monument known as the Statue for the Children of the A-bomb located in Peace Memorial Park in Hiroshima. Students will find it interesting and worthwhile to compare one or both of Coerr's books with *My Hiroshima,* written and illustrated by Junko Morimoto (Viking, 1987), and *Hiroshima No Pika,* written and illustrated by Toshi Maruki (Lothrop, Lee & Shepard, 1982), which was named the 1993 Mildred Batchelder Award book for the best book in translation.

95   de Paola, Tomie

THE FIRST CHRISTMAS   *3–8 YEARS*

Illustrated by Tomie de Paola. New York: Putnam, 1984

This version of the nativity is retold through a minimal text and six beautiful three-dimensional pop-up scenes that change as the reader moves the parts indicated by strategically placed arrows. The book is sturdy in its construction and stunning in appearance; it most certainly will be a family keepsake or a treasure in the professional book collector's library.

96   de Paola, Tomie, *Reteller*

THE LEGEND OF THE POINSETTIA   *4–9 YEARS*

Illustrated by Tomie de Paola. New York: Putnam, 1994

This picture book is a retelling of the Mexican legend of how the poinsettia, a weed that bears red starlike blossoms, came to be called *flor de la Nochebuena* ("flower of the Holy Night") and why this red and green flowering plant is traditionally associated with Christmas and called *poinsettia* in the United States. In the Author's Note de Paola explains that in Mexico this plant is a wildflower and is known by several names: *flor de fuego* (fire flower), *flor de Navidad* (Christmas flower), and *flor de la Nochebuena* (flower of the Holy Night). In the United States this plant is called *poinsettia* after Dr. Joel Roberts Poinsett, who served as the United States Minister to Mexico from 1825 to 1830. He called the plant "painted leaves" and brought cuttings of it when he returned to his home in South Carolina at the end of his assignment in Mexico. The illustrations, done in the naive art style, depict the story of a little girl named Lucinda who, at Mass on Christmas Eve, presented a bundle of weeds to the Christ Child figure lying in the manger. Not only did the weeds Lucinda placed in the manger promptly burst into flaming red star-shaped flowers, but when everyone went outside after the Mass, all of the weeds throughout the town were also aflame with these beautiful red flowers the people thereafter called *la flor de la Nochebuena*—the flower of the Holy Night.

97   De Regniers, Beatrice Schenk

DAVID AND GOLIATH   *7–10* YEARS

Illustrated by Scott Cameron. New York: Orchard, 1996

De Regniers describes how the boy David, who was small for his age, killed the Biblical giant Goliath when the one stone he slung from his slingshot struck the evil warrior on the forehead, cut off the giant's head, and brought it to Saul, King of Israel. The death of Goliath ended the war between the men of Israel and the Philistines. David went to live with King Saul, who raised him as his son and rewarded him with gold and silver, robes of linen and wool. David fought in the king's army when there were battles, and when the king was sad David sang and played his harp to give him comfort. David married King Saul's daughter and became king when Saul died. As king he usually wore a crown of gold bedecked with rubies, but when he recalled the days when he was a young shepherd who wore a crown of red poppies, he would play his harp and sing a song of rejoicing in the Lord as King and His presence. De Regniers artfully includes two songs from the Bible in this story about David: the first is Psalm 138, the song David sang on the way to the army camp; the second is the song of rejoicing, which comes from the First Book of Chronicles, Chapter 16. The oil paintings reproduced in full color firmly establish aspects of the time and place of this biblical tale. The vegetation, the stretches of arid and parched land, and the rolling hills are indicative of the geography around Jerusalem and Bethlehem. The era during which the battles between the men of Israel and the Philistines occurred, the reign of King Saul, and the boyhood years of David, son of Jesse, are reflected in the clothes they wore, the weapons and armor they used. Close-up and distance scenes are effectively dispersed throughout the book, and the flow of the lines, the points of interest, and the effects of light and shadows vary from picture to picture, creating a vitality in the overall visual effects of the page designs and format throughout the book.

98   Downes, Belinda

SILENT NIGHT: A CHRISTMAS CAROL SAMPLER   *ALL AGES*

Illustrated by Belinda Downes. New York: Knopf, 1995

Twelve traditional Christmas carols with lyrics and musical score are beautifully enhanced with full-page pictures made of swatches of woven fabric and embroideries stitched in colorful thread with gold highlights mounted on woven linen-like fabric. At first glance the artist's use of bright colors and perspective suggests illuminations, but closer examina-

ILLUSTRATION 18   From *Silent Night: A Christmas Carol Sampler* by Belinda Downes. Copyright © 1995 by Belinda Downes. Reprinted by permission of Alfred A. Knopf, Inc.

tion reveals that the shapes of the figures are done in an expressive naive art style. (See illustration 18.) This beautiful picture book would prove to be a treasured gift item that might well be handed down from generation to generation. Its appeal should be quite timeless.

99   Early, Margaret, *Reteller*

WILLIAM TELL   *8–11* YEARS

Illustrated by Margaret Early. New York: Abrams, 1991

When the people who lived along the shores of Lake Lucerne in the three tiny countries of Schwyz, Uri, and Unterwalden lost their freedom to Austria, they were ruled by an evil governor named Gessler. A harsh dictator, Gessler ordered his Austrian soldiers to destroy the animals, crops, and houses of anyone who disobeyed his commands. Typical of his commands was the edict that anyone who passed by a pole on which his hat was mounted was to bow down before the hat as though the hat were Gessler himself; failure to do reverence to the hat meant imprisonment or death. When William Tell, who was respected for his skill as an archer and hunter, came to town with his son, Tell refused to show reverence to the governor's hat. After hearing Tell's son brag that his father could shoot an apple from a tree at fifty paces, Gessler challenged Tell to shoot an apple from his son's head. They agreed that if Tell succeeded both he and his son would both go free; if he failed their punishment was death. Tell hid one arrow in his jerkin and with the other arrow he pierced the apple. As he had promised, Gessler freed the boy, but vowed to imprison Tell in the dungeon of his castle for life. A fierce storm came up while Tell was being taken by boat to the prison in Gessler's castle. Acknowledging Tell's great strength and skill as a helmsman, Gessler promised Tell his freedom if he got them all safely ashore. Tell steered the boat toward a large rock which protruded from a cliff, leaped on to the rock, shoved the boat back into the stormy lake, and climbed to the top of the cliff to safety. From his hiding place, Tell watched Gessler and his men arrive home safely and saw Gessler strike a woman who begged the cruel governor to release her husband who was unjustly imprisoned. Tell shot his second arrow through Gessler's heart. The townspeople celebrated and cheered Gessler's demise and honored Tell for his courage and bravery and for having restored freedom to their land. The people decided to make the three small countries that bordered Lake Lucerne into one free, united country, one that was big enough and strong enough to regain and protect its freedom. They named that new country Switzerland. The stylized pictures in this oversized book are done in rich full color and a generous amount of gold; they highlight the lush valleys and lakes as well as the beauty and grandeur of mountainous terrain that surrounds them. The medieval era during which the action of this well-known legend occurred is suggested quite aptly in the clothes the villagers and soldiers wear, the weapons the warriors use, the architecture of the castles and peasants' homes, and the meticulously designed borders with which each picture is framed. Compare Margaret Early's verbal and visual retelling of this legendary hero with that created by Leonard Everett Fisher in *William Tell* (Farrar, Straus, & Giroux, 1996).

100   Everett, Gwen

LI'L SIS AND UNCLE WILLIE   *7–11+ YEARS*

Illustrated with photographs and reproductions of paintings
by William H. Johnson. New York: Rizzoli and National
Museum of American Art, Smithsonian Institution, 1991

> Told from the viewpoint of his niece, six-year-old Li'l Sis, this is a fictional
> story based on the life and artistic accomplishments of noted African-
> American expressionist painter William H. Johnson (1901–1970). It is il-
> lustrated with a few black-and-white photographs and numerous full-color
> reproductions of his bright, bold paintings. In spite of its brevity, this very
> special picture-book biography competently puts forth the opinion of cur-
> rent art historians: William H. Johnson left a legacy in American art that
> clearly recognizes him as a significant and major figure in the development
> of American modernism. Richard J. Powell's *Homecoming: The Art and
> Life of William H. Johnson,* with an introduction by Martin Puryear (Riz-
> zoli and National Museum of American Art, Smithsonian Institution,
> 1991), was published on the occasion of the exhibition of Johnson's work
> at the National Museum of American Art in 1991 and 1992. It chronicles
> Johnson's advancement from a student to professional painter of American
> and European importance and offers considerable information and insight
> about how his awareness of his cultural roots served to formulate the au-
> thentic, self-locating, artistic expression that ultimately typified so much
> of his work. Educators might want to refer to this excellent resource to help
> children understand how important Johnson is as a modern expression-
> istic painter and as an African-American painter, in particular.

101   Feelings, Tom

THE MIDDLE PASSAGE: WHITE SHIPS/   *9 YEARS–ADULTHOOD*
BLACK CARGO

Introduction by John Henrik Clarke. New York:
Dial, 1995

> The artwork was rendered in pen-and-ink and tempera on rice paper.
> Each and every illustration in this visual chronicle is a marvel; one can
> only imagine how magnificent the original paintings must be. It is not
> surprising that it took Tom Feelings almost twenty years to complete
> them. Each piece of artwork, which portrays wrenching, passionate im-
> ages of the cruel, horrendous journeys that millions of captured Africans
> experienced aboard the slave ships as they traveled the Atlantic to the
> Americas, is exquisitely assembled and bound in this book. In his intro-
> ductory comments, Feelings says that engaging in the process of creating
> this historical narrative entirely through pictures was a long "psycho-
> logical and spiritual journey" for him. Let us hope that the journey ex-
> perienced by the readers of this book will increase their awareness of the
> nightmarish and devastating journeys many contemporary Africans and

African Americans are still experiencing. Feelings and his editor should be congratulated for publishing such an important book. Tom Feelings received the 1996 Coretta Scott King Award for his illustrations in *The Middle Passage: White Ships/Black Cargo.*

102   Freedman, Russell

BUFFALO HUNT   *8–12+ YEARS*

Illustrated. New York: Holiday House, 1988

A wealth of facts about the buffalo in the 1800s is presented in this excellent informational book. It tells of how the Indians of the Great Plains considered the buffalo a sacred animal and praised its spirit. When they hunted and killed it, they used all of its parts from head to tail, using its meat, hide, and bones to subsist; in later years they used only the buffalo hides and tongues, selling them to white people at considerable profit. It tells also that the white hunters (pioneers traveling westward in covered wagons, professional hunters hired by the U.S. Army, and railroad construction crews) killed the buffalo for food. Thus, eventually there remained literally no buffalo roaming the Great Plains. This book is illustrated with reproductions of a few traditional Indian paintings as well as reproductions of paintings and drawings by artist-adventurers who also traveled westward in the 1800s; e.g., George Catlin, Karl Bodmer, and Albert Bierstaat.

103   Gallaz, Christopher, and Roberto Innocenti

ROSE BLANCHE   *8–12+ YEARS*

Translated from the French by Martha Coventry and Richard Graglia. Illustrated by Robert Innocenti. Mankato, Minn.: Creative Education, 1985

Rose Blanche, who lived in a small town in Germany during World War II, describes incidents that give evidence of the War: the presence of German soldiers, their tanks and trucks in the town, the herding of people by the soldiers at gunpoint into the trucks. She tells also of how she followed the tracks of one of the trucks loaded with these people into the forest and discovered many children, emaciated and starving and wearing gold stars, imprisoned behind electric barbed wire. The text changes to third-person narration and the reader is told how each day Rose Blanche sneaked food to the children in the camp—first her own lunch, then more and more food from home, yet each day she herself grew thinner and thinner because she was saving her food for the young prisoners. One day Rose Blanche did not come home from school, and the reason for her failure to return is devastating. The illustrator's portrayal of the fog on the day she "disappeared" and the use of the lily and other flowers to symbolize what happened to the girl and the end of the war only serve to emphasize the haunting theme of this story. The detailed surrealistic paintings must be examined very carefully; they offer a number of profound visual comments about war in general and children as victims of war in particular which were omitted or briefly alluded to in the sparse text. Compare the theme of *Hiroshima No Pika,* written and illustrated by Toshi Maruki (Lothrop, Lee & Shepard, 1982), with the theme in this book. *Rose Blanche* received the 1983 Batchelder Award for the best book in translation.

104   Garland, Michael

DINNER AT MAGRITTE'S   *6–10* YEARS

Illustrated by Michael Garland. New York: Dutton, 1995

Pierre, a young boy, is invited by his neighbors, Rene and Georgette Magritte, to have dinner with them and their guest Salvador Dali. While waiting for Mr. Dali, Pierre watches Magritte paint and the artist tells him a bit about his approach to painting. After Dali arrives, the Magrittes, Dali, and Pierre go for a walk in the woods behind Magritte's house, play a bit of croquet which is interrupted by rain, go inside for dinner, and then play a game of charades. All this sounds rather dull and quite lacking in imagination and originality, except that most of the pictures depicting these activities are full-color surrealistic oil paintings in the tradition of Magritte and Dali; some, in fact, are copies of paintings by these two well-known surrealist painters. (See illustration 19.) Children will most likely notice that somewhere within each picture, including the title page, appears the statement "Kevin is Pierre." (Kevin is said to be the name of Garland's son.)

105   Goble, Paul

DEATH OF THE IRON HORSE   *6–10* YEARS

Illustrated by Paul Goble. New York: Bradbury, 1987

On August 7, 1867, a group of Cheyenne Indians derailed a Union Pacific freight train traveling from Omaha to Fort McPherson in North Platte, Nebraska. The accomplished artwork which effectively illustrates this account of their brave and defiant act against the white men who encroached on their territory is done in India ink and watercolor. It is important to notice the special beauty and graphic accomplishment of the illustrations in this book as well as the authenticity of their content; i.e., aspects of the terrain, the flora and fauna of the region where the action occurred, and the details seen on the Indians' clothes, headpieces, hairstyles, etc.

ILLUSTRATION 19   From *Dinner at Magritte's* by Michael Garland. Copyright © 1995 by Michael Garland. Used by permission of Dutton Children's Books, a division of Penguin USA.

106 Harrison, Ted

CHILDREN OF THE YUKON   *8–14* YEARS

Illustrated by Ted Harrison. New York:
Tundra Books, 1977

> A rare informational book! Bright, flat colors illustrate these stylized
> paintings, suggestive of the naive school of art, offering a childlike charm
> and considerable depth and feeling to the emotional yet informative and
> authoritative array of facts which the author offers about the history and
> way of life throughout the year in the various settlements of the Yukon.
> In the main, the author/artist has emphasized how the Yukon, which is
> in the northwest corner of Canada and east of Alaska, differs from other
> parts of North America.

107 Harrison, Ted

A NORTHERN ALPHABET   *6–11+* YEARS

Illustrated by Ted Harrison. Plattsburgh, N.Y.:
Tundra Books, 1982

> This unique alphabet book depicts cultural aspects of people living
> across North America north of the 55th and, in some cases, the 60th par-
> allel. Each of the flat, bright, full color, naive-style paintings is filled with
> things beginning with a single letter of the alphabet that pertain to life
> in the Yukon. The text, in large primary-sized type, offers a literal-level
> statement about the picture and is intended to serve only as a story starter,
> for each picture tells much more than the text suggests. Thus, children are
> likely to look more closely at each picture, find more things in it begin-
> ning with that letter, and use them to create a more elaborate story. For
> those who need help with the names of things in the pictures, they are
> listed in the back of the book. Also, each picture is framed with a strip
> of many more words pertaining to the Yukon, but not shown in the pic-
> ture. This serves to arouse the curiosity of the readers so they can seek out
> other books that provide information about these "enrichment words."

108 Harvey, Brett

CASSIE'S JOURNEY: GOING WEST IN THE 1860's   *7–10* YEARS

Illustrated by Deborah Kogan Ray. New York:
Holiday House, 1988

> A little girl describes her family's journey by wagon during the 1860s
> from Illinois to California. The black grease-pencil sketches offer a dra-
> matic impressionistic glimpse of the hardships, dangers, and pleasantries
> experienced by one family as well as by some other members of the
> wagon train during their overland journey to the Pacific. The very simple
> topographical map at the beginning of the book shows the route followed

by Cassie and her family; it should help readers appreciate further the distance and varied terrain these travelers covered during their migration westward.

109   Hooks, William H.

FREEDOM'S FRUIT   *7–10* YEARS

Illustrated by James Ransome. New York: Borzoi/
Knopf, 1996

Mama Marina, a conjure woman and a slave, vowed to buy the freedom of her daughter Sheba and Joe Nathan, the young man who loved Sheba. Master Alston asked her to conjure the master's grapes so the slaves would not eat them off the vine when they ripened; she agreed to do what he asked of her, but she charged him a piece of gold, adding to the small amount she had already managed to save. When word spread among the slaves that the grapes were conjured, the slaves stopped eating them. Mama Marina picked two bunches of bitter, green grapes from the conjured vine, gave Sheba and Joe Nathan a bunch of the grapes and told them to eat them. She also told them that they would "go down through the valley of the shadow of death," but they would not die, instead they would "come out of that valley two free souls." Shortly after the harvest there was an early frost. Soon the leaves of the vine shriveled up and turned brown and both Sheba and Joe Nathan became very ill. "By Christmas time the grapevines were dark brown branches, lifeless, gnarled and twisted" and the two young people were weak and couldn't eat; Sheba's hair was turning gray and she walked like an old woman and Joe Nathan was thin, his face looked old and wrinkled, and his fingers were so gnarled he could no longer work the leather he used to be so good at. At this point, Master Alston became quite concerned about Joe Nathan, because he rented out the young black slave to a plantation nearby to make leather harnesses and shoes for the owner's slaves. He brought in a doctor to examine Joe, but the doctor said he could not find any medical reason for the young man's condition. When it seemed as if Sheba and Joe Nathan were dying, Mama Marina asked Master Alston if she could buy their freedom with what little money she had been able to save. Knowing he could not sell "dying" slaves to anyone else, he sold them to the woman and also gave her their papers of freedom. In early spring when the grapes were just about ready to burst into buds, Sheba and Joe Nathan devoured the cornmeal gruel Mama Marina made for them and seemed to get healthier and stronger with each passing day. A week later, in the morning before daylight, Mama Marina gave Sheba and Joe Nathan their freedom papers and her friend old Johnnycake, who went to Charleston each month to pick up supplies for Master Alston, stopped at Mama Marina's cabin, picked up the two young people and took them straight to a Quaker meeting house in Charleston. Mama Marina said she would take the spell off the grapes when they ripened, for she knew that by then

Sheba and Joe Nathan would be healthy and free. James Ransome's brightly colored, full-page pictures add exactly the right amount of reality to this moving tale that portrays the miseries of slavery and the "miracles" that love can accomplish.

110 Hort, Lenny, *Reteller*
THE BOY WHO HELD BACK THE SEA   *6–10* YEARS
Illustrated by Thomas Locker. New York: Dial, 1987

Originally this well-known Dutch legend about an irresponsible boy who plugged the leaking hole in the dike and thereby saved his low-lying village from being destroyed by the raging sea was told by Mary Mapes Dodge in her classic novel *Hans Brinker, or, The Silver Skates,* but on this occasion it has been adapted and retold as a story within a story in the personal and informal style of a storyteller. The full-page illustrations that provide an authentic setting in terms of time and place for this legend are full-color oil paintings done in the style of the seventeenth-century Dutch masters (Rembrandt and Vermeer) known for their use of sunlight and torchlight in their landscapes and seascapes. A fine picture book. Compare the Hort's retelling and Locker's illustrations in *The Boy Who Held Back the Sea* with *The Hole in the Dike,* retold by Norma Green and illustrated by Eric Carle (Crowell, 1974).

111 Kipling, Rudyard
GUNGA DIN   *9–12+* YEARS
Introduction by Kingsley Amis. Illustrations by Robert
Andrew Parker. San Diego: Harcourt Brace, 1987

An informative commentary about Kipling and his background explains why he wrote poetry about the British military serving in India, especially the classic narrative poem "Gunga Din," which is based on the Indian Meeting of 1857 and a heroic water carrier at the siege of Delhi in that year. The language of the poem is suggestive of the British cockney with its rhythms of the music halls in the late 1800s. The illustrations are expressionistic drawings done in pen-and-ink line and full-color watercolor and gouache wash. They can give the reader a fine sense of place as well as a genuine feel for the characters involved in this incident, be they the officers, the enlisted men, or like Gunga Din, the native crew who served as water carriers and tended the wounded under fire.

112 Langstaff, John, *Compiler*
WHAT A MORNING! THE CHRISTMAS STORY   *5–10+* YEARS
IN BLACK SPIRITUALS
Musical arrangements by John Andrew Ross. Illustrated by
Ashley Bryan. New York: Margaret K. McElderry/Macmillan, 1987

A collection of Bible verses illustrated with expressionistic paintings done in tempera and reproduced in rich, full color are alternated with five black spirituals to tell the story of the Nativity. The presence of African motifs in all of the illustrations in this unique picture book featuring a black Holy Family will prove an inspiration to blacks and nonblacks alike. The musical arrangements are for singing and piano as well as for suggested guitar cords. The "Note to Teachers, Parents and Instrumentalists" at the back of the book offers helpful suggestions for interpreting the text and illustrations and for using this book.

113   Lasky, Kathryn
THE LIBRARIAN WHO MEASURED THE EARTH   *8–11+ YEARS*
Illustrated by Kevin Hawks. Boston: Little, Brown, 1994

A very important readable introduction to the life story of a Greek scholar, poet, and librarian who left an important legacy still relevant to astronomers, mathematicians, and geographers born some two thousand years later. Lasky has provided thoroughly solid and understandable explanations of the strategies Eratosthenes devised for determining the circumference of the earth. She also provides the readers with insightful glimpses of lifestyles and attitudes toward education and literature during Eratosthenes' lifetime. The full-color expressionistic acrylic paintings Hawkes created to illustrate this picture book biography are the work of an illustrator who is obviously knowledgeable about the historical aspects of Eratosthenes' world and expressed that knowledge creatively in accomplished visual images. (See illustration 20.) Hawks most aptly supports what the author has expressed so effectively in words, but also effectively extends relevant information about Eratosthenes' world and the people with whom he lived: how students of all ages and walks of life were educated and what the schools looked like, the way people of all ages dressed, traveled, and played as well as what the harbors, villages, and markets looked like.

114   Lawrence, Jacob
HARRIET AND THE PROMISED LAND   *8–12+ YEARS*
Illustrated by Jacob Lawrence. New York: Simon & Schuster, 1994

The story of Harriet Tubman, the legendary African-American heroine born a slave in 1820 in Maryland who in nineteen trips on the Underground Railroad helped more than three hundred slaves reach freedom in the northern states and Canada, is movingly told in spare, deceptively simple verse and sophisticated expressionistic paintings rendered in poster paint and reproduced in full color. The stylized drawings (some suggestive of Goya), the exaggerated features of the characters, the brilliant and flat shades of

ILLUSTRATION 20   From *The Librarian Who Measured the Earth* by Kathryn Lasky. Text Copyright © 1994 by Kathryn Lasky; Illustrations Copyright © 1994 by Kevin Hawkes. By permission of Little, Brown and Company.

color all contribute to make this painter's work beautifully artistic and noteworthy. Through skillful use of metaphors and symbolism Lawrence alludes to aspects of black history, the Old Testament, and the human condition to comment on the brutal conditions black persons endured as slaves and the intolerable, dehumanizing circumstances many present-day African Americans face daily. This book was originally published by Windmill in 1968.

115   Le Tord, Bijou

A BLUE BUTTERFLY: A STORY ABOUT CLAUDE MONET   *7–10+ YEARS*
Illustrated by Bijou Le Tord. New York: Doubleday, 1995

A recognized minimalist artist in her own right, Bijou Le Tord has created an elegant tribute to the famous impressionist painter Claude Monet. She describes Monet's approach to painting in spare poetic prose, and using Monet's own palette of only eight colors has fashioned pictures of Monet himself painting, studying the effects of the light, and walking in a snow-storm. In a style somewhat suggestive of that used by Monet, she has painted numerous pictures of the same subjects he painted (flower garden scenes at different times of the day, as well as cityscapes, seascapes, and boats in various weather conditions), each one delicate and exquisite yet unpretentious and somewhat naive. Supplement this charming study of Monet with *What Makes a Monet a Monet?* by Richard Mühlberger (Metropolitan Museum of Art/Viking, 1993). Also compare *A Blue Butterfly* with *A Painter: How We Work,* written and illustrated by Douglas Florian (Greenwillow, 1993), and *An Artist,* written and illustrated by M. B. Goffstein (Harper, 1980).

116   Lewis, J. Patrick

THE CHRISTMAS OF THE REDDLE MOON   *6–9 YEARS*
Illustrated by Gray Kelley. New York: Dial, 1994

This picture book is memorable for at least two reasons, if not more. First, because it tells a haunting story of how two children lost in a blizzard on Christmas Eve are saved by the legendary and mysterious Wee Mary Fever, the last of the reddle-sellers in England who died around 1920. (Reddle is a red clay dug from the ground in rural England and sold to sheep farmers for marking their sheep.) Second, the illustrations, which are striking, ethereal realistic pastel drawings in rich full color, enhance the feelings of fear and tension the children experienced when they were lost in the snow and when they realized they were in the home of the strange reddlewoman who was reputed to crush bones of people who happened by, mixing them with other ingredients to make a magic powder. The narrator points out to his readers that stories about Wee Mary Fever grew into legend. "Each year the story grew until it was nothing but half-truths. And no telling which half the truth might be." No doubt some readers will not find it difficult to determine which aspects of *The Christmas of the Reddle Moon* are fact or fiction, reality or fantasy, but they will probably enjoy this story anyway. Compare this story with *The Polar Express,* the 1986 Caldecott Medal Award–winning picture book written and illustrated by Chris Van Allsburg (Houghton Mifflin, 1985).

117 Livingston, Myra Cohn
KEEP ON SINGING: A BALLAD OF MARIAN ANDERSON   *5–9* YEARS
Illustrated by Samuel Byrd. New York: Holiday House, 1994

A brief, competently crafted ballad combined with watercolor paintings offers a glimpse at the life of the celebrated singer. Referring students to the author's notes about the allusions in this poem to events in Marian Anderson's life should prove helpful to those who have not yet heard of her.

118 Maruki, Toshi
HIROSHIMA NO PIKA   *8–12* YEARS
Illustrated by Toshi Maruki. New York: Lothrop, Lee & Shepard, 1982

A stirring story of what happened to a little girl, the members of her family, and the residents of Hiroshima when "the Flash of Hiroshima" (the atomic bomb) was dropped on that city by the Americans on the morning of August 6, 1945. The full-color impressionistic and expressionistic paintings can evoke deep emotional response on the part of the reader and are in sharp contrast to the very simple understated, almost emotionless text, making the theme "it can't happen again if no one drops the bomb" even more forceful. Notice how the illustrations and the narration move from the child, to the family, to the multitudes, then back to the child, family, and multitudes repeatedly. An effective persuasive technique, whether or not it was a conscious one on the part of the author/illustrator. This book, which was originally published in Japan in 1980 by Komine Shoten Co., Ltd., under the same title, received the Nippon Award for the most excellent picture book of Japan, given by the Yomiuri Shimbun Press in 1981. The publisher of the English translation was awarded the 1983 Mildred Batchelder Award for the best book in translation.

119 McCully, Emily Arnold
THE PIRATE QUEEN   *7–10* YEARS
Illustrated by Emily Arnold McCully. New York: Putnam, 1995

Loosely based on biographical and historical fact, this is a fictional story of the female pirate Grania O'Malley who lived in the last half of the sixteenth century. She was raised in a seafaring and pirating family and married into another; she was a sea queen and warrior throughout her long lifetime. She sided with the British or with the Irish, depending on her purpose, but whether she was acting as a sea captain, warrior, mercenary, or landowner she was always courageous, cunning, and competent. Many of the illustrations are full pages or double-page spreads. The landscapes and seascapes depicting the serenity and beauty of Ireland's rich green and rolling countryside and its rocky shores are especially noteworthy. McCully has captured the nuances of Grania's feisty personality, which were evident in her childhood and through her years as a seafaring "dowager" of the sea. Supplement this picture-book biography with *The Ballad of the Pirate Queens,* written by Jane Yolen and illustrated by David Shannon (Harcourt Brace, 1995).

120   Merrill, Linda, and Sarah Ridley

THE PRINCESS AND THE PEACOCKS: OR, THE STORY   *7–10* YEARS
OF THE ROOM

Illustrated by Tennessee Dixon. New York: Hyperion/
Freer Gallery of Art, Smithsonian Institution, 1993

This story is "narrated" by the subject of James McNeill Whistler's portrait titled *The Princess of the Land of Porcelain.* In it she "relates" how, in 1876 and 1877, this American artist decorated the dining room of the British businessman Frederick Richards Leyland's London townhouse, where this painting was hung. Full-page pictures done in pen-and-ink and watercolors are filled with authentic details of what Whistler actually painted on the walls, ceiling, and fixtures of what eventually became known as the Peacock Room. This account of how Whistler created his only surviving interior decorative art was inspired by the art-historical research and discoveries made in preparation for the restoration of the Peacock Room, presently installed in the Freer Gallery of Art, Smithsonian Institution in Washington, D.C. Full-color photographs showing two views of the Peacock Room as it actually looks are included at the back of this picture book; one shows the portrait of *The Princess from the Land of Porcelain* as she reigns over Whistler's *Harmony in Blue and Gold: The Peacock Room.*

121   Mitchell, Margaree King

UNCLE JED'S BARBERSHOP   *5–9* YEARS

Illustrated by James Ransome. New York: Simon &
Schuster, 1993

One of the most accomplished picture books published in the 1990s is *Uncle Jed's Barbershop.* Set in the segregated South, where most people were sharecroppers, this is the story of the many hurdles Uncle Jed, the only barber in the county, managed to overcome before he opened up his own barbershop at age seventy-nine. First he gave his niece Sarah Jane's family the money the white doctors demanded before they would perform the necessary emergency operation needed to save her life, then there were the bank failures of the Great Depression. The realistic, brightly colored oil paintings which illustrate this story of dreams deferred and ultimately realized are spectacular. Ransome should be complimented on his ability to depict the range of emotions experienced by each of the characters in this story as well as to convey a definite sense of time and place and ethnicity.

122   Morrison, Taylor

ANTONIO'S APPRENTICESHIP: PAINTING A FRESCO   *9–12+ YEARS*
IN RENAISSANCE ITALY

Illustrated by Taylor Morrison. New York: Holiday House, 1996

What a fine book to use to introduce children to the process of painting frescoes and help them appreciate the roles an apprentice played in this process! The illustrator's full-color paintings and sketches superbly depict aspects of this historical setting and the action involving the characters, especially in showing how they prepared the fresco plaster and laid it on the brick walls; gathered the tools, equipment, and materials; and processed them so they could be used to sketch, draw, and color the twenty-two illustrations depicting the life of Christ that eventually appear in the mural on these wall surfaces. (See illustration 21.) The story is set in Florence, Italy, during the fifteenth century when fresco painting was very much in vogue, and the author and illustrator authentically depict Florence as the cultural capital of the world. However, the characters in this book and the Chapel of San Francesco at Castellino in Florence where painters, sculptors, and carpenters shared their skills and competed for the favor of patrons are fictitious. For an in-depth glimpse of what the life of an artist's apprentice was like during this same era in Florence, teachers and librarians might want to read aloud or encourage children to read independently the novel *The Apprentice,* an excellent novel written by Pilar Molina Llorente, translated by Robin Longshaw and illustrated by Juan Ramon Alonso (Farrar Straus & Giroux, 1989).

123   Oppenheim, Shulamith L.

THE LILY CUPBOARD   *7–9 YEARS*

Illustrated by Ronald Himler. New York: Charlotte
Zolotow/HarperCollins, 1992

During the German occupation of Holland, Miriam, a young Jewish girl, is sent by her parents to live in the country with a gentile family. The

ILLUSTRATION 21   Illustration copyright ©1996 by Taylor Morrison. Reprinted from *Antonio's Apprenticeship* by permission of Holiday House, Inc.

impressionistic paintings, executed in watercolor and gouache, express the intense sadness Miriam and her parents feel as they prepare for her departure, the warmth and kindness of the Dutch family (a little boy by the name of Nello and his parents) with whom she is sent to live, the joyful camaraderie Miriam and Nello develop as they play together around the family's farm and with the small black rabbit Nello gave her, as well as the intense fear they all experience when they realize the soldiers are approaching their house and they manage to hide Miriam and her rabbit in the lily cupboard just in time. One might think this is a rather grim story for children within the age range of what apparently is the intended audience, but the focus is on the love and security Miriam's biological parents and her foster parents tried to and actually did provide for her, rather than on the details of the horror and physical suffering that the Nazi soldiers could inflict on the characters in this story.

124 Picó, Fernando
THE RED COMB   *7–10* YEARS
Translated and adapted by Argentina Papacios.
Illustrated by Mariá Antiona Ordóñez. Mahwah, N.J.:
BridgeWater, 1991.

> A satisfying, romantic tale of how a little girl and her next door neigh-
> bor, an elderly widow, schemed to prevent a runaway slave from being
> captured and turned over to the authorities for a handsome reward. The
> vibrant, radiant full-color expressionist illustrations enhance aspects of
> the strong characters and colorful locales of this historically grounded
> tale which is set in Caimito, a rural district of Rio Piedras, Puerto Rico,
> in the mid-nineteenth century. *The Red Comb* was the winning entry in
> the children's literature contest organized by Ediciones Huracan of
> Puerto Rico in 1987 to encourage authors to write historical fiction for
> young readers. This picture-book version of this tale was published origi-
> nally in Spanish as a co-edition with Ediciones Ekaré-Banco del Libro
> of Caracas, Venezuela.

125 Podwal, Mark, *Reteller*
GOLEM: A GIANT MADE OF MUD   *7–10+* YEARS
Illustrated by Mark Podwal. New York: Greenwillow, 1995

> Podwal does not cite the actual names of the rabbi or the emperor in his
> retelling of this well-known Jewish legend about what happened when a
> rabbi created a golem out of mud and brought it to life through his mystic
> understanding of the secrets of human history. He does, however, indi-
> cate in the credits on the copyright page that it is based on a historical event
> which occurred during the late sixteenth century in the city of Prague,
> involving a scholar and mystic named Rabbi Judah Loew ben Bezalel,
> who created a golem that came alive and prevented Emperor Rudolf II
> from burning the holy books of the Jews. Full-color, rather simple ex-
> pressionistic paintings rendered in gouache, colored pencil, and ink ac-
> company this unpretentious and forthright retelling of this legend.
> Compare Podwal's verbal and visual version of this legend with the 1977
> Caldecott Honor Award–winning version of *The Golem* written and il-
> lustrated by Beverly Brodsky McDermott (Lippincott, 1976) and *Golem*
> written and illustrated by David Wisniewski (Clarion, 1996).

126 Polacco, Patricia
PINK AND SAY   *7–10* YEARS
Illustrated by Patricia Polacco. New York: Philomel, 1994

> This is a true and sad tale about two injured Yankee Civil War soldiers:
> Say, a fifteen-year-old Caucasian Yankee deserter, who lies alone and

wounded in a Georgia pasture, and Pink, a black youth separated from his company, the Forty-eighth Colored. Pink manages to get Say to his (Pink's) home, and his mother, who nurses the two boys back to health, is killed trying to stave off plunderers. On their way to rejoin Pink's company, the youths are captured by the Confederates and taken to Andersonville, where they are separated at the gate; Pink is promptly sentenced to be hanged and Say is imprisoned but released months later in poor health. The line-and-watercolor-wash expressionistic pictures coupled with a competently crafted text add up to a haunting tale that offers glimpses of the pain and great suffering of war as well as admirable acts of kindness and personal sacrifice people willingly offer others in need.

127   Raschka, Christopher

CHARLIE PARKER PLAYED BE BOP   *9–13* YEARS

Illustrated by Christopher Raschka. New York:
Richard Jackson/Orchard, 1992

> Full color, uninhibited, bold, expressive cartoon sketches done in charcoal and watercolor accent the lyrical verse that offers young readers a fine introduction to Charlie Parker, nicknamed "Bird" (1920–1955), the celebrated saxophonist, composer, and his revolutionary style of modern jazz known as be bop. Obviously, it would be wise to play some recordings of Parker's music to help the readers appreciate how the illustrations and text of this picture book capture the spirit of his music, but one might also obtain a copy of the book entitled *Jazz: My Music, My People,* written and illustrated by Morgan Monceaux and accompanied by a brief, insightful forward by the celebrated jazz trumpeter Wynton Marsalis (Knopf, 1994). *Charlie Parker Played Be Bop* was named a 1993 Notable Children's Book.

128   Ringgold, Faith

AUNT HARRIET'S UNDERGROUND RAILROAD   *7–10* YEARS
IN THE SKY

Illustrated by Faith Ringgold. New York: Crown, 1992

> In this companion picture book to *Tar Beach* (Crown, 1991), Be Be and Cassie, the characters we all met in that award-winning book, travel one of the same routes the runaway slaves took on the Underground Railroad. Faith Ringgold's brief but informative and significant text and her emotionally revealing and dramatic naive paintings in rich full color make it possible for young children to understand better and appreciate more fully how amazing and important the accomplishments of Harriet Tubman and others associated with the Underground Railroad actually were. (See illustration 22.) The brief biographical sketch, the bibliography for further reading at the back of the book, and the map showing some of the

ILLUSTRATION 22   From *Aunt Harriet's Underground Railroad in the Sky* by Faith Ringgold. Copyright © 1992 by Faith Ringgold. Reprinted by permission of Crown Publishers, Inc.

many routes taken by the runaway slaves traveling on the Underground Railroad should prove helpful to young readers interested in learning more about aspects of this important element in United States history. Supplement the reading of this fine picture book with Mary E. Lyons' *Stitching Stars: The Story Quilts of Harriet Powers* (Scribner, 1993).

129   Ringgold, Faith

MY DREAM OF MARTIN LUTHER KING   *7–12+ YEARS*

Illustrated by Faith Ringgold. New York: Crown, 1995

With large, stark naive-style paintings in shades of purples, blues, grays, black, and white (in contrast with the warm and vibrant hues we tend to associate with her art), Faith Ringgold recounts important incidents in King's life and the history of the Civil Rights Movement within the framework of her own dreams. Especially provocative, however obvious its message, is her dream of people of all colors, races, and religions meeting after King's death to burn bags containing their "prejudice, hate, ignorance, violence, and fear." The bags are emptied into a pile and it explodes into a fire that lights the sky with words: "Every good thing starts with a dream." A time line and bibliography about Dr. King's life are included at the back of the book and both should prove helpful to children who want to find out more about him.

130   Schroeder, Alan

CAROLINA SHOUT!   *6–9* YEARS

Illustrated by Bernie Fuchs. New York: Dial, 1995

A stunning glimpse of some culturally rich aspects of African-American social life and customs in Charleston, South Carolina, before World War II is found in this picture book. It is written in lyrical prose and illustrated with exquisite, full-page impressionistic paintings done in full oils on canvas. The illustrator has magnificently achieved the use of light and shading to highlight the time of day, location, and conditions under which each of the street vendors typically promoted their wares and services, and as a body of work these paintings in-and-of themselves constitute a first-class visual record of the cultural history of African Americans living in this part of South Carolina in the first quarter of the 1900s. According to the Author's Note, some of the vendors' songs or "shouts" recorded in this story were used or are comparable to those included in George and Ira Gershwin's opera *Porgy and Bess,* in "Street Cries," a chapter in *Gumbo Ýa-Ýa,* a collection of Louisiana folklore compiled by Lyle Saxon, Edward Dreyer, and Robert Tallant (The Louisiana State Library, 1945), and in a collection of shouts entitled *The Book of Negro Folklore* edited by Langston Hughes and Arna Bontemps (Dodd, Mead, 1958). I would encourage teachers and librarians to use a recording of *Porgy and Bess,* the publications cited above, or others more accessible to them to supplement the songs included in *Carolina Shout!* I would also recommend playing the piano solo entitled "Carolina Shout," composed by James P. Johnson, to demonstrate the role played by ragtime and jazz during the era in which this story takes place.

131   Sills, Leslie

INSPIRATIONS: STORIES ABOUT WOMEN ARTISTS   *8–12+* YEARS

Illustrated. Niles, Ill.: Albert Whitman, 1989

The lives of four accomplished women artists, all of whom persevered against many obstacles and pursued their work as they wanted to, are described briefly. These four women artists are Georgia O'Keefe, Frida Kahlo, Alice Neel, and Faith Ringgold. In each case, photographs of the women and copies of their work, in both full color and black-and-white, are included. A very informative and inspiring book.

132 Smucker, Barbara
SELINA AND THE BEAR PAW QUILT   *5–9* YEARS
Illustrated by Janet Wilson. New York: Crown, 1995

Throughout their history, Mennonites have believed violence was contrary to the teachings of their church; thus, they would never take up arms and tried to avoid war and killing. Because they would not side with either the North or the South during the Civil War they were considered disloyal by both and were persecuted and harassed, their property and farmlands were ruined, and some of their meeting houses were burned. Selina's parents decided to move to Upper Canada where they had many relatives and friends and her father could work at the sawmill. As the family was preparing to leave, Selina's grandmother, who said she was too old to start a new life again, gave Selina a Bear Paw quilt top she had just finished making, telling the child to take it to her new home and to spread it over her bed when it was quilted so she would remember her whenever she looked at it. Each full-page picture, done in rich colors and detailed floral and geometric designs, is framed in close-up views of fifteen real quilt patterns. The patterns pictured and named on the back cover of the book include Friendship Star, Log Cabin, Bear Paw (also called Duck's Foot in the Mud), Four Patch, Flying Geese, Grandmother's Fan, and others. Each picture in this picture book is interesting, but the picture of the quilting bee showing the women sitting around the quilting frame, laughing, chatting, and sewing the layers of quilt together seems to capture best the simple life and the camaraderie of these people. Supplement *Selina and the Bear Paw Quilt* with Raymond Bial's *With Needle and Thread: A Book about Quilts* (Houghton Mifflin, 1996.)

133 Spedden, Daisy Corning Stone
POLAR, THE TITANIC BEAR   *8–11* YEARS
Introduction by Leighton H. Coleman III. Illustrated by
Laurie McGaw and with photographs. Boston: Madison/
Little, Brown, 1994

Polar, a beautiful white mohair Steiff teddy bear that belonged to a little boy named Douglas Spedden, relates his and the boy's experiences as they and the boy's family traveled from the family homes in Tuxedo Park, New York, and Bar Harbor, Maine, to such places as Europe, Panama, Bermuda, and Algiers. For one of their return trips from France to New York, Polar, "Master" (the bear's name for Douglas), and the boy's parents embarked on the first voyage of the *Titanic*. The experiences the Sedden family and the bear had on the fifth night of the ill-fated voyage, when the *Titanic* hit an iceberg and sank, are described in considerable detail in this unique historical picture book. The full-color impressionistic paintings done in watercolor and the copies of old photographs reproduced in sepia add considerably to helping children understand something of the era in which these events occurred and the social status of the family focused on throughout the book. They also tend to elucidate the swings in moods and emotions related to the various events involving the boy and the bear that are described in the text.

134   Towls, Wendy

THE REAL McCOY: THE LIFE OF AN AFRICAN-AMERICAN INVENTOR   *7–10 YEARS*

Illustrated by Wil Clay. New York: Scholastic, 1993

A credible biography of Elijah McCoy (1844–1929), a Canadian-born African-American who patented over fifty inventions, the most notable of which was his automatic oil cup, which eventually became standard equipment on most locomotives and heavy machinery. It is thought the expression "the real McCoy" began when engineers, wanting an oil cup based on the model designed by McCoy rather than one of the many imitations that existed, asked for "the real McCoy," meaning they wanted the genuine article or the real thing. The full-color, realistic paintings were done with acrylic paint and add considerable vitality and authentic detail to this inspiring story about the life, challenges, and accomplishments of this brilliant African-American pioneer in engineering.

135   Tsuchiya, Yulio

FAITHFUL ELEPHANTS: A TRUE STORY OF ANIMALS, PEOPLE AND WAR   *9–12 YEARS*

Translated by Tomoko Tsuchiya Dykes. Illustrated by Ted Lewin. Boston: Houghton Mifflin, 1988

This is a highly emotional and disturbing portrayal of grief, fear, and sadness produced by war. The zookeeper at the Ueno Zoo in Tokyo relates a grim account of why and how three famous performing elephants at the zoo were allowed to starve to death and all of the other animals in the zoo were poisoned to death. This true story is illustrated with expressive watercolor paintings, most of them double-page spreads. (Notice the effect used by the illustrator when he dramatically dwarfs the humans in relation to the elephants, thus emphasizing the animals' vulnerability to them.) This tragic tale was first published as a narrative poem in Japan in 1951 by Kin-no-Hoshi-Sha Co., Ltd. under the title *Kawaiso No Zo*. It is read on the Japanese radio every year to mark the anniversary of Japan's surrender in World War II. A tomb on the grounds of the Ueno Zoo contains the remains of the three elephants and other animals that were killed by command of the Japanese army because they were worried about what would happen if the bombs hit the zoo and the animals escaped from their cages. Children still decorate the monument with semba-tsuru (paper cranes). Compare and contrast how the author and illustrator of *Faithful Elephants* made the antiwar statement and portrayed innocent victims of war with the ways these same themes were made in the 1983 Batchelder Award book *Hiroshima No Pika,* written and illustrated by Toshi Maruki (Lothrop, Lee & Shepard, 1982), and the 1986 Batchelder Award book *Rose Blanche,* written by Christopher Gallaz and Roberto Innocenti and illustrated by Roberto Innocenti (Creative Education, 1985).

136 Watson, Amy, and the staff of the Abby Aldrich
Rockefeller Folk Art Center

THE FOLK ART COUNTING BOOK   *5–10+ YEARS*

Illustrated with photographs and reproductions of three
centuries of American folk art. Based on a concept by
Florence Cassen Mayers. New York: Abrams/The Colonial
Williamsburg Foundation of Williamsburg, Va., 1992

> Each page of this counting book consists of a large, plain number from 1 to 20, illustrated with an outstanding example of a full-color photograph or reproduced image of a folk art painting, carving, or household items produced in America during the last three centuries. A descriptive listing of objects illustrated in this book is presented at the back of the book.

137 Winter, Jeanette

THE CHRISTMAS TREE SHIP   *6–9 YEARS*

Illustrated by Jeanette Winter. New York: Philomel, 1994

> Jeanette Winter's competently crafted and candid text, enhanced by her rich, full-color expressionistic paintings, describes a memorable story of loss, courage, and purpose. Based on a true story, *The Christmas Tree Ship* tells how Captain Herman Schuenemann and the crew of his schooner, the *Rouse Simmons,* on their way from Manistique, Michigan, to Chicago with a load of spruce trees for Christmas, were lost in the icy waters of Lake Michigan during a winter storm in 1912 and how his widow, their three daughters, and some other women continued to bring spruce trees from Michigan to Chicago for twenty-two more years.

138   Wolkstein, Diane

ESTHER'S STORY   *7–10+ YEARS*

Illustrated by Juan Wijngaard. New York: Morrow, 1996

A thoroughly polished retelling of the Old Testament story of how Esther, a humble and shy Jewish orphan girl originally called Hadassah, became the wise and courageous queen of all Persia and ingeniously saved her people from being killed by Haman and his followers. In appreciation for what Esther did for them, Jews throughout the world still celebrate on the 14th and 15th of the month of Adar, which falls in either February or March. This holiday is called the Feast of Purim, which means "lots," because of the lot that Haman cast to determine the date for the destruction of the Jews. The full-page jewel-toned gouache paintings make the action and the point of the story perfectly clear; in fact, each illustration is a picture with a story. The human figures, animals, and natural objects are conventionalized and idealized in a manner suggestive of traditional Persian paintings. Every detail seems to be as perfect as human skill can make it. In fact, perfection seems to be the major characteristic of the traditional Persian paintings, yet none are complicated or pretentious. And these are the same characteristics of the illustrations Juan Wijngaard created for this stunning picture book: the males are handsome and the females are all beautiful, the renderings of the tiles on the walls and archways of buildings, patterns of carpets, clumps of flowers or the trees, the details on the jewelry and in the embroidery and fabric designs of the women's and men's garments are amazing. Worthy of note is the richness of the colors; vivid and pure gold, malachite, ultramarine, and vermilion are used generously throughout.

The World
I Live In

*T*he picture books in this section are those books in which the writer sets out to help the reader to acquire knowledge, and the techniques the writer uses, which may well include storytelling, will be subordinate to that end. In other words, formally or informally, the writer of an informational book sets out to inform or to teach. We have available to us a vast number of informational books that have the potential to sharpen children's sense of wonder about themselves, about others, and about their many worlds, worlds near and far, past, present and future. We have a vast number of informational books that have the potential to make children feel comfortable with, and indeed welcome, change and the unknown rather than fear them or even remain oblivious to them. Children of all ages can and should be taught to read informational books critically if they are to become independent and lifelong learners, so that they will not only delight in learning but will continue to learn even when their formal education has been completed.

139   Ada, Alma Flor, *Reteller*

MEDIOPOLLITO/HALF-CHICKEN   *5–9* YEARS

Illustrated by Kim Howard. New York: Doubleday, 1995

> This picture book is a bilingual retelling of a folktale that traveled from Spain to Latin American countries; the author has chosen colonial Mexico as the setting. The last of thirteen chicks to hatch was born with one wing, one leg, one eye (because he had only half a head), and half as many feathers as the other chicks; obviously, then, he was named Half-Chicken. He thoroughly enjoyed the attention his uniqueness attracted, so when Half-Chicken overheard the sparrows say that not even the court of the viceroy in Mexico City had seen anything so "different," he decided to travel to Mexico City to show his unique self to the viceroy. During the course of his travels he stopped briefly to help those in need: he moved the branches that blocked a stream, he prevented a small fire from burning out by fanning it with his one wing, he untangled the wind that was caught in the branches. He arrived at the viceroy's palace, but the guards laughed at him and told him to go through the kitchen. When the cook saw him, he threw Half-Chicken into a kettle of hot water. Each of the natural elements (fire, water, and wind) Half-Chicken had helped came to his aid in its own way: The fire (which was heating the water in the cooking pot) told the little rooster to ask the water to put out the fire (which it did most willingly), and when the frustrated cook threw the little rooster out the window, the wind lifted him up into the air until he landed on one of the towers of the palace. It is there that Half-Chicken and all weathercocks from that day to the present have stood on their only leg, seeing everything that goes on below and pointing to the direction the wind blows. The lively line-and-wash illustrations, in the vibrant shades of red, green, and gold so prevalent in the traditional Mexican folk arts and crafts, are done in a rather unsophisticated expressionistic style, suggestive of the patterns and textures of Mexican murals. In her afterword, the author expressed the hope that the dual-language format used in this picture-book retelling of a story which is so repetitive would "give children a greater appreciation of and interest in acquiring the gift of an additional language."

140   Agaard, John, and Grace Nichols, *Editors*

A CARIBBEAN DOZEN: POEMS FROM   *5–12+* YEARS
CARIBBEAN POETS

Illustrated by Cathie Felstead. Cambridge, Mass.:
Candlewick, 1994

> The poetry by thirteen ("a baker's dozen") Caribbean poets collected in this picture book reveals each poet's love of life on the Islands (be it Trinidad, Guyana, Jamaica, or the Bahamas). It also shows their obvious sensitivity to and love for the power of language. The poets whose works are included

in this very special collection speak rhythmically and lyrically and most vividly of relationships between themselves and significant others, the images of themselves growing up, the familiar sights, sounds, and smells that surrounded them. In short essays preceding their selections, the poets describe their own childhood memories and the bases and influences of their poetry. Vibrant, lively pictures, done in collage, watercolor, pastel, gouache, oils, and ink, not only artfully highlight, but astutely extend and enrich each of these finely crafted sensory- and imagery-filled poems.

141   Baker, Jeannie

THE STORY OF ROSY DOCK   *6–10* YEARS

Illustrated by Jeannie Baker. New York: Greenwillow, 1995

These exquisitely detailed, accomplished collage illustrations resemble photographic stills of suffocating heat hanging over a sun-drenched, almost barren desert, rushing flood waters and strong wind sweeping over the desert, and barren, high, red, rocky cliffs. A succinct, at times poetic text coupled with these beautiful visual images documents the life cycle of the plant commonly called "rosy dock" *(Rumex vesicarius)* and its rapid spread throughout Australia shortly after a nineteenth-century immigrant from North Africa or western Asia settled by a river and planted some rosy dock seeds she had brought with her. The last picture in the book depicts a vast range of land covered with this plant's beautiful red seed pods and looking very much like a huge red blanket, making dramatically explicit the author/illustrator's message: some nonnative plants multiply so quickly and profusely that they not only change whole landscapes, they push many native plants to extinction. Children and adults will want to allow plenty of time to look at the details in these pictures, for they are loaded with many kinds of creatures and plants native to much of Australia, especially in the remote or sparsely populated areas.

142   Banyai, Istvan

ZOOM   *6–10+* YEARS

Illustrated by Istvan Banyai. New York: Viking, 1995

This slick, yet clever wordless book is bound to challenge and delight the careful "reader" of visuals. Gradually, frame by frame, the perspective of the subject "zooms" away from the small portion of the subject until that portion is seen within the context of the whole. More specifically, the first thing we see is a red, spiky thing; when we turn the page, our view is broadened further and that "thing" is found to be the comb of a rooster. And so it goes; each time we turn a page our view of the subject is enlarged and more about it is disclosed. We realize the rooster is being watched by two children, whom we eventually discover are standing on a bench that is in a farm building surrounded by other buildings. Eventually we learn these are toys that belong to a girl pictured on the cover of a book being read by a boy on a ship that is shown on an advertisement on the side of a bus moving through a crowded city street, and that bus is captured on camera for a television program being watched by a cowboy. The scenes enlarge until we are in outer space and we see earth only as a minuscule object surrounded by a gigantic universe. Given an opportunity to offer their ideas about what the "message" of this book might be, thoughtful children and adults will no doubt come up with some interesting ones. Each would probably be quite correct, for *Zoom* is a fine example of a multidimensional book. See *Re-Zoom* (Viking, 1995) for another, even more sophisticated wordless book created by Istvan Banyai.

143   Baylor, Byrd

GUESS WHO MY FAVORITE PERSON IS?   *5–9* YEARS

Illustrated by Robert Andrew Parker. New York:
Scribner, 1977

A unique approach to alerting young readers to the many facets of their surroundings and to respecting the varied responses each of us brings to them. Via a fluid conversational text and evocative impressionistic watercolor paintings, readers are introduced to two friends playing a game in which they name their favorite things: favorite colors, things to touch, sounds, places to live, dreams, tastes, and much more.

144   Baylor, Byrd

I'M IN CHARGE OF CELEBRATIONS   *8–12+* YEARS

Illustrations by Peter Parnall. New York: Scribner, 1986

In beautiful descriptive poetic prose the author shares with her readers a number of special experiences in the Southwest desert country that she said warranted her private celebrations—"besides the ones they close school for." The sophisticated expressionistic painting and the use of negative space to form the shapes, characteristics we so readily identify with the name of this notable book artist, are as unique and picturesque as is the author's use of language. A fine model to motivate children (and adults) to be more aware and appreciative of their surroundings, no matter where they live.

145   Baylor, Byrd

THE OTHER WAY TO LISTEN   *7–12+* YEARS

Illustrated by Peter Parnall. New York: Scribner, 1978

This is a *very* sophisticated picture book. Imagery-filled prose combined with black and yellow abstract expressionistic drawings, many of which employ the negative space technique, details how the narrator hears the hills singing, a feat which she said "seemed like the most natural thing in the world." Readers are encouraged to listen for the sounds made by the stars in the sky, the rocks murmuring, the wildflower seeds bursting open, the cactus blooming in the dark, and much more. They are cautioned that it takes a long time learning and lots of practice. Compare this picture book and the video film version, *The Other Way to Listen,* narrated by Will Rogers, Jr. (Tucson: Southwest Series, 1988).

146   Behfel, Tages

. . . I NEVER SAW ANOTHER BUTTERFLY   *9–18 YEARS*

Second ed. Illustrated with children's drawings. New York: McGraw-Hill, 1978

An anthology of poems and full-color drawings created by children confined in the Terezin Concentration Camp from 1942 to 1944, commenting on life in the camp or life in general. Also included is a biographical sketch of each child whose poem or painting appears in the anthology, indicating where the child was born, when she or he arrived at Terezin, and the date of her or his death or departure from the camp.

147   Bonners, Susan

PANDA   *5–9 YEARS*

Illustrated by Susan Bonners. New York: Delacorte, 1978

A fascinating and authentic portrayal of the panda's life cycle in watercolor paintings done on wet paper. A wild panda of southwestern China is depicted from birth until she is six years old, fully grown, and awaiting the birth of her first cub. The reader of this picture book will want to look again and again at the pictures of the antics of the pandas and the scenes of the icy mountains, wildflower fields, and bamboo thickets.

148   Brent, Isabelle

AN ALPHABET OF ANIMALS   *4–9 YEARS*

Illustrated by Isabelle Brent. Boston: Little, Brown, 1995

This is an elegant book to hold, read, and look at carefully many times over! Full-page, detailed portrait paintings of twenty-six animals are in gold leaf and jewellike colors; they are done in a romanticized and fanciful art style. Each picture is framed in precise and ornate geometric patterns reminiscent of medieval illuminated manuscripts. A brief, well-written statement informs the reader of an array of interesting, sometimes humorous facts about each animal: its history, habits, habitat, and distinctive physical characteristics, such as its size, shape, and markings.

149   Brett, Jan

ARMADILLO RODEO   *5–8* YEARS

Illustrated by Jan Brett. New York: Putnam, 1995

Bo, a curious and myopic armadillo, got distracted and separated from his
mother and three brothers as they traveled across the Texas hill country. Bo
noticed a cowgirl, Harmony Jean, who was deliberately scuffing up her
brand new cowboy boots by sliding down the bank over rocks and sand,
tramping about in the mud, and splashing in the creek so she would not
have to ride in a barrel race "looking like a tenderfoot in new boots." When
he saw her boots through his myopic eyes he thought he found a new
friend, a shiny red armadillo, and he followed the cowgirl (and his new

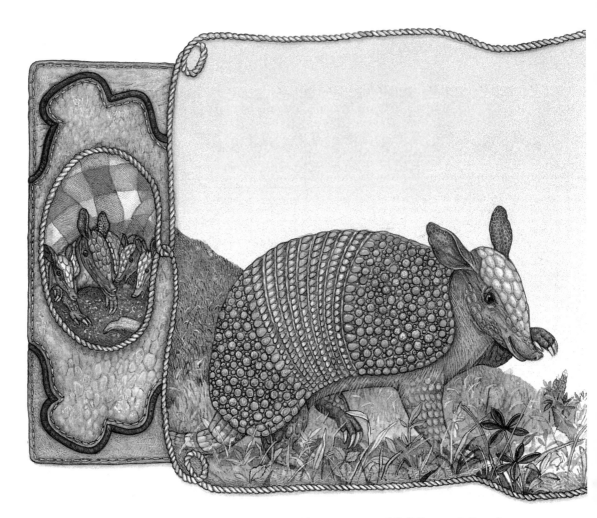

ILLUSTRATION 23   Illustration by Jan Brett reprinted by permission of G. P. Putnam's Sons from
Armadillo Rodeo, copyright © 1995 by Jan Brett.

"armadillo" friend) to the rodeo. When the girl swung her leg over the pony, Bo thought he saw the red "armadillo" leap on the pony, and so did he. The pony bucked when he felt Bo jump on his back and Bo fell off. The adventures that follow prove exciting, but not catastrophic. Typical of Brett's approach to illustrating, there is always a subplot or series of related events depicted in the side panels, and in this book the observant reader will notice that Bo's mother and brothers are always close by asking the other animals if they have seen her curious son. (See illustration 23.) How Bo discovers that Harmony Jean's boots are not and never were an armadillo will surely make the reader feel quite smug, for each one could have told him that early in the course of his wild adventures. All ends happily, for Bo and his family are reunited and head home together. Jan Brett's

realistic line and wash paintings, done in clean, rich colors, are intricately designed and contain an abundance of flora and fauna indicative of the place in which the action occurs. She also includes numerous events, clothes, and motifs traditionally associated with the Western rodeos.

150 Brown, Rick

WHAT RHYMES WITH SNAKE? *3–6* YEARS

Illustrated by Rick Brown. New York: Tambourine, 1994

An array of delightful surprises is offered in this clever lift-the-flap word and picture book. When the flap is lifted, the initial consonant or consonant blend of the word is changed and, of course, so is the word: goose becomes moose, crane becomes plane, bell becomes shell, frog becomes log; lift the flap that covers only a portion of the creature or object pictured and an absolutely unexpected creature or object will appear: a point of the star becomes the fin of a car, the goose's wing becomes the moose's antlers, the beak of the hen becomes the tip of the pen, the tip of the handle of the rake becomes the back end of the snake. The large, bright full-color pictures, outlined in heavy black lines, make a perfect match for this refreshingly creative and amusing play with words and lines.

151 Brown, Ruth

COPYCAT *4–9* YEARS

Illustrated by Ruth Brown. New York: Dutton, 1994

Children are bound to delight in the antics of Buddy, the kitten that copied the pets with whom he lived: Holly the lazy mother cat, Baby the shy kitten, and especially Bessie the dog. Buddy even copied squirrels and birds. Unfortunately, when he tried to chew on Bessie's bone like she did, he broke three teeth and had to go to the veterinarian, for, as the author tells her readers, "Cats teeth aren't made for chewing bones." The realistic line-and-wash illustrations in this oversized picture book are created by alternating full and half pages; by turning each half page and full page a wonderful surprise is unveiled. This approach to creating pictures is used most cleverly in this picture book, especially the one showing what poor Buddy looked like when he got back from the veterinarian minus the three teeth he broke chewing on Bessie's bone!

152 Calhoun, Mary

CROSS-COUNTRY CAT *5–10* YEARS

Illustrated by Erick Ingraham. New York: Morrow, 1979

A tension-filled saga about a cat that found his way home on cross-country skis after his owners inadvertently left him behind at their mountain cabin. The realistic illustrations make this high-spirited fantasy about a persistent and agile cat thoroughly convincing and memorable. See other stories about this clever cat: *Henry the Sailor Cat* (Morrow, 1994), *High-Wire Henry* (Morrow, 1991), and *Hot-Air Henry* (Morrow, 1981).

153   Cannon, Annie

THE BAT IN THE BOOT   *5–8 YEARS*

Illustrated by Annie Cannon. New York: Orchard, 1996

Based on an actual incident, this is a credible, authentic portrayal of how a mature Big Brown Bat rescued a baby Big Brown Bat "trapped" inside the home of a family that did not view bats as enemies and was not repulsed by them as so many people tend to be. The full-color realistic illustrations are rendered in watercolor, tempera, and pencil.

154   Carle, Eric

THE VERY LONELY FIREFLY   *4–8 YEARS*

Illustrated by Eric Carle. New York: Philomel, 1995

In the dark of a summer night a very lonely newborn firefly searches for his fellow fireflies. He flies toward each light he notices, only to discover the light actually comes from such things as a lightbulb, a candle, a flashlight, the eyes of an owl, and a car's headlights. Eventually he sees a group of fireflies flashing their lights and is no longer lonely, for he will now have many companions. No matter how many times they reach the last page of *The Very Lonely Firefly,* children and adults are bound to be delighted when they see the lights from the many fireflies twinkle off and on. (When the battery wears out, simply replace it with a new one.) Eric Carle indicated on the book jacket that the theme of this special concept book is friendship, but perhaps some budding entomologist will inform his or her classmates that when this soft beetle, which is commonly called a firefly, is "flashing its light" it actually is sending out its "mating call." Alerted to the various sources by which light is emitted, children's curiosity might well be aroused, encouraging them to identify many other sources of light within their surroundings. *The Very Lonely Firefly* is the last of a quartet of multidimensional concept books about the "basic needs" of lonely creatures written and illustrated by this highly respected and prolific collage artist. The first one in this series (published by Philomel) is the classic *The Very Hungry Caterpillar* (1981), one theme of which Mr. Carle said is "hope." Others are *The Very Busy Spider* (1984), in which a theme is "work," *The Very Quiet Cricket* (1990), in which a theme is "love," and the latest in the series, *The Very Lonely Firefly,* in which a theme is "belonging." Two other stunning picture books one might combine with the reading of *The Very Lonely Firefly* are *Fireflies for Nathan,* written by Shulamith L. Oppenheim and illustrated by John

Ward (Tambourine, 1994), and *Ten Flashing Fireflies,* written by Philemon Sturges and illustrated by Ann Vojtech (North-South Books, 1995).

155   Carlstrom, Nancy White
NORTHERN LULLABY   *5–8 YEARS*
Illustrated by Leo and Diane Dillon. New York: Philomel, 1992

On each page is a short poem in free verse, rather simple and spare in style and form. Each poem, evocative and filled with sensory images of the terrain and the weather conditions in Alaska, is embellished by an oversized, double-spread picture that is a sophisticated anthropomorphized representation of the aspects of nature in winter at night mentioned in the verse. Together the verses form a lyrical lullaby that is calming and soothing. The paintings, done with watercolors and shaded with airbrush, look like collages or stencils. (See illustration 24, pages 136–137.) The decorations on the bowls, masks, persons' clothes and headbands, and even on the endpapers reflect the designs of a number of different Native-American groups living throughout Alaska.

156   Chapman, Cheryl
SNOW ON SNOW ON SNOW   *3–6 YEARS*
Illustrated by Synthia Saint James. New York: Dial, 1994

Be prepared; children may ask you to reread this picture book again and again, even when the snow is long gone and perhaps well through the heat of the summer. The playful use of words is enhanced by the full-color paintings executed in oil and acrylic on canvas in a crisp, bold, flat, and pared-down style. Younger children might ask why the faces of all the characters, except Clancy the dog, are without features, but I am certain their attention will quickly be diverted from this visual technique by the action pictured and the precise, playful language; they can and probably will quickly create visual images of their own to "fill in" the missing physiognomies.

157   Cole, Joanna
MY NEW KITTEN   *5–9 YEARS*
Photographs by Margaret Miller. New York: Morrow, 1995

A little girl watches her Aunt Bonnie's Maine Coon cat whelp five kittens. When she visits her aunt a week later, she notices how much bigger, furrier, and "cuter" the kittens are and is allowed to choose one of them for her own. She chooses the one that was the first to open his eyes and names him Dusty because he is gray. The twenty crisp and clearly focused colored pictures were taken over an eight-week period. These photographs, combined with an easy-to-read text that is printed in clean, large type, document the development of Dusty and his littermates. They are depicted as being curious about practically everything in sight, and by copying the mother cat, they learn how to eat cat food and to use the litter box. When Dusty is eight weeks old, he goes to his new home to live.

158   Cunningham, David

A CROW'S JOURNEY   *5–10* YEARS

Illustrated by David Cunningham.
Morton Grove, Ill.: Albert Whitman, 1996

In response to the curious crow's question, "Where does the mountain snow go in spring?" Cunningham has created spare verse and amazingly realistic gouache paintings in full color. These pictures of uncluttered landscapes look quite like professional photographs; they show the crow (and the reader) the path of the water from melted mountain snow as it trickles downhill, joins a stream and then a shallow rushing brook, goes on to a strong rapid, then to a waterfall which ends below in a collection of calm water, flows into a stream that flows into a river, which widens and meets the ocean. *A Crow's Journey* offers the reader a truly memorable and satisfying aesthetic experience!

159   Day, Alexandra

FRANK AND ERNEST ON THE ROAD   *6–10* YEARS

Illustrated by Alexandra Day. New York: Scholastic, 1994

In response to their advertisement in the "Yellow Pages," offering to take care of someone's business while the owner is away, Frank and Ernest are hired to deliver a truckload of fruit. In order to carry out this temporary job, the two animal pals must learn the specialized language of the trucker. Some of the specialized terms and the meanings they learned were: "double nickels" means 55-mile-an-hour speed limit, "green stamps" means a speeding ticket, "magic mile" means the final mile of a long trip, and "ulcer gulcher" means traffic jam. A glossary including these terms and many more appears on the front and back endpapers. Two other books about the specialized language these two friends had to learn in order to carry out a temporary job are *Frank and Ernest* (Scholastic, 1988) and *Frank and Ernest Play Ball* (Scholastic, 1990). All of the books about Frank and Ernest are illustrated with crisp and clean, realistic paintings done in oils and watercolor and printed in full color.

ILLUSTRATION 24   Illustration by Leo and Diane Dillon reprinted by permission of Philomel Books from *Northern Lullaby* by Nancy White Carlstrom, illustrations copyright © 1992 by Leo and Diane Dillon.

160 Delafosse, Claude, and Gallimard Jeunesse, *Creators*

ANIMALS   *8–12+ YEARS*

Illustrated by Tony Ross and with reproductions
of gallery art. New York: Scholastic, 1995

> Through the clever use of plastic overlays and astute questions, readers
> of this unique picture book are encouraged to participate and to think
> about various kinds of art in ways that help them to look at, recognize,
> and appreciate some techniques artists have used in their art. Reproduc-
> tions of art by such artists as Henri Matisse, Alberto Giacometti, Alex-
> ander Calder, Breughel the Elder, and M. C. Escher, as well as a tapestry,
> cave paintings, and sculptures are focused on in this book. Tony Ross's
> cartoon-style sketches done in pen-and-ink line and watercolor wash add
> a bit of levity throughout, but they do not demean the fine art included
> in this book. Instead they tend to encourage participation on the part of
> the readers and enhance the objectives the creators apparently intended
> to accomplish, namely introducing children to great art and making it
> more accessible to them. *Animals* was originally published in France un-
> der the title *Le Bestiaire* by Éditions Gallimard Jeunesse in 1993 and is
> included in A First Discovery Art Book series. Other titles in this series
> are *Portraits, Paintings,* and *Landscapes;* all were published by Scholas-
> tic in 1993.

161 de Regniers, Beatrice Schenk, Eva Moore,
Mary Michaels White, and Jan Carr, *Compilers*

SING A SONG OF POPCORN   *4–12+ YEARS*

Illustrated by nine Caldecott Medal artists.
New York: Scholastic, 1988

> A real gem! One hundred twenty-nine poems culled from the work of
> renowned poets are grouped within nine themes: "Fun with Rhyme,"
> Weather, Spooky Poems, Story Poems, Animals, People, Nonsense
> Rhymes, "Seeing, Thinking and Feeling" poems, and Free Verse. Each
> section is illustrated with original artwork by one of nine different
> Caldecott-winning artists. *Sing a Song of Popcorn,* an expanded and up-
> dated edition of *Poems Children Will Sit Still For* (Scholastic, 1969), is a
> must for every teacher or librarian serving children and for families. At
> the back of the book one will find indexes of titles, first lines, and authors
> as well as biographical sketches of each of the award-winning illustrators
> whose work appears in this book.

162   Dotlich, Rebecca Kai

SWEET DREAMS OF THE WILD: POEMS FOR BEDTIME   *4–8* YEARS

Illustrated by Katharine Dodge. Honesdale, Pa.:
Wordsong/Boyds Mills, 1996

> Children are certain to be fascinated with these verses that tell them
> where a variety of creatures sleep. Depending on where they live, some
> readers will probably be quite familiar with some of the creatures dis-
> cussed, such as the squirrel, cat, spider, or cow; they are less likely to
> have seen or even heard about some of the other creatures discussed, such
> as the bat, hummingbird, brown bear, mountain goat, or sea otter. The
> full-page colored-pencil drawings are in soft hues and each depicts the
> creature sleeping in its typical position in its natural habitat (except the
> domesticated and tamed cat, which is curled up sound asleep on a win-
> dow seat). This book contains a charming collection of poems and illus-
> trations for bedtime!

163   Ehlert, Lois

COLOR ZOO   *3–6* YEARS

Illustrated by Lois Ehlert. New York: Lippincott, 1989

> Faces of zoo animals are depicted in simple geometric shapes on flat,
> brightly colored paper; each is named in large black bold type. When one
> turns the page, the geometric shape that formed an animal's face stands
> alone and the name of this shape also appears in large black bold type.
> This entire picture book is an intriguing exercise in graphic art and paper
> engineering. For other fine concept books by this author/artist (published
> by Harcourt Brace) see: *Eating the Alphabet: Fruits and Vegetables from
> A to Z* (1989), *Growing Vegetable Soup* (1987), and *Planting a Rainbow*
> (1988).

164   Geisert, Bonnie, and Arthur Geisert

HAYSTACK   *5–8* YEARS

Illustrated by Arthur Geisert. Boston: Houghton
Mifflin, 1995

> The title suggests that the haystack is the focal or dominant point of this
> beautiful book. In actual fact, the haystack is a clever literary and visual
> device the creators of this book used to document the cyclical nature of
> farm work on the prairies and to cite the variety of animals one would be
> likely to find on a farm in the heartland of America in the early 1930s. The
> exquisitely defined etchings touched up with soft, clean watercolors

combined with brief, but informative text provide a realistic, yet rather quaint and somewhat bucolic portrait of farm life. Compare the images of farm life on this prairie in a less technological era with those depicted by William Kurelek's award-winning picture books *A Prairie Boy's Winter* (Houghton Mifflin, 1975) and *A Prairie Boy's Summer* (Houghton Mifflin, 1973), and Thomas B. Allen's *On Granddaddy's Farm* (Knopf, 1989).

165   Gundersheimer, Karen
       SPLISH SPLASH BANG CRASH   *6 MONTHS–3 YEARS*
       Illustrated by Karen Gundersheimer. New York:
       Scholastic, 1995

   The four-color, exuberant cartoon-style, line and clean, crisp watercolor-wash illustrations depict nursery-school-age children representing various racial groups playing with everyday objects and toys, accompanied by tongue-tickling words describing the sounds of each thing. Conjointly they provide delightful read-aloud fare. There is little doubt (to the delight of both adults and children!) that children will quickly be "reading" this book along with or independent of their parent, teacher, babysitter, or older sibling.

166   Haldane, Suzanne, and Maude Sallinger
       TEDDIES & TRUCKS   *9 MONTHS–3 YEARS*
       Illustrated with photographs. New York: Dutton, 1996

   Soft-looking, fuzzy, cuddly teddy bears attend commonly known trucks in this wonderfully uncluttered informational board book that is sturdy and easy for the very young to handle. The text, printed in bold, heavy primary-sized type, identifies the kind of truck pictured below it (e.g., garbage truck, livestock truck, car transporter, tow truck). Some of the pictures are full pages or double-page spreads; the photographs of vehicle replicas are reproduced in crisp, solid full colors; the teddy bears attending the trucks are photographs of teddies provided by Wang International. Haldane and Sallinger also created a companion book *Teddies & Machines* (Dutton, 1996).

167   Harrison, Ted
       O CANADA   *7–10 YEARS*
       Illustrated by Ted Harrison. New York:
       Ticknor & Fields, 1993

   Accomplished expressionistic paintings, done in acrylics and reproduced in flat, rich, vibrant full color, are coupled with an insightful commentary to depict this award-winning author/artist's personal impressions of the landscapes characteristic of each of the provinces and territories in Canada as well as the diverse cultures that populate them. Following a brief introduction in which Harrison briefly explains how Canada and the United States are really quite different from each other, he provides a map that is attractive, colorful, and easy for children to interpret. The map shows clearly the location and size of each province and territory in proportion and in relation to the others. He leaves no doubt about the vastness of Canada and the significance of the fact that it is a country surrounded by three oceans (the Pacific Ocean, Arctic Ocean, and Atlantic Ocean) and is contiguous with the United States on the fourth side. The score and words (in English and French) of "O Canada," the national anthem, are included at the end of the book.

168   Heller, Ruth

COLOR   *6–10* YEARS

Illustrated by Ruth Heller. New York: Putnam, 1995

Some basic concepts about color, in relation to the media used to create them and the processes used to reproduce them, are described in slight verse. Transparent overlays help children (and a good many adults) to understand the process by which multicolored pictures are printed. Heller's illustrations, done in rich, clean colors, are perky and each page is formatted differently, all of which should serve to attract children's attention and keep them engaged from the beginning through to the very last page. One might also use the following books to supplement and expand upon the concepts Heller has aptly put forth in this very fine concept book: *The Adventures of the Three Colors,* written and illustrated by Annette Tison and Talus Taylor (World, 1971); *From Pictures to Words: A Book about Making a Book,* written and illustrated by Janet Stevens (Holiday House, 1995); and *See What I Am,* written and illustrated by Roger Duvoisin (Lothrop, Lee & Shepard, 1974).

169   Higginson, William J., *Editor*

WIND IN THE LONG GRASS: A COLLECTION OF HAIKU   *5–10+* YEARS

Illustrated by Sandra Speidel. New York: Simon & Schuster, 1991

This is truly a very special book in every respect. The haiku collected in it are written by people from all over the world, and each poem seems to capture something precious or at least worthy of note about most ordinary happenings, especially one person's response to some aspect of nature. The impressionistic illustrations were done in pastels and reproduced in full color. (See illustration 25.) Each illustration takes the reader well beyond the literal level of interpretation. It seems the more often one reads the poems aloud and looks at the illustrations, the more intensely

ILLUSTRATION 25   Reprinted with the permission of Simon & Schuster Books for Young Readers from *Wind in the Long Grass* by William Higginson, illustrated by Sandra Speidel. Illustrations copyright © 1991 by Sandra Speidel.

one responds to the ethereal aura created by the wonderful match of the content and tones or moods depicted in the poems and the subtle and exquisite use of texture, choice of colors and hues, and content that characterize the illustrations individually and as a whole.

170   Hodges, Margaret, *Reteller*
HIDDEN IN THE SAND   *6–10* YEARS
Illustrated by Paul Birling. New York: Scribner, 1994

This well-told story, enhanced and enriched with accomplished full-color impressionistic paintings, results in a picture book that offers rich images of the great desert between India and the Middle East: the desert is portrayed as fierce and harsh during the day; fiery sun high in the sky blinds the eyes and parches the lips and mouth, the sea of sand is so fine and dry that the hooves of the oxen sink deep into it at every step and all tracks of the oxen and the wagons they pull are immediately swallowed so there are no roads on which to travel or to follow; the sand becomes too hot during the day for man or animal to walk on. In contrast, at night the waves of sand and air are cool and the sky is clear and filled with bright, shining stars. This retelling of the tale from the Buddhist classic *The Jataka* is bound to impress children with how important knowledge of the stars is when traveling across land as barren as this great desert and how one can find a source of water in a wilderness of sand. One might bring to the students' attention how the story of *Hidden in the Sand* parallels the Old Testament story of Moses striking water in the rock in the wilderness (Book of Numbers).

171   Hughes, Shirley

OUT AND ABOUT   *3–7* YEARS

Illustrated by Shirley Hughes. New York: Lothrop, Lee & Shepard, 1988

> Simple, zestful rhymes combined with animated action-filled drawings done in mixed media and reproduced in full color depict the wonders and pleasurable activities of the outdoors with family and friends or alone in all kinds of weather through the four seasons of the year. A truly beautiful book for family sharing! This book is good for reading aloud to all children, but particularly to those who are visually impaired, for the rhymes focus on the physical senses of hearing, touch, and smell in response to one's surroundings.

172   Jenkins, Steve

BIGGEST, STRONGEST, FASTEST   *4–8* YEARS

Illustrated by Steve Jenkins. New York: Ticknor & Fields, 1995

> Large, full-color paper collage pictures depict the record holders among fourteen members of the animal kingdom, including mammals, insects, birds, reptiles, and crustaceans. In addition to telling the reader what record each animal holds (the biggest and smallest, fastest and slowest, strongest and longest animal, and so on), information is also given about habitat, diet, and its size in relation to some object in the child's world. All this information is summarized in a readable chart at the back of the book. Also provided is a selective bibliography of sources children can refer to if they want more information about the animals mentioned in this book as well as other animals.

173 Johnson, Paul Brett, and Celeste Lewis
LOST *5–10* YEARS
Illustrated by Paul Brett Johnson. New York: Orchard, 1996

> This heart-wrenching story begins with a double-page sketch of a girl and her father setting up their camp in the barren desert. They do not seem to notice that Flag, their pet beagle, is standing alert and wagging his tail, looking at something beyond the scope of the page. This picture, done in brown and yellow pencil and printed on sand-colored paper, appears on the copyright page and foreshadows what is to follow. On the next left-hand page is a full-color picture showing Flag running after a rabbit. Unfortunately, neither the girl nor her Dad are privy to what is depicted in this or in any of the full-color pictures that follow; thus, they do not become aware until some time later that Flag has run off. The harrowing experiences Flag had while he was lost for a month in the desert of Tonto National Forest north of Cave Creek, Arizona, are depicted in full-color acrylic paintings reproduced on the left-hand pages. Juxtaposed on the right-hand pages, the attempts of the girl and her father to find their beloved beagle are depicted in colored-pencil sketches printed on sandy colored paper. This thoroughly engrossing survival story is based on a real dog that was lost in this harsh desert for over a month and amazingly was found alive. Compare and contrast the images of the desert depicted in this book with those in *Desert Trip,* written by Barbara A. Steiner and illustrated by Ronald Himler (Sierra Club Books for Children, 1996).

174 Johnson, Stephen T.
ALPHABET CITY *6–9* YEARS
Illustrated by Stephen T. Johnson. New York: Viking, 1995

> What at first glance appear to be photographs of city sights that seem to form the capital letters of the alphabet are actually masterfully rendered full-color realistic paintings done with pastels, watercolors, gouache, and charcoal. Johnson's practice of noticing these images of aspects of his city could effectively motivate people of all ages to look at their environment, wherever and whatever that may be, and discover unexpected shapes, colors, and ideas of their own in combinations and arrangements of scale, effects of shadows, and designs and motifs in surface textures. *Alphabet City* was named a 1996 Caldecott Award Honor Book.

175 Keats, Ezra Jack
THE SNOWY DAY *2–4* YEARS
Illustrated by Ezra Jack Keats. New York: Viking, 1962, 1996

This sturdy board book edition of the 1963 Caldecott Medal Award picture book will help children see many times over how young Peter celebrates the wonders of fresh fallen snow.

176   Krupinski, Loretta, *Compiler*

A NEW ENGLAND SCRAPBOOK: A JOURNEY THROUGH   *ALL AGES*
POETRY AND PICTURES

Illustrated by Loretta Krupinski. New York:
HarperCollins, 1994

> Children and adults will find much of interest in this fine collection of poems, informative prose, and calendar-like paintings in full color done with gouache and colored pencil. It makes a glowing statement about the unique qualities of the New England climate, terrain, flora and fauna, history, and architecture, especially the houses, farms, churches, and lighthouses.

177   Larrick, Nancy

CATS ARE CATS   *3–10+ YEARS*

Illustrated by Ed Young. New York: Philomel, 1988

> This is an absolutely top-notch picture book in every respect! The forty-two poems about the many aspects of "catness" constitute a superb collection; they are by some of the best poets of our time and of times past (e.g., John Ciardi, Lillian Moore, Karla Kuskin, Elizabeth Coatsworth, and Aileen Fisher). Each of the illustrations, done on wrapping paper in charcoal and pastel, captures and extends the themes and aura of the poem for which it was created; each is worthy of framing and hanging in one's own home or in the best of art galleries.

178   Little Simon Merchandise

GUESS WHO'S MY MOTHER?   *1–4 YEARS*

Illustrated. New York: Simon & Schuster, 1995

> This tiny interaction board book has split pages; the half page at the top pictures a mature female animal, the bottom half page pictures a baby animal. The challenge for the child is to flip the half pages until he or she can match the baby animal with the half page that pictures the same kind of animal in its mature stage. Because the book is small (3½″ × 4¾″), the pictures in it are small, but each one, done in what looks like ink line and watercolor wash prepared on four-color acetate overlays, depicts an entire animal in a style that is a bit quaint, but is readily recognizable. Another book in this Mix and Match miniature board book series is *Guess*

Where I Live? (Simon & Schuster, 1996), but because more background knowledge about the habits and habitats of each animal depicted is required to find the picture that shows the kind of "home" each animal lives in, the intended audience is more likely to be a little older (around 3–6 years).

179 Locke, Ann

I CAN SAY APPLE   *6 MONTHS–2 YEARS*

Illustrated by Louise Batchelder. New York:
De Agostini, 1996

The cartoon-style illustrations in this board book are done in line and watercolor wash and depict a toddler wearing, holding, or just looking at things common to its environment, such as an apple, cup, shoes, book, or table. Other board books in this series created for the toddler by Locke and Batchelder are *I Can Say Blanket* and *I Can Say Teddy* (De Agostini, 1996).

180 MacKinnon, Debbie

CATHY'S CAKE   *1–3 YEARS*

Illustrated with photographs by Anthea Sieveking.
New York: Dial, 1996

Cathy's Cake and three other board books *(Billy's Boots, Ken's Kittens, Meg's Monkey)* are included in the series A First Lift-the-Flap Book: Hide-and-Seek-Surprises. The infants and toddlers pictured in these delightful board books are of Caucasian, African, Asian, and Hispanic heritage and they are shown playing with or looking for/at/under ordinary toys, a pet kitten (but no puppy?), and household furnishings. The text in each book consists of complete declarative sentences and questions and was written by Debbie MacKinnon; Anthea Sieveking took the photographs which are reproduced in crisp, bright, full colors and printed as full-page, uncluttered pictures. (See illustration 26.) The series was published by Dial in 1996. Children (and adults) are in for a good time, for a surprise greets them each time they lift a flap. Even though the children will probably remember after the first reading what lies behind each flap, they are certain to ask to have this book and the others in this series reread countless times and most assuredly will continue to be delighted each and every time they lift up the flaps. Undoubtedly the flaps will eventually have to be reinforced with a sturdy transparent tape.

Is the cake in here?

No. It's a birthday present.

ILLUSTRATION 26   Photographs by Anthea Sieveking, copyright © 1996 by Anthea Sieveking. From *Cathy's Cake* by Debbie MacKinnon, photos by Anthea Sieveking. Used by permission of Dial Books for Young Readers, a division of Penguin Books USA, Inc.

181   Marshak, Samuel

HAIL TO MAIL   *5–9* YEARS

Illustrated by Vladimar Radunsky. Translated from the
Russian by Richard Pevear. New York: Holt, 1990

> Spare and witty narrative verse reports the succession of cities around the
> world to which a certified letter addressed to Mr. John Peck traveled. It
> journeyed by land, sea, and air as conscientious postal carriers (from New
> York City to Boise, to Zurich and Griesernweg, to the Amazon in Brazil,
> and back to New York City) attempted to deliver it. Children are bound
> to be amused and intrigued by Radunsky's droll and exaggerated, sophis-
> ticated expressionistic paintings which so cleverly enhance this saga of
> how a letter just misses Mr. Peck as he travels around the world. *Hail to
> Mail* was originally published in 1990 in Russia under the title *Pochta*.
> Children would have great fun comparing the story, illustrations, and the
> succession of cities the letter in *Hail to Mail* was sent to with the stories,
> illustrations, and letters sent by the protagonists in *Around the World in
> Eight Days,* written and illustrated by John Burningham (Jonathan Cape,
> 1972), and *Dear Santa,* written by Elisabeth Borchers and illustrated by
> Wilhelm Schlote (Greenwillow, 1977).

182   Miller, Cameron, and Dominique Falla
WOODLORE   *7–10+* YEARS
Illustrated by Cameron Miller and Dominique Falla.
New York: Ticknor & Fields, 1995

> Simple couplets identify the kind of wood that frames each picture and
> state the traditional purposes that kind of wood best serves: maple and
> spruce for lutes and violins, the longbow made of yew, the Windsor chair
> made of beechwood, ship decks made of Burmese teak, rocking horses
> made of yellow pine, and so on. The stunning, exquisitely detailed
> realistic illustrations were done on plywood primed with gesso, using
> acquareles (water-soluble pencils). Each picture depicts woodworkers
> engaged in their craft. This book could serve as a fine introduction to the
> history of woodworking and the varied uses of wood, but it is a fine pic-
> ture book in-and-of itself to read and look at many times over. At the back
> of the book, in "Notes on Illustrations" the authors provide a brief state-
> ment explaining the setting pictured as well as the process used to pre-
> pare the wood and the nationality and occupation of the people who first
> made the wooden objects depicted in the illustrations.

183   Moss, Lloyd
ZIN! ZIN! ZIN! A VIOLIN   *5–10* YEARS
Illustrated by Marjorie Priceman. New York: Simon &
Schuster, 1995

> Illustrated with zany, expressionistic line and full-color gouache wash
> paintings which extend the rhythmic verse, this picture book serves as a
> counting book as well as a way to introduce children to ten musical in-
> struments and the groups that use these instruments to play primarily
> classical music. The close observer will most likely notice and delight in
> the antics of two cats, a dog, and a mouse who respond to each other, to
> the sounds an individual instrument makes, and to the sounds made
> when all the instruments are played together in a orchestral arrangement.
> *Zin! Zin! Zin! A Violin* was named a 1996 Caldecott Award Honor Book.

184   Naraheshi, Keiko
I HAVE A FRIEND   *4–7* YEARS
Illustrated by Keiko Naraheshi. New York: Margaret K.
McElderry/Macmillan, 1987

> A young boy refers to his shadow as "yesterday's night left behind for the
> day" and in perky prose tells of the diverse shapes it takes as it appears
> in many common and unusual places in both daytime and nighttime. The
> large watercolor paintings in the naive art style reflect the openness and
> vitality of the little boy's response to this natural phenomenon and to life

in general; furthermore, they encourage the readers to look for their own shadows wherever and whenever they can.

185   Oates, Eddie Herschel

MAKING MUSIC: SIX INSTRUMENTS YOU CAN CREATE   *7–10 YEARS*

Illustrated by Michael Koesch. New York: HarperCollins, 1995

> Realistic line and watercolor-wash paintings enhance the precise and easy-to-understand directions provided for making six different kinds of musical instruments: balloon tom-tom, wrench xylophone, and xylo-drum, examples of percussion instruments; garden-hose trumpet and spoon roarer, examples of wind instruments; and singing sitar, an example of a string instrument. Full-page watercolor paintings of children playing each of these instruments serve to demonstrate to young readers that they, too, can actually make and play these instruments.

186   Olson, Arielle North

THE LIGHTHOUSE KEEPER'S DAUGHTER   *5–10 YEARS*

Illustrated by Elaine Wentworth. Boston: Little, Brown, 1987

> Combining incidents that actually happened in lighthouses along the Maine coast, the author has created a thoroughly credible and moving story about a young girl who kept the lighthouse lamps burning for weeks while her father was forced to remain ashore by a violent winter storm. The oversized full-color watercolor paintings provide truly beautiful scenes of the seascape, the interior of the lighthouse, and the family's home alongside the lighthouse on the rocky island. Compare the experiences of the young girl, the writing style, and the illustrations in *The Lighthouse Keeper's Daughter* with these same literary aspects in *Celia's Island Journal,* written by Celia Thaxter and illustrated by Loretta Krupinski (Little, Brown, 1992).

187   Ormerod, Jan

COME BACK, PUPPIES   *3–6 YEARS*

Illustrated by Jan Ormerod. New York: Lothrop, Lee & Shepard, 1992

> Originally published in Great Britain, this "hide-and-seek book" is an absolute delight, certain to be enjoyed by everyone, especially the very young, but also the older, experienced readers and even sophisticated adults! Mother Scottie or cairn terrier (it is hard to tell which) asks where her ten puppies are. By turning the see-through acetate pages, each of which has a flat, colorful picture of one or more of the puppies painted on

it, the reader will eventually find all ten puppies, be they cream, golden, brown, or black. Only the very alert reader will notice that the spotted puppy was with its mother all the time! See Ormerod's *Come Back, Kittens* (Lothrop, Lee & Shepard, 1993) for another round of fun.

188 Oxenbury, Helen

I HEAR   *6 MONTHS–2 YEARS*

Illustrated by Helen Oxenbury. Cambridge, Mass.:
Cambridge, 1985

On each left-hand page, a simple word labels something an infant or toddler might hear in its immediate environment (bird, rain, dog, telephone, watch, and so on); on the right-hand page facing it, a unisex child is shown listening to that thing. Typical of Oxenbury's books for the youngest audience, the line-and-wash illustrations are amusing, precise, and easily recognizable. Other board books in this series designed to alert children to their senses and help them to be responsive to their immediate world through these senses are *I See, I Touch,* and *I Can.* All of these charming books are available in two different sizes, 6″ × 6″ and as a boxed set of four miniature (3⅛″ × 3¼″) books (Candlewick, 1996).

189 Paterson, Bettina

WHO'S AT THE FIREHOUSE?   *6 MONTHS–2 YEARS*

Illustrated by Bettina Paterson. New York:
Grosset & Dunlap, 1996

Unsophisticated cartoon-style drawings in flat, bright primary colors depict a spotted puppy exploring a firehouse. Readers who lift the flaps as the puppy encourages them to do will discover what the curious little puppy saw: a fire engine is in the garage, a fireman is driving the fire truck, a hose is stored in the side of the fire truck, and the firemen are wearing special hats and coats and boots when they rush away in the truck to put out a fire. Other titles in this Lift-and-Look board book series include *Hide-and-Seek Bunnies, Peek-a-Boo Baby, Peek-a-Boo Kitty, Peek-a-Boo Moon,* and *Peek-a-Boo Teddy* (Grosset & Dunlap, 1996.)

190 Paul, Ann Whitford

THE SEASONS SEWN: A YEAR IN PATCHWORK   *7–10+ YEARS*

Illustrated by Michael McCurdy. San Diego:
Browndeer/Harcourt Brace, 1996

Expertly executed scratchboard illustrations printed in full color, together with brief but informative statements, make quite clear to children how the names of patchwork quilt patterns so often stemmed from actual items or occurrences in the United States during the nineteenth century; e.g., flora and fauna commonly observed during different seasons of the year, qualities or interests of political leaders and/or members of their families, modes of transportation, and significant events. Compare this fine informational book with *Selina and the Bear Paw Quilt,* written by Barbara Smucker and illustrated by Janet Wilson (Crown, 1995), and Raymond Bial's *Needle and Thread: A Book about Quilts* (Houghton Mifflin, 1996). In his illustrations for *The Night Before Christmas* by Clement C. Moore (Holiday House, 1980), Tomie de Paola included patchwork designs which were used in antique quilts. One might examine these pictures to determine which quilt designs he included are also discussed and pictured in *The Seasons Sewn: A Year in Patchwork.*

191   Penn, Malka

THE MIRACLE OF THE POTATO LATKES: *5–9+ YEARS*
A HANUKKAH STORY

Illustrated by Giora Carmi. New York: Holiday House, 1994

The belief that "God will provide" gives solace to many and it certainly did for Tante Golda even when a poor harvest left her with no potatoes, which meant that she would be unable to make her famous latkes for her friends and neighbors at Hanukkah. Tante Golda was always generous with whatever little or much she had, and when an old beggar, tired and hungry, knocked at her door and asked for food, she took pity on him, inviting him to share the batch of golden, crispy latkes she had made with her last small potato. Thereafter, each morning during Hanukkah when she woke up there was one more potato sitting next to the menorah. So each night she invited one more guest to share her latkes. On the last day of Hanukkah she noticed there were eight potatoes and just as it had always been, there were eight candles, eight potatoes, and eight guests to celebrate and eat her famous latkes. Then, she found that her wooden barrel was filled to the very top with potatoes, enough to last the entire winter. Since neither Tante Golda nor her guests could account for the miracle of the appearance of the potatoes, the only conclusion she could come to was that indeed it was God who provided. Expressionistic illustrations, done in line and wash, capture the spirit of this joyful story. I "tested" the recipe for Tante Golda's famous potato latkes the author provided at the end of the story and they were not only golden and crispy, but very tasty! Compare the text, setting, and illustrations of this variant of the Hanukkah tale with that entitled *Just Enough Is Plenty* retold by Barbara Diamond Goldin and illustrated by Seymour Chwast (Kestrel/ Viking, 1988).

192   Radin, Ruth Yaffe

HIGH IN THE MOUNTAIN   *7–11+* YEARS

Illustrated by Ed Young. New York: Macmillan, 1989

> Lyrical poetic prose and elegant abstract impressionistic paintings in full
> color express a child's sense of wonder from the time she wakes up early
> in the morning as the mist lifts from the mountains, through the day as
> she runs in the meadow among the alpine flowers and sees a deer among
> the trees, until dusk when she and her grandfather follow a mountain
> road up and down among the clouds, then pitch their tent and build a
> campfire for the warmth and light it provides. Read this picture book
> aloud to get the full benefit of the imagery-filled and mood-enhancing
> text. In each and every way, this picture book is a real gem!

193   Rand, Gloria

SALTY DOG   *5–8* YEARS

Illustrated by Ted Rand. New York: Holt, 1989

> The well-written, straightforward text and the expressionistic paintings
> in traditional watercolor and liquid watercolor chronicle the growth and
> adventures of a dog and the step-by-step construction of a wooden sail-
> boat. Children are bound to enjoy the challenge of finding in the illus-
> trations the parallels that show the plucky and clever puppy become a
> plucky and clever full-grown dog and the progress of the sailboat from the
> construction of the frame, to the fitting out, to the maiden voyage. Other
> titles about this valiant dog are *Salty Sails North* (1990), *Salty Takes Off*
> (1992), and *Aloha, Salty* (1996).

194   Rikys, Bodel

RED BEAR   *1–3* YEARS

Illustrated by Bodel Rikys. New York: Dial, 1992

> Oil pastels, with the line drawn in brush and India ink, were used to
> prepare the crisp, somewhat restrained pictures highlighting specific col-
> ors that appear throughout Red Bear's day, from the moment he wakes up,
> gets dressed in colorful clothes, feeds his black cat, goes outdoors and
> chats with a green caterpillar, indulges in a pink ice cream cone, plays
> with an orange balloon, rides a gray elephant, and goes to bed covered
> with a quilt made of patches in all the colors he saw during his busy day.
> The names of the colors are given on each page except the last, a tech-
> nique that will challenge the very young child to recall what he or she has
> learned, but serves as a nice way to summarize and conclude this pleas-
> ant little concept story.

195   Riley, Linda Capus

ELEPHANTS SWIM   *5–9* YEARS

Illustrated by Steve Jenkins. Boston: Houghton Mifflin, 1995

> Accomplished, full-color collage pictures combined with simple rhymes
> depict how sixteen animals swim. More detailed information about each
> animal's behavior in the water is provided in the "Notes" at the back of
> the book. Unfortunately, the title does not do justice to the wealth of in-
> formation and vast amount of fun this concept book offers young readers.

196   Robbins, Ken

AIR: THE ELEMENTS   *7–12* YEARS

Illustrated with photographs. New York: Holt, 1995

> Striking hand-colored photographs and refined poetic prose add up to a
> fairly comprehensive, thought-provoking, multilevel picture book that is
> actually a photo essay about some major concepts pertaining to air. *Air*
> is the third book in Robbins' series about each of the four classical ele-
> ments. Unfortunately there is no table of contents or index included, but
> each aspect of the element discussed is clearly labeled, so the reader may
> choose to read the book from beginning to end or to read only those parts
> he or she is most interested in. Some aspects of air touched upon are quite
> profound and technical (e.g., convection, moisture, oxidation, evapora-
> tion, seed dispersal, pollution, and prevailing winds), but without being
> the least bit condescending Robbins defines and discusses the concepts
> underlying the aspects and technical terminology in a manner the age
> group that seems to be his intended audience would find readable, un-
> derstandable, and certainly very relevant. Just as he did in the earlier
> books in this series, Robbins instills a sense of respect for this element;
> he leaves little doubt in the minds of the reader that clean, "fresh air is
> a precious natural resource." Other books in this series about each of the
> four classical elements written and illustrated by Robbins and published
> by Holt are *Earth* (1994), *Water* (1994), and *Fire* (1996).

197   Rylant, Cynthia

ALL I SEE   *5–9* YEARS

Illustrated by Peter Catalanotto. New York: Orchard, 1988

> Thought-provoking concepts about an artist are offered in this oversized
> picture book about how a friendship developed between a young man
> who painted only whales because that was all he saw and a little boy who
> painted whatever he saw. Large impressionistic watercolor paintings
> (many of them double-page spreads) show the same setting but from dif-
> ferent perspectives. They also offer the careful reader of the visuals ex-
> cellent lessons in the study of light. A special picture book! Compare the

authors' definition of an "artist" as well as the style of art used in the illustrations of this book with those in *An Artist,* written and illustrated by M. B. Goffstein (Harper & Row, 1980).

198   Sabuda, Robert

THE CHRISTMAS ALPHABET   *ALL AGES*

Concept, design, and paper engineering by
Robert Sabuda. New York: Orchard, 1994

> A sophisticated, comprehensive celebration of the religious and secular aspects of the Christmas season, this unique pop-up book might well be designated a family heirloom or a "special-treat" book in a classroom or school library collection. Behind each colored door labeled with a letter one finds an amazing crisp white object that pops up, amazing because it embodies a masterpiece in paper engineering and is typified by restrained and tasteful elegance. For another truly creative pop-up book by Sabuda see *The Twelve Days of Christmas* (Simon & Schuster, 1996).

199   Sadie Fields Production

THE TRAIN: WATCH IT WORK!   *7–11+ YEARS*

Illustrated by John Bradley. Design and paper engineering
by Ray Marshall. New York: Kestrel/Viking, 1986

> This unique informational book should delight train enthusiasts of all ages and could serve as an excellent introduction to the history of trains for the neophyte. Information about the internal workings and the development of trains over more than 100 years, from nineteenth-century locomotives to the latest high-speed electric trains, is presented through various means: a brief, but comprehensive text; three-dimensional pop-up pictures; moving diagrams and lift-up flaps, etc. The discussion and illustrations related to railroad signaling are excellent; signals used in the United Kingdom, France, Italy, Germany, and the United States are depicted so the reader can easily compare and contrast them. An easy-to-assemble model of the French TGV, the world's fastest electric train, is included in a pocket at the back of the book.

200   Sandeved, Kjell B.

THE BUTTERFLY ALPHABET   *7–14+ YEARS*

Illustrated with photographs by Kjell B. Sandeved.
New York: Scholastic, 1996

> Striking, distinct photographs in rich, full color dramatize the amazing colors and patterns of the wings of butterflies and moths from around the

world, arranged in alphabetical order. Each of these amazing insects, which Sandeved has described as "a caterpillar in a wedding gown," is shown from two perspectives—in flight with wings spread out as well as in a close-up and greatly magnified view of a portion of its wing.

201   Seymour, Tres

THE GULLS OF THE EDMUND FITZGERALD   *7–9 YEARS*

Illustrated by Tres Seymour. New York: Orchard, 1996

This simple narrative very briefly describes in unsophisticated poetic prose how the mighty SS *Edmund Fitzgerald,* a 700-foot-long freighter, split in half and sank in the turbulent waters of Lake Superior during a storm on November 10, 1975, and a crew of twenty-nine men met their demise. The gulls that followed the *Edmund Fitzgerald* warn the boy on the beach of the power and "hunger" of this Great Lake by telling him repeatedly not to go near the water. Their message about this treacherous lake is reiterated when they name some of the other ships that went down in its waters during storms in late fall or winter, namely, the SS *Sunbeam,* the SS *Manistee,* and the SS *City of Bangor.* In the main, the style of paper collage the illustrator used in the pictures seems a bit too sweet and quaint for this tragic story. There are some instances in which his pictures actually do reflect the mood and the action quite appropriately; these are storm scenes depicting the *Edmund Fitzgerald* being tossed about in the turbulent waters and split amidship and in the process of sinking. This is a particularly timely publication for the states along the shores of Lake Superior, for just recently (in the spring of 1995) the *Edmund Fitzgerald's* bell was brought up from the waters of Lake Superior, refurbished by the staff of the Michigan State University Museum, and exhibited there in late August 1995. The bell was taken to northern Michigan where it tolled at a memorial service. It is now on permanent exhibit in the Great Lakes Shipwreck Museum in Whitefish Point, Michigan.

202   Shannon, George

TOMORROW'S ALPHABET   *6–9 YEARS*

Illustrated by Donald Crews. New York: Greenwillow, 1996

This is a refreshingly unique, mind-stretching, and informative alphabet book! Each letter of the alphabet refers to what the object, animal, or plant will change into or amount to over a block of time. For example, for the letter *A* the seed is "tomorrow's" apple, for the letter *G* a clump of bulbs is "tomorrow's" garden (of daffodils), for the letter *Q* scraps of fabric are "tomorrow's" quilt, and for *R* grapes are "tomorrow's" raisins. Bright, clean watercolors were used to create the striking full-color pictures.

203   Siebert, Diane

HEARTLAND   *6–10* YEARS

Illustrated by Wendell Minor. New York: Crowell, 1989

> The central theme of this celebration of the Midwest in the American
> Heartland is "a land where, despite man's power, nature reigns." Real-
> istic paintings in brilliant, lush colors and fine rhymed verse are effec-
> tively combined to convey this theme. Also, see *Mojave* (Crowell, 1988),
> by this author-artist team.

204   Sills, Leslie

VISIONS: STORIES ABOUT WOMEN ARTISTS   *9–12+* YEARS

Illustrated. Morton Grove, Ill.: Albert Whitman, 1993

> A critical biography accompanied by reproductions or photographs of
> each artist's works in full color and black-and-white as well as photo-
> graphs of each woman give the reader some understanding as to how their
> life experiences, the circumstances and expectations of the times in
> which they lived, their educational opportunities (especially in terms of
> how their talents were recognized and nurtured), and the nature of their
> relationships with family and friends tended to inhibit or nurture the
> development of their artistic talents. The artists focused on in this second
> volume about women artists are Mary Cassatt (1844–1926), an American
> who explored and experimented in printmaking and pastels and impres-
> sionist painting, especially depicting relationships between mothers and
> their children; Leonora Carrington (1917–), an English surrealist painter
> who often used fairy tales, legends, myths, religious teachings, and the
> women's rights activist movement in Mexico as the sources of her cre-
> ative power; Betye Saar (1926–), an African American whose box sculp-
> tures and erudite installations (large art pieces that people can enter and
> participate in) are often inspired by the occult; and Mary Frank (1933–),
> an English-born American citizen who is a sculptor (in wood, but more
> often in clay), painter (monoprints), sketcher, and printmaker. An invalu-
> able bibliography of references for further reading is provided. An earlier
> book by Leslie Sills containing critical biographies of women artists, en-
> titled *Inspirations: Stories about Women Artists* (Albert Whitman, 1989),
> focuses on Georgia O'Keefe, Frida Kahlo, Alice Neel, and Faith Ringgold.

205   Simon, Norma

WET WORLD   *3–6* YEARS

Illustrated by Alexi Natchev. Cambridge, Mass.:
Candlewick, 1995

> The title tells it all! In spare rhythmic text and simple impressionistic
> grease-pencil line and watercolor wash reproduced in clean, clear full

color a little girl is depicted making an exuberant upbeat comment about a very wet day. She starts the gray, cloudy, rainy day with a healthful, warm breakfast, dresses in just the right kind of bright yellow rain slicker, hat, and shiny red boots, and delights in romping about in this wet world: walking in the rain as the raindrops sprinkle and drip on her waterproof clothes, splashing in the puddles, watching the cars with their windshield wipers rhythmically swishing away the water as they move down the wet road, and finally going home to her warm mother and father and crawling into her warm, dry bed wondering what kind of weather tomorrow will bring.

206   Simon, Seymour

WINTER ACROSS AMERICA   *6–10* YEARS

Illustrated with photographs. New York: Hyperion, 1994

Exquisite colored photographs and Seymour Simon's poetic prose emphasize the wonder and beauty of winter, its harshness, new beginnings, a time of rest and renewal. The reader gets a memorable glimpse of winter in the Arctic Circle where the sun may not rise above the horizon for weeks or months and the shaggy musk ox (looking something like giant goats) dig beneath the snow to search for mosses and dead grasses to eat; in the Florida Everglades which are thousands of miles of freshwater marshes, small ponds, and tree-covered islands where winter is mild and warm compared to the icy winters in the North, so that the fish, birds, insects, and other animals are active all winter; and throughout other parts of North America, such as the Midwest where blizzards and ice storms are relatively common and "snowbirds" like small flocks of plucky black-capped chickadees are seen all winter long.

207   Sky-Peck, Kathryn, *Editor,* and
Boston Museum of Fine Arts

WHO HAS SEEN THE WIND? AN ILLUSTRATED   *4–9+* YEARS
COLLECTION OF POETRY FOR YOUNG PEOPLE

Illustrated. New York: Rizzoli, 1991

A exquisite book in every respect! Thirty-seven classic poems for children, thirty-five of them illustrated with full-color reproductions of famous paintings from the Boston Museum of Fine Arts. Some of the great poets whose works are included in this book are George MacDonald, Henry Wadsworth Longfellow, Amy Lowell, Robert Louis Stevenson, Rudyard Kipling, Kenneth Grahame, Ogden Nash, and Hilaire Belloc. Some of the painters whose works bring the worlds depicted in the poems to life with color and brushstrokes are Mary Stevenson Cassatt, Paul Gauguin, Samuel F. B. Morse, Winslow Homer, Pierre Auguste Renoir, Arthur Rackham, Oscar Claude Monet, Jean François Millet, Jacob Maris,

John Singer Sargent, and Edouard Manet. Aspects of children's here-and-now world depicted in the poems and pictures, appealing to one or more of their senses (sight, sound, touch, smell, and taste), are fish, dogs, cats, flowers, babies, seasons of the year, sailing, and much more.

208 Steiner, Barbara A.

DESERT TRIP   *6–9* YEARS

Illustrations by Ronald Himler. San Francisco: Sierra Club Books for Children, 1996

A mother and her daughter backpack overnight in the desert, observing aspects of its terrain, climate, flora, and fauna. Ronald Himler's multimedia expressionistic illustrations, reproduced in full color, reaffirm the awesome beauty and variety that so impressed this mother and daughter during their jaunt through the desert. Noteworthy are the paintings depicting a number of desert flowers; each one is labeled with its common, rather than its scientific, name. Compare and contrast the tone and mood evident in the text and illustrations depicting the mother's and daughter's impressions and experiences in *Desert Trip* with the experiences of others depicted in *Lost,* written by Paul Brett Johnson and Celeste Lewis and illustrated by Paul Brett Johnson (Orchard, 1996), and *One Night: A Story from the Desert,* written by Christiana Kessler and illustrated by Ian Schoenherr (Philomel, 1995.)

209 Stevens, Janet, *Adapter*

TOPS & BOTTOMS   *4–8* YEARS

Illustrated by Janet Stevens. San Diego: Harcourt Brace, 1995

Hare has neither money nor land, but he knows he must plant crops to feed his hungry family; he is also ambitious and clever. Bear has plenty of land but is lazy and rather dull-witted. Hare proposes to Bear that he (Hare) will plant the crops and share half of the harvest his labor yields with Bear; all Bear needs to do is donate the land and decide if he wants the tops or bottoms of whatever crops Hare has planted. During each of the repeated readings children are certain to ask for, they will delight in the series of events that follow Bear's decisions. The large, detailed and realistic full-color paintings done in watercolor, colored pencil, and gesso add immeasurably to the hilarity and liveliness inherent in this trickster tale of one-upmanship. *Tops & Bottoms* was named a 1996 Caldecott Award Honor Book.

210   THE STORY OF FLIGHT   *8–12+ YEARS*

Scholastic Voyages of Discovery Series. Translated from
the French. Illustrated. New York: Scholastic, 1995

> Originally published in France in 1994 under the title *Voler comme
> l'oiseau* by Éditions Gallimard Jeunesse, *The Story of Flight* takes the
> reader on a voyage of discovery through time and through space. It con-
> tains a wealth of short, fairly easy-to-read texts designed to capitalize on
> what is relevant to today's youth and to extend their knowledge about
> many historical, social, and cultural aspects of flight and to develop an
> understanding of significant scientific and technological concepts. The nu-
> merous aspects of flight covered in this attractive and interactive book are
> arranged in a manner that allows the reader to concentrate on those aspects
> most relevant to his or her immediate interests (and attention span). The
> graphics, overlays, and special effects in this book are absolutely amazing;
> there are many durable pieces the reader can manipulate, actively partici-
> pating in the explorations and discovery related to the cultural history and
> cross-cultural relationships described in this remarkable story of flight.
> Noteworthy are the helpful and rather extensive study aids to motivate
> acquisition of more advanced knowledge: table of contents, time line, bib-
> liography for further reading, addresses of museums, people important be-
> cause of their connections with this field (including brief biographical
> sketches of each person named), and an index. In addition to this unique
> and visually striking book on flight as an aspect of science and technology
> there are also Voyage of Discovery nonfiction series books on aspects of
> natural history, performing arts, and visual arts, and in each the same
> imaginative approach is used to make complex topics understandable.

211   Walsh, Ellen Stoll

MOUSE PAINT   *2–4 YEARS*

Illustrated by Ellen Stoll Walsh. San Diego: Harcourt
Brace, 1991

> Three white mice discovered jars of red, blue, and yellow paint. Thinking
> it was "mouse paint" in the jars, each mouse climbed right into a jar and
> one became a red mouse, another became a yellow one, and the third
> became a blue one. Once out of the jars of paint, each mouse dripped in
> its path a puddle of the colored paint it was covered with. The mice soon
> discovered that the red mouse's feet turned orange when it pranced about
> in the yellow puddle, the yellow mouse's feet turned green when it strut-
> ted about in the blue puddle, and the blue mouse's feet turned purple
> when it danced in the red puddle. The simple collage illustrations are in

ILLUSTRATION 27   Illustration by Ruth Tietjen Councell reprinted by permission of Philomel Books from *Old Dame Counterpane* by Jane Yolen, illustrations copyright © 1994 by Ruth Tietjen Councell.

bright, flat colors. After the readers have had a chance to listen to and examine *Mouse Paint* several times (for they will most certainly want to hear and look at it many times over), they might enjoy being introduced to *Play with Paint,* written by Diane James and illustrated by Sara Lynn (Carolrhoda, 1993), which offers them a little more sophisticated introduction to primary colors and demonstrates what happens when they are mixed.

212   Weiss, George David, and Bob Thiele

WHAT A WONDERFUL WORLD   *ALL AGES*

Illustrated by Ashley Bryan. New York: Jean Karl/
Atheneum, 1995

> Children of many ethnic, cultural, and racial backgrounds and the great Satchmo himself are shown performing in a puppet-show interpretation of this upbeat song celebrating wonderment, love, and hope in the world. The talented, award-winning artist's brilliantly colored tempera and gouache expressionistic paintings provide a perfect background for the hand-written lyrics and invite joyful singing from all who are lucky enough to be able to hold a copy of this book in their hands. Be certain to play a recording of Louis Armstrong's classic trumpet and vocal interpretation of this song.

213   Yolen, Jane

OLD DAME COUNTERPANE   *4–7 YEARS*

Illustrated by Ruth Tietjen Councell. New York:
Philomel, 1994

> In precise, lilting verse, Jane Yolen describes how Old Dame Counterpane works from dawn to dusk to make a quilt consisting of ten squares. Each square represents an aspect of our world: the sun, the sky, the seas, the flowers, the animals, buildings, and the people in it. On the tenth day Old Dame Counterpane finishes sewing the tenth square of her unusual quilt, but she and probably her readers know that when the night is over she will start anew to make another quilt. The cartoon-style watercolor paintings in soft, muted colors enhance the whimsical and fanciful aura of this engaging counting book. (See Illustration 27, pp. 160–161.)

The Imaginative World

*I*t should be emphasized that all good literature, regardless of its genre, has the potential to stimulate children's imaginative thinking power, for the reader creates his or her own images of sight, sound, smell, taste, and touch depicted in a story, poem, or informational piece through the author's use of language and the book artist's illustrations. The reader can also envision (create images of) the characters' feelings and emotions depicted or alluded to in a quality literary selection. Thus all good literature calls for imaginative thinking. "Imaginative literature" tends to be interpreted more commonly as fanciful literature, thus using imaginative thinking in a more limited sense than described above. The picture books included in "The Imaginative World" are primarily literary selections in which the reader is taken into a world where the impossible becomes convincingly possible. In other words, the reader is taken into the world of make-believe, into a fanciful world.

214 Aksakov, Sergei
THE SCARLET FLOWER   *5–10* YEARS
Translated from the Russian by Isadora Levin. Illustrated by
Boris Diodorov. San Diego: Harcourt Brace, 1989

> This is a retelling of the Russian variant of "Beauty and the Beast." The
> illustrations, beautifully crisp and detailed, are done in ink, colored pen-
> cil, and paint. They can be likened to those in Lucy Maxym's book
> *Russian Lacquer: Legends and Fairy Tales* (Manhasset, N.Y.: Siamese
> Imports, 1981).

215 Andersen, Hans Christian
THE NIGHTINGALE   *6–12* YEARS
Translated by Eva Le Gallienne. Illustrated by Nancy
Ekholm Burkert. New York: Harper, 1965

> Exquisite jewel-toned, double-spread paintings in three colors, in a style
> suggestive of Chinese art, illustrate the enduringly popular story of the
> emperor and the nightingale, a drab, ordinary-looking bird that sang so
> beautifully.

216 Andersen, Hans Christian
THUMBELINA   *5–10* YEARS
Translated from the Danish by Richard and Clara Winston.
Illustrated by Lisbeth Zwerger. New York: Morrow, 1980

> The full-page, meticulously detailed, representational illustrations in
> richly colored ink and wash highlight the sensuous imagery and contrast-
> ing moods expressed in this romantic story of how a tiny girl exploited
> by creatures stronger and more aggressive than herself eventually found
> happiness in the world of flowers. This picture book is an elegant and
> artistic achievement!

217 Auch, Mary Jane
EGGS MARK THE SPOT   *5–9* YEARS
Illustrated by Mary Jane Auch. New York: Holiday House, 1996

> Pauline was a hen that could lay eggs decorated with images that looked
> exactly like the images of what she saw in her mind. She was invited by
> the director of the Big City Art Gallery to make copies of the famous paint-
> ings exhibited there at that time. Unfortunately, when she saw them she
> could not lay eggs decorated with images that duplicated these famous
> paintings; she could only lay eggs decorated with original images these
> paintings inspired her to create. Luckily for the Gallery, however, when

Pauline observed a thief stealing a Degas painting, she was able to concentrate on that experience to lay eggs detailing how he got into the gallery, his escape route, and what he looked like without his mask. The humor in this story is developed with some very witty play on and play with words, slapstick incidents, and delightfully clever cartoon-style illustrations done in bright cheerful colors. For another story about Pauline, see Mary Jane Auch's *The Easter Egg Farm* (Holiday House, 1992).

218   Auch, Mary Jane
HEN LAKE   *5–8 YEARS*
Illustrated by Mary Jane Auch. New York: Holiday House, 1995

A fun-filled, far-out fantasy about Poulette, an extraordinary hen who wanted only to be recognized for her accomplishments as a ballerina, accomplishments belittled by Percival, an obnoxious and arrogant peacock who lived in the same barnyard as she and bragged about his singing and dancing prowess. Poulette talked Percival into competing against her in a talent show. In preparation for the competition Poulette taught her fellow hens how to dance the routines for the ballet "Hen Lake." Children are certain to be surprised and delighted to see how this chicken ballet company managed to win and what they all learned about Percival. Auch's rather flippant tone and clever play with language coupled with her action-filled cartoon-style illustrations done in clean, bright colors are a perfect blend for this kooky animal fantasy.

219   Bang, Molly
DAWN   *5–8 YEARS*
Illustrated by Molly Bang. New York: Morrow, 1983

In this variant of the Japanese folktale "The Crane Wife," the story takes place in nineteenth-century New England. A wounded Canada goose, rescued by a poor shipbuilder, returns as a beautiful woman; the two are married and a little girl is born to them. The woman surprises her husband with a set of beautiful and strong sails for the sailboat he has made for his family. When a man asks the shipbuilder to make him a racing schooner equipped with sails like those the woman made for their sailboat, the woman most reluctantly agrees to weave them—on the condition that her husband never come into the room while she is weaving the sails. Fearful his wife will not finish them in time, he breaks his promise and looks in on her, finding that she is the Canada goose he had rescued years before. She disappears after that and only their daughter remains with him. The full-page realistic illustrations alternate with those in full-color paintings and black-and-white pencil and ink drawings. If one looks carefully at the details in the full-color illustrations and their frames, one will see any number of clues that the woman is a Canada goose. Seek and thou shalt find! The text is done in accomplished hand calligraphy by G. G. Laurens. Compare Molly Bang's variant of the Japanese folktale with *The Crane Maiden,* retold by Miyoko Matsutani, English translation by Alvin Tresselt and illustrated by Chihiro Iwasaki (Parents, 1968), and *The Crane Wife,* retold by Sumiko Yagawa, translated from the Japanese by Katherine Paterson, and illustrated by Suekichi Akaba (Morrow, 1981).

220   Barber, Antonia

THE ENCHANTER'S DAUGHTER   *5–10* YEARS

Illustrated by Errol LeCain. New York: Farrar, Straus &
Giroux, 1987

Lavish, full-page fantasy paintings place this fairy tale in ancient China. They add an aura of elegance and charm to this well-told story of the Enchanter's beautiful daughter, tired of living alone, with no companionship except her father who was too busy to talk to her because he was trying to find in his books the secret of eternal youth before age and death robbed him of all his power and possessions. How she managed to escape from this sterile and lonely place and was reunited with her mother and brother should fascinate and satisfy most of the young readers of this very beautiful picture book.

221   Brett, Jan

THE WILD CHRISTMAS REINDEER   *5–9* YEARS

Illustrated by Jan Brett. New York: Putnam, 1990

This is an unusual multi-faceted picture storybook! The borders on each page document the activities of Santa's elves in the workshop of Winterfarm, his home in the Arctic tundra, from December first through December twenty-fourth. The elves are busy baking sweets, knitting, sawing, hammering, or painting the toys and gifts they have created for delivery on Christmas Eve. The humorous story of how Teeka gets Santa's rambunctious reindeer ready to fly on Christmas Eve is detailed in the large center portion of each double-page spread. Traditional Ukranian folk motifs are evident throughout: in the designs on the blankets that cover the reindeer and the figures on the hand-knit socks, in the architectural style of the buildings on Santa's Winterfarm and in the area surrounding it, in the designs on the door and window frames and the pillars inside these buildings, and in the decorations painted on the toys and woven into the fabrics or embroidered on the dolls' and Teeka's clothes. Be certain to take the jacket off of the hardbound edition to see the visual treat the decorations on the cover provide.

222   Burningham, John
AVOCADO BABY   *4–7 YEARS*
Illustrated by John Burningham. New York: Crowell, 1982

> This is a refreshingly humorous tall tale about the amazing feats the Hargraves' baby can do because he lives on a diet of avocado pears. The full-color expressionistic drawings done in ink and watercolor wash add just the right amount of credibility. (See illustration 28.) Be certain to notice the endpapers, which depict the baby engaging in even more escapades that exhibit his unusual strength and agility among a maze of botanically accurate stages of the avocado plant—from the sprouted seed through to the mature flowering plant, the fruit, and another sprouting seed. Compare with *Swamp Angel,* written by Anne Isaacs and illustrated by Paul O. Zelinsky (Dutton, 1994).

223   Burningham, John
CLOUDLAND   *5–7 YEARS*
Illustrated by John Burningham. New York: Crown, 1996

> This oversized picture book is illustrated with expressive action-filled drawings done in multimedia, i.e., collage, ink line with watercolor wash, and ink line and pastel. These illustrations, typical of those done by this award-winning British creator of children's books, add considerable credibility to this fantasy about the adventures little Albert has on the clouds with some cloud children who caught him when he fell off a cliff while he was walking on a high mountain with his parents. Children are certain to be charmed with the way Albert "magically" finds his way back to his own bed in his own room to be reunited with his parents.

224   Carr, Jan
THE NATURE OF THE BEAST   *5–8 YEARS*
Illustrated by G. Brian Kras. New York: Tambourine, 1996

> Isabelle bought a big, friendly, furry beast that is on special for one dollar at a pet store. Her father said she could keep the beast if she used its presence in their home to observe it "scientifically." That meant she was to record everything she could about the beast—what he liked, what he didn't like, and how he behaved in general. When the beast got too noisy Isabelle's mother phoned the pet store to say she was going to return the beast. Upon overhearing that he was going to have to go back to the pet store, the beast's behavior changed dramatically. Not only was he unusually quiet and lethargic, but he became so weak he could hardly talk, and when he did speak, which became less frequently with each passing day, his voice was weak and quavering. Worried and concerned, the family

The baby would help
carry the shopping,
move the furniture
and push the car
when it would not start.

ILLUSTRATION 28   Unabridged text and illustrations from *Avocado Baby* by John Burningham reprinted by permission of HarperCollins Publishers. Copyright © 1982 by John Burningham.

took him to a veterinarian, who confirmed that the beast was very ill and they had brought him to the clinic just in time. That the beast survived and remained with the family is perhaps quite predictable for adults, but not for children, and the conditions under which he was allowed to stay with the family are likely to surprise and delight everyone. The expressive, action-filled cartoon-style sketches, done in acrylic, gouache, and pencil, accentuate the humour and pathos expressed so competently in the text.

225   Cech, John

DJANGO   *5–8* YEARS

Illustrated by Sharon McGinley-Nally. New York:
Four Winds, 1994

> This is a story of how a young boy's talented playing of his grandfather's violin during a frightening hurricane not only calmed the members of his family, but "called" the birds and animals in from the woods and the fields to wait out the storm on the high grounds where his home stood. The vivid, perky watercolor paintings are in the naive style and illustrate perfectly the moods and actions of this original fantasy inspired by a legend set in the cypress swamps of northern Florida.

226   Clément, Claude

THE PAINTER AND THE WILD SWAN   *8–12* YEARS

Translated from the French by Robert Levine. Illustrated by
Frédéric Clément. New York: Dial, 1986

> Teiji, a famous Japanese painter, stopped painting after he saw a flock of exquisitely beautiful swans fly overhead, for he insisted that he had to see the birds again in order to capture their beauty on canvas. As he followed the birds across a treacherous lake to the island where the birds rested a block of ice hit his boat and it capsized. Teiji managed to swim to the shore of the island and he did see the beautiful swans again, but he died of exposure to the icy water and the winter elements. Although he lost his brush and paints when his boat capsized and thus never did paint them, he died knowing that just seeing the beautiful birds was enough, for he said, "Such beauty is rare and impossible to capture on canvas." The ice and snow that cover his body gradually change to feathers and large wings, and he flies away "with his brothers" where winter is milder. This transformation, elegantly depicted in words and pictures, is thoroughly hypnotic in its effect. The acrylic paintings, in tones of blue-gray and white with hints of red and yellow, are breathtaking in their beauty and are strongly suggestive of the classic Japanese brush paintings. The entire format of this book is a work of art; the crisp type, the delicate Japanese calligraphy which tells one swan's story, the studied and varied placement of the paintings which are of different sizes and shapes, the effects of the cold colors and shading all add up to an example of elegant bookmaking. Originally published by Duculot Paris-Gembloux in 1986, it was entitled *Le Peintre et les cygnes sauvages*. It received the French Foundation Grand Prize for Children's Literature.

227   Cohen, Caron Lee

THE MUD PONY   *5–10+* YEARS

Illustrated by Shonto Begay. New York: Scholastic, 1988

> Based on an ancient "boy-hero story" told among the Skidi band of the
> Pawnee Indians of the Great Plains, this folktale tells of how a boy, ac-
> cidentally left behind by his family when they broke camp to hunt for buf-
> falo, was reunited with them, saved them and other members of his tribe
> from an approaching enemy, and helped them capture buffalo that pro-
> vided the food they needed to survive through the winter months. The
> symbolism evidenced in the Skidi people's lore and their oneness with
> nature, in addition to their emphasis on virtues of persistence and the
> spirit of humility, are all authentically reflected in the text and the superb
> full-color expressionistic paintings which are combined to tell this folk-
> tale. Compare and contrast this picture book retelling of the Skidi "boy-
> hero story" with that retold in the 1982 Caldecott Honor Award–winning
> book *Where the Buffalo Begin,* retold by Olaf Baker and illustrated by
> Stephen Gammell (Warne, 1981).

228   Craft, Marie Charlotte, *Reteller*

CUPID AND PSYCHE   *7–10* YEARS

Illustrated by Kinuko Y. Craft. New York: Morrow Junior
Books, 1996

> This picture book is a unique interpretation of the ancient Greek myth
> which tells how Cupid, the god of love, fell in love with Psyche, the beau-
> tiful mortal who was the daughter of a king and queen. Forty lavish, ro-
> mantic, full-color paintings, done in oil over watercolor, firmly establish
> and enrich the details of the cultural and geographical aspects of the time
> and place in ancient Greece implied in the carefully crafted text, reflect-
> ing the understated, yet elegant style of a talented and experienced sto-
> ryteller. The beautiful and detailed designs in the borders that surround
> each full page also suggest the original source of this well-known myth.

229   Day, Alexandra

FRANK AND ERNEST   *5–10+* YEARS

Illustrated by Alexandra Day. New York: Scholastic, 1988

> Anyone interested in language, especially "a secret language" or play
> with and on words, will thoroughly enjoy this story of what happened
> when Frank and Ernest agreed to run a restaurant while its owner was on
> holiday. Examples of their restaurant language and its counterpart in
> "Standard English" include: "burn one, take it through the garden and
> pin a rose on it" for a hamburger with lettuce, tomato and onion; "Eve
> with a lid and moo juice" for a piece of apple pie and a glass of milk; and

"Paint a bow-wow red [and] . . . a nervous pudding" for a hot dog with ketchup and jello. The large full-page, realistic illustrations done in full-color wash add to the humor of this unique picture book. Be certain to notice each of the four endpapers, for they contain a full glossary of the restaurant language used by Frank and Ernest when they call the orders out to their cook.

230   Day, Edward C., Reteller

JOHN TABOR'S RIDE   *6–9 YEARS*

Illustrated by Dirk Zimmer. New York: Knopf, 1989

This retelling of John Tabor's far-fetched tale of his meeting with a mysterious old man and his fantastic ride on a whale is based on an entry in a journal written by seaman J. Ross Browne, published in *Etchings of a Whaling Cruise* (1846), and used later by Herman Melville in his novel *Moby Dick*. The cartoon-style pen-and-ink line and crosshatching and full-color wash illustrations are action filled and reflect perfectly the humorous and hair-raising aura of this fantastic yarn. Notice the map on the endpapers designating the route taken by John Tabor when he was on the whaling ship and on the whale.

231   de Beaumont, Madame

BEAUTY AND THE BEAST   *6–12 YEARS*

Translated from the French and adapted by Diane Goode.
Illustrated by Diane Goode. New York: Bradbury, 1978

Delicate, beautifully structured watercolor paintings on parchment, alternating between full color and black-and-white, dramatize the imaginative language of this version of the well-known tale of magic, kindness, and love.

232   Demi, *Adapter*

THE FIREBIRD   *6–10 YEARS*

Illustrated by Demi. New York: Holt, 1994

Demi's ornate, oversized picture-book adaptation of this well-known Russian folktale is based on Arthur Ransome's translation and retelling of it in *Old Peter's Russian Tales* (London: Thomas Nelson, 1916). With the help of his wise and magical Horse of Power, Dimitri, the hero of this fantasy, is able to meet the demands of the greedy and vain Tsar Ivan who wants the Firebird instead of just its feather, which Dimitri originally brought to him. Dimitri captures the magical Firebird and in the process finds Vasilissa, the fairy princess, in the Land of Never on the edge of the world; he also finds her wedding dress hidden in a golden casket in the

ILLUSTRATION 29 Illustration copyright © 1994 by Demi. Reprinted from *The Firebird* by permission of Henry Holt and Company, Inc.

depths of the sea. The tsar meets his demise when he jumps into a magical cauldron filled with boiling water, thinking it will make him handsome as it did Dimitri. Dimitri is proclaimed the new tsar, and he and Vasilissa are married; they "lived together for many years in love and happiness." The meticulously detailed, highly decorative illustrations which harmonize with and enrich the competently written text so well were created with traditional Chinese paints, inks and brushes, and watercolor on acetate and paper. (See illustration 29.) The generous use of gold throughout the book enhances perfectly the opulence with which the greedy tsar surrounded himself. Contrast the text, setting, and illustrations of Demi's version of this fairy tale with Rachel Isadora's adaptation of *Firebird* (Putnam, 1994) and Robert D. San Souci's retelling of *The Firebird,* illustrated by Kris Waldherr (Dial, 1992). It might be helpful to play a musical recording of Igor Stravinski's "The Firebird" in connection with the reading of any or all of these versions.

233 Demi

THE STONECUTTER   *5–9* YEARS

Illustrated by Demi. New York: Crown, 1995

The decorative paintings Demi made for her retelling of the old Chinese folktale about a stonecutter who wants to be something he is not until he learns the hard way that he wants to be himself are fine-line pen-and-ink drawings colored with traditional Chinese paints on backgrounds made of Chinese silk. Compare Demi's verbal and visual retelling of the Chinese variant of *The Stonecutter* with the Japanese variant of *The Stonecutter* adapted and illustrated by Gerald McDermott (Viking, 1975).

234 Diamond, Donna, *Adapter*

SWAN LAKE   *6–10* YEARS

Introduction by Clive Barnes. Illustrated by
Donna Diamond. New York: Holiday House, 1980

The elements of good and evil that are focused on in the Russian fairy tale of the tragic love of Odette, the graceful Swan Queen, and Siegfried, the handsome prince, have been retained in this picture-book adaptation of the classical ballet version of that story. The six double-page and two full-page pencil drawings are strongly suggestive of the great master Monet. Each picture provides a stunning interpretation of a major incident in this fantasy; together they give one the feeling of watching an accomplished performance of this ballet by a professional troupe.

235 Esbensen, Barbara Juster, *Reteller*

THE STAR MAIDEN: AN OJIBWAY TALE   *5–9* YEARS

Illustrated by Helen K. Davie. Boston: Little, Brown, 1988

The Star Maiden, tired of wandering in the sky, came to earth to live among the people as a water lily. The full-page expressionistic watercolor paintings in full color are framed with designs and symbols suggestive of those used traditionally by the Ojibway, or Chippewa, people. The traditional clothes worn by these Native Americans in past times and aspects of the terrain, flora, and fauna of the Mid-States region where the Ojibway lived (Michigan, Minnesota, etc.) are also authentically portrayed in the pictures of this retelling of "The Star and the Lily" from *The Traditional History and Characteristic Sketches of the Ojibway Nation,* an 1850 work by Ojibway Chief Kah-ge-ga-gah-bowh, who later took the name George Copway.

236   Fisher, Leonard Everett

THESEUS AND MENOTAUR   *5–9* YEARS

Illustrated by Leonard Everett Fisher. New York:
Holiday House, 1988

> Superbly executed dramatic and sophisticated expressionistic paintings in rich full color are perfectly suited to illustrate this carefully written retelling of the well-known Greek myth about the hero Theseus and his fierce battle with Menotaur, a monster that was half man and half bull. The combination of fine language and accomplished graphics bring characters and action to life!

237   Freeman, Don

A POCKET FOR CORDUROY   *4–7* YEARS

Illustrated by Don Freeman. New York: Viking, 1978

> Pen-and-wash illustrations in full color highlight the adventures of the appealing, lovable toy bear. Corduroy, as resourceful as always, decided to find something with which to make a pocket for his green pants after he heard Lisa's mother tell her to take everything out of her pockets before putting her clothes into the washing machine at the laundromat. Corduroy's adventures at the laundromat and the fact that he did get a pocket will please his many young fans. See the many other books about Corduroy in English and in Spanish.

238   Garfield, Leon

THE WEDDING GHOST   *12–16+* YEARS

Illustrated by Charles Keeping. New York: Oxford, 1987

> In this very clever blend of elements from Shakespeare's *Twelfth Night* and "Sleeping Beauty," one will find a haunting, multilevel comment about people's concept of the real and the ideal, the homely and the

romantic. The expressionistic black-and-white line and wash drawings embellish the nineteenth-century English setting and the mysterious and sinister overtones of this fantasy. To say this picture book is a memorable read would be a gross understatement.

239   Goble, Paul

ADOPTED BY THE EAGLES: A PLAINS INDIAN   *7–12* YEARS
STORY OF FRIENDSHIP AND TREACHERY
Illustrated by Paul Goble. New York: Bradbury, 1994

Two young men, White Hawk and Tall Bear, formed a sacred friendship with each other. They were what the Lakota people called *kolas,* which Paul Goble explains in the "Author's Note" meant they were friends who were expected "to guard each other from all errors and share their strengths while walking life's Good Red Road together." The two young men set out to capture some horses of their enemies, but their hunting expedition proved unsuccessful. On their way back home White Hawk betrayed Tall Bear, leaving him stranded on a rocky ledge when he tried to capture two young eagles. Tall Bear soon realized that White Hawk did this because he wanted to marry Red Leaf, a young maiden they both liked. Often in American Indian literature we find the idea of birds or animals helping people in need, and so it is in this Lakota story. The young eagles saved Tall Bear's life, they made him their brother and shared their nest with him, their parents adopted him and brought him food. When the eagles were ready to leave their nest, Tall Bear grabbed them by the legs, and they carried him to earth. White Hawk fled the village when Tall Bear returned home and was never seen again. Red Leaf and Tall Bear were married and as he had promised the eagles, he and Red Leaf returned to the lonely butte to give them gifts of appreciation for saving his life. The large, brightly colored illustrations, done in India ink and watercolor, capture the essence of the vast stretches of flat land and the lonely high buttes of South Dakota, where this story takes place. Like the many other book illustrations created by this award-winning artist over twenty years, the illustrations of the flora and fauna of the region, the traditional clothing of the people, their hair styles, and the stylized portraits of their horses and other animals are meticulously detailed and thoroughly authentic.

240   Goble, Paul

THE GIRL WHO LOVED WILD HORSES   *6–9* YEARS
Illustrated by Paul Goble. New York: Bradbury, 1978

A distinguished book in every sense: fine use of language, excellent design, and accomplished illustrations are expertly combined in this 1979

Caldecott Award Medal winner to tell the story of a Native-American maiden who loved horses and understood them in a special way. The maiden accepted the invitation of the Appaloosa stallion to live with his herd and eventually, because she communicated with them and understood them so well, she turned into a horse. This original fairy tale is illustrated with colorful, full-page, stylized paintings, containing authentically characteristic details suggestive of the Plains Indians–the "Horseback Indians" of the Plains area of North America.

241   Goble, Paul, *Reteller*

HER SEVEN BROTHERS   *6–10* YEARS

Illustrated by Paul Goble. New York: Bradbury, 1988

Illustrated with full-color paintings made with pen and India ink and watercolor, these pictures are filled with many allusions and direct references to the folk art, the cultural traditions, and the flora, fauna, and terrain associated with the Cheyenne Indians and the Great Plains region of the United States where they lived. This story is an authentic retelling of the Cheyenne legend that tells how a girl and her seven brothers became the stars that make up the Big Dipper.

242   Greenstein, Elaine

MRS. ROSE'S GARDEN   *4–8* YEARS

Illustrated by Elaine Greenstein. New York: Simon & Schuster, 1996

Each year Mrs. Rose entered her vegetables in the competition at the county fair, but she never won a a blue ribbon, for someone else's vegetables were always larger. The spring she combined several kinds of fertilizer and put the mixture on the vegetables growing in her garden, the results were more than she ever imagined possible. There was no doubt that her vegetables would win all the blue ribbons. At first she was thrilled with this realization, but her enthusiasm about that prospect soon waned. The action Mr. and Mrs. Rose took assured that she would be awarded only one blue ribbon and delighted Mrs. Rose, friends and neighbors, and is certain to please the readers of this tale as well. The author tells the readers that Mrs. Rose's vegetables were "the biggest ever," "gigantic," and "huge," but the illustrations more aptly depict the fanciful aspects of this satisfying story. Large full-color expressionistic illustrations, done in casein paint, suggest more convincingly than the text how immense the vegetables actually were.

243 Grimm, Jacob and Wilhelm

THE BROTHERS GRIMM: POPULAR FOLK TALES   *6–12* YEARS

Translated by Brian Alderson. Illustrated by Michael
Foreman. Garden City, N.Y.: Doubleday, 1978

> This not a picture book, but it is a stunning illustrated book with a full-
> page painting in full color and a small black-and-white sketch for each of
> the thirty-one popular folktales retold in it. And, as Alderson states in his
> Afterword, he offers his readers "something of the unselfconscious
> directness and the colloquial ease" so characteristic of the nineteenth-
> century storytellers from whom the Grimm brothers originally collected
> the tales. See also "the mate" of this collection, *Hans Andersen: His Clas-
> sic Fairy Tales,* translated by Eric Haugaard and illustrated by Michael
> Foreman (Doubleday, 1978). Both are just the thing for the family library.

244 Grimm, Jacob and Wilhelm

RUMPELSTILTSKIN   *5–8* YEARS

Retold by Paul O. Zelinsky. Illustrated by Paul O. Zelinsky.
New York: Dutton, 1986

> This is a fine retelling in words and pictures of the well-known German
> folktale of how the miller's daughter, brought to the castle because her
> father falsely bragged to the king that she could spin straw into gold, out-
> witted the little man (an imp-like creature) who did the spinning for her
> on the condition that when she became queen she would give him her
> firstborn child. It is illustrated with accomplished detailed oil paintings
> done in a style suggestive of the Renaissance masters. Especially notewor-
> thy is the artist's use of color and shading to designate the opulence of the
> setting and the texture of the costumes worn by the characters. Zelinsky
> was the recipient of the 1987 Caldecott Award Medal for the illustrations
> he created for this book. Compare and contrast aspects of this retelling with
> other variants: Cornish—*Duffy and the Devil,* retold by Harve Zemach and
> illustrated by Margot Zemach (Farrar, Straus & Giroux, 1973) and named
> the 1974 Caldecott Award Medal winner; British—*Tom Tit Tot,* retold and
> illustrated by Evaline Ness (Holt, 1965) and named a 1966 Caldecott Honor
> Book; and German—*Rumpelstiltskin,* by the Brothers Grimm, retold and
> illustrated by Donna Diamond (Holiday House, 1983).

245 Hodges, Margaret, *Adapter*

COMUS   *6–10* YEARS

Illustrated by Trina Schart Hyman. New York:
Holiday House, 1996

> This enchanting story of how two brothers, with the help of the Good Spirit
> of the forest and Sabrina, a gentle nymph whose magic was as powerful as

Comus's, rescued Alice, the boys' sister, from the spell of the evil magician, known as Comus. It is based on "A Masque at Ludlow Castle," John Milton's adaptation of "Childe Roland," which is thought to be the oldest of all the old English fairy tales. Stunning oil paintings highlight both the aura of doom and evil that permeates the forest at night and Comus's hidden palace inhabited by monsters who were elegantly dressed and had the faces of beasts "never known on land or sea" and the aura of goodness, peace, and happiness whenever the Good Spirit, Sabrina, and Alice are present. (See illustration 30.) Since Milton's adaptation of this fairy tale was performed as a masque (a short allegorical dramatic entertainment of the sixteenth and seventeenth centuries performed by masked actors), it might be fun for students to make paper-bag masks (or any other easy-to-make mask) and dramatize Hodges' adaptation of it.

ILLUSTRATION 30   Illustration copyright © 1996 by Trina Schart Hyman. Reprinted from *Comus* by permission of Holiday House, Inc.

246   Hong, Lily Toy, *Reteller*

TWO OF EVERYTHING   *4–7* YEARS

Illustrated by Lily Toy Hong. Morton Grove, Ill.:
Albert Whitman, 1993

> Stylized illustrations in airbrushed acrylics and gouache add a humorous
> touch to this Chinese folktale about the series of events that occur after
> a poor old farmer finds a brass pot that possesses the magical power to
> double whatever is placed in it.

247   Hooks, William H.

MOSS GOWN   *4–12* YEARS

Illustrated by Donald Carrick. New York: Clarion/
Houghton Mifflin, 1987

> This romantic story blends aspects of "Cinderella" and *King Lear:* Can-
> dice is forced to work as a scullery maid in a white-pillared mansion
> owned by the handsome Young Master, whom she eventually marries.
> Her benefactor is the gris-gris woman, a swamp witch who gives her a
> magical moss gown which changes into a golden gown; when the Morn-
> ing Star fades the gown turns back into a dull gray moss. The expertly
> executed, full-page line and watercolor paintings in full color suggest
> elements of the Victorian era in the tidewater section of eastern North
> Carolina. An excellent read-aloud selection for primary-grade children as
> well as for independent reading by transitional readers. Fine fare for the
> study of narrative literary conventions by students in the middle and
> upper elementary grades.

248   Hooper, Patricia   *5–9* YEARS

HOW THE SKY'S HOUSEKEEPER WORE HER SCARVES

Illustrations by Susan L. Roth. Boston: Little, Brown, 1996

> The housekeeper wore a different colored scarf each day throughout the
> week and each day she engaged in a different housekeeping task. When the
> rain knocked on her window and asked her to come out and cheer him up
> with her colored scarves, this industrious housekeeper, fearful she might
> get lost in his downpour, disappointed the lonely rain by refusing him. She
> hid from the rain and neglected all her work; soon everything in the sky
> became dusty and dull. When the sun demanded that she resume her
> housekeeping tasks, she realized she had badly neglected her duties and
> resolved to do them all regardless of the weather. How she surmounted her
> fear of getting lost in the rain and the ramification of her efforts surprised
> and delighted both the sun and the moon, as most assuredly they will the
> readers. Together, the carefully scripted text and the energetic collages and
> paintings amount to a charming and memorable fantasy.

249   Isaacs, Anne

SWAMP ANGEL   *5–9 YEARS*

Illustrated by Paul O. Zelinsky. New York: Dutton, 1994

> What a great tall tale! Beautifully crafted prose with just the right amount of colloquial phrases and clever use of words by a talented storyteller, matched with expertly executed expressionistic oil paintings on wood veneers from Tennessee (maple, cherry, and birch), relates the spectacular exploits of Angelica Longrider, alias "Swamp Angel," so convincingly children will have little trouble suspending disbelief. They are certain to be impressed by the fact that as a newborn this heroine was scarcely taller than her mother and needed help in climbing a tree, as a twelve-year-old she lifted covered wagons mired in the mud as if they were twigs in a puddle and set them on high ground, and as a young woman she scuffled with and ultimately killed Thundering Tarnation, a gargantuan and cunning bear known throughout Tennessee because he gobbled up over half the winter food supply stored in settlers' root cellars and his fur was so thick a gunshot could never penetrate his skin. Compare with John Burningham's *Avocado Baby* (Crowell, 1982).

250   Kellogg, Steven

THE MYSTERIOUS TADPOLE   *4–8 YEARS*

Illustrated by Steven Kellogg. New York: Dial, 1977

> Each year Louis receives a birthday present for his nature collection from his Uncle McAllister who lives in Scotland. In this thoroughly fantastic tale, Alphonse, the tadpole the lad's generous relative caught in Loch Ness and sent to Louis for his birthday, grows into a Loch Ness monster during the course of a year. On his next birthday Louis receives another present, an egg, for his collection. Shortly after its arrival a strange-looking ducklike animal is hatched from it. So, new fantastic adventures may be imagined by the readers of this refreshingly original tale. Kellogg's delightful, cartoon-style illustrations are filled with wonderfully zany details.

251   Kellogg, Steven

PREHISTORIC PINKERTON   *5–8 YEARS*

Illustrated by Steven Kellogg. New York: Dial, 1987

> Cartoon-style illustrations done in full color with ink and pencil line and watercolor wash add considerable depth to a brief, easy-to-read story about Pinkerton's chaotic visit to the dinosaur section of the museum. Other books about this nutty Great Dane (all published by Dial) include *Tallyho, Pinkerton!* (1982); *Pinkerton, Behave!* (1979); and *A Rose for Pinkerton* (1981).

252 Kimmel, Eric A.

COUNT SILVERNOSE: A STORY FROM ITALY *6–9 YEARS*

Illustrations reconstructed by Omar Rayyan. New York:
Holiday House, 1995

> Children are quite likely to find it interesting to compare this retelling of
> a tale from Italo Calvino's classic collection *Italian Folktales* with vari-
> ants of the Blue Beard motif: One is obviously "La Barbe Bleue" ("Blue
> Beard") which first appeared in *Histoires, ou Contes du temps Passe* col-
> lected and retold by Charles Perrault (Paris, 1697) and more recently in
> *Andrew Lang's Blue Fairy Book,* edited and adapted by Brian Alderson
> and illustrated by John Lawrence (Kestrel/Viking, 1995). The other is
> found in "Captain Murderer," the macabre story Charles Dickens' nurse
> told him when he was a child and which he included in a book of remi-
> niscences, *The Uncommercial Traveller* and published as a novella en-
> titled *Captain Murderer,* adapted by George Harland and illustrated by
> Rowan Barnes-Murphy (Lothrop, Lee & Shepard, 1986). The illustrations,
> many of them double-page spreads, are reconstructions of those Kim-
> melino diPerugia made in his sketchbook (1504), purportedly to explain
> the disappearance of many of Italy's washerwomen at the turn of that
> century. The illustrator uses several techniques to suggest that the pic-
> tures are study sketches an artist who lived hundreds of years ago made
> for a work in progress. For example, the edges of each illustration are
> ragged and the backgrounds are yellowed and stained to indicate the
> pages of the sketchbook have dried out and are badly deteriorated. Many
> of the illustrations even have the artist's notes written on them. Some of
> the illustrations are executed in pencil and a thin, layered full-color wa-
> tercolor wash, others are limited to pencil sketches, and in others only
> portions of the pencil sketches are painted in full color. This is a very
> special picture book!

253 Kurtz, Jane

MIRO IN THE KINGDOM OF THE SUN *6–10 YEARS*

Illustrated by David Frampton. Boston: Houghton
Mifflin, 1996

> Skillfully executed woodcut prints reproduced in full color and a mod-
> ernized version of an Inca folktale told in the style of an accomplished
> and relaxed storyteller tell the tale of heroism. Miro, a spirited young Inca
> heroine, saved the dying prince's life by bringing him some water from
> the lake located at one of the corners of the earth, known as the "pachap
> chucun chucun," for the only way the prince's health would be restored
> was to drink this water from a special golden flask made by the high
> priest. Accomplishing this task was indeed an achievement; in fact, nei-
> ther the soldiers and knights throughout the Inca kingdom nor Miro's two

brothers had been able to find the lake at "pachap chucun chucun." With two drops of water splashed into the prince's mouth his strength was regained and after consuming the rest of the water from the golden flask, his health was fully restored. The Sun King invited Miro to stay forever in his palace and live out her days as one of the "daughters of the sun," but she rejected the offered reward. Instead, she asked for two things: first, that the king free her brothers from the dungeon in which they had been thrown when, unable to find the special lake at the "pachap chucun chucun," they brought ordinary water to the ailing prince and pretended it was the healing water. Second, that he allow her to go so that she might travel his great kingdom to see all the things she had only had a glimpse of during her journey to his palace with the healing water. The Sun King granted her wishes. Miro and her brothers returned to the grassland, riding on white llamas loaded with riches from the king's bounty.

254   Lattimore, Deborah Nourse

THE DRAGON'S ROBE   *6–10* YEARS

Illustrated by Deborah Nourse Lattimore. New York: Harper, 1990

In-and-of itself Lattimore's text is an example of storytelling at its best, but combined with her superb illustrations, she has created a fascinating original fairy tale about a young Chinese girl who saves her people from drought and invasion by foreign enemy forces by weaving an imperial dragon's robe. Perseverance is the major theme of this story about ancient China during the twelfth century (Northern Sung dynasty), and there is considerable evidence in the competent writing and exquisite illustrations that the creator of this elegant picture book, like the young heroine of the story, went to great lengths and put forth a great deal of effort to create something of beauty. The illustrations strongly suggest the art that the Emperor Hui Tsung, who ruled during this era, is so famous for; they are nonetheless very appropriate in the framework of a contemporary picture book. The essence of a specific landscape as well as the social history of this time period is captured in the details included in the pictures: the architecture, the wood and tile work, the Mongolian clothing, the ceramic armor of the Khan, even the embroidered insignia panels worn by the lords. Notice that the small vignettes at the top of each frame not only have a texture that suggests the girl's weaving, but they also carry part of the text or focus on an important element in the text. The miracle of Lattimore's illustrations is that her use of split-perspective architecture and inside-outside views of the world suggest a gestalt which focuses on all aspect of life at the same time, a stance that is typical of the traditional Chinese attitude.

255 Louie, Ai-Ling, *Reteller*
YEH-SHEN   *5–10* YEARS
Illustrated by Ed Young. New York: Philomel, 1982

The complete Hsueh Chin T'oo Yun edition of the Chinese "Cinderella" story recorded from the Ch'ing dynasty (1644–1912) is shown in the Chinese characters on a block-printed page. Following this is a portion of that story retold in English and accompanied by Ed Young's illustrations done in pastels and watercolors and set in panels like those of the Chinese folding painted screen. One can tell from the details in the pictures (the style of clothing and jewelry worn by the characters, their hairstyles, etc.) that the story is set "before the time Chin (222–206 BC)." Be certain to notice that an image of a fish appears in each illustration, for in this variant of the Cinderella motif the magic comes from the bones of the fish that Yeh-Shen loved and her stepmother killed. Compare aspects of the Chinese "Cinderella" story (the source of magic, how the heroine meets and eventually marries the hero, how the heroine and the slipper are "reunited," and what happens to the heroine's stepmother and stepsister[s]) with other variants, such as: Vietnamese—*In the Land of Small Dragon,* retold by Ann Nolan Clark and Dang Manh Kha and illustrated by Tony Chen (Viking 1979); French—*Cinderella,* adapted from Perrault's "Cendrillon" of 1697, retold by John Fowles and illustrated by Sheila Beckett (Little, Brown, 1974); German—*Cinderella,* by the Brothers Grimm, retold and illustrated by Nonny Hogrogian (Greenwillow, 1981); English—*Tattercoats,* retold by Flora Annie Steel, illustrated by Diane Goode (Bradbury, 1976).

256 Macaulay, David
SHORTCUT   *7–9* YEARS
Illustrated by David Macaulay. Boston: Houghton
Mifflin, 1995

This picture book is an original tall tale which consists of several "chapters"; its cause-and-effect, linearly structured plot starts in Chapter One, when Albert and June, his housemate and horse, decided to take a shortcut to the market. The shortcut proved to be too steep for the horse, so Albert took off his coat, hung it on a signpost, and pushed the wagon as June pulled it up the hill. Albert went back to get his coat, and they resumed their travels until Albert decided to stop for lunch at a cafe while June grazed on the tasty clover. Then they traveled a bit more until their path was blocked by a heavy rope tied around a tree stump. June gnawed through the rope and they proceeded to the market, where they quickly sold all their melons, and got home before dark. What happens in the succeeding eight chapters proves quite catastrophic to the cast of characters introduced in the frontispiece, but as luck would have it, we learn via the Epilogue all turns out happily for everyone. This zany tale is not as convoluted as Macaulay's *Black and White,* the 1992 Caldecott Medal winner, but the reader does have to look carefully for the clues to recognize the cause-and-effect sequence of events. The line and watercolor-wash illustrations are perfect for this clever tall tale.

257   Martin, Rafe

THE BOY WHO LIVED WITH THE SEALS   *7–9 YEARS*

Illustrated by David Shannon. New York: Putnam, 1993

Experienced and talented storytelling combined with striking full-color realistic acrylic paintings reproduced in full color effectively dramatize this Chinook Indian legend about a lost boy who grew up in the sea with seals, but was eventually found and forced to return and live with his people. (See illustration 31.) He did everything the way the seals did: instead of talking like people, he grunted and barked like a seal; instead of eating the food people eat, he ate only raw fish, seaweed, and clams; instead of walking upright on his feet, he crawled and slid along the surface. Eventually he learned to do things the way people do, but he was always mindful of the sea and the creatures of the sea. This preoccupation with the sea was evident in the designs the boy carved and painted on the canoes and paddles he made for his people, in his habit of sitting on the shore of the river while he made bows and arrows, and in the stories he told his people and the manner in which he told these stories about his life under the sea with the seals. Realizing that their son was not happy living away from his beloved sea and seals, his parents were eventually able to take some solace and even find joy in the fact he chose to return to his home with the seals. Each spring, when his parents returned to the spot where the boy left them to join the seals, a new canoe and paddle more wonderfully crafted, painted, and carved than the last were always waiting for them.

258   Martin, Rafe

THE ROUGH-FACE GIRL   *6–10 YEARS*

Illustrated by David Shannon. New York: Putnam, 1992

In this abbreviated version of the Algonquin Indian "Cinderella" variant, the heroine is Rough-Face Girl, forced by her two cruel and hardhearted older sisters to sit by the fire and feed the flames. The sparks that pop from the burning branches fall on her, so that soon her hands, arms, and face become burnt and scarred; even her beautiful long black hair is charred and ragged. In their village, there lives a great Indian warrior whose name is Invisible Being; he can be seen only by his sister. Rough-Face Girl, like her sisters and all of the other maidens in the village, knows that Invisible Being will marry the first maiden who can see him as he comes home to his tent near the shores of Lake Ontario at night.

ILLUSTRATION 31   Illustration by David Shannon reprinted by permission of G. P. Putnam's Sons from *The Boy Who Lived with the Seals* by Rafe Martin, illustrations copyright © 1993 by David Shannon.

Only a truthful maiden can see him. To prove she has actually seen Invisible Being, the maiden must be able to tell the warrior's sister what his bow and the runners of his sled are made of. Rough-Face Girl's sisters fail this test. Everyone laughs at Rough-Face Girl when she resolves to marry Invisible Being. Because the warrior is indeed visible to her, she is able to answer to the questions his sister asks her. When Invisible Being sees Rough-Face Girl in their wigwam, he sees only her inner beauty. Later, when Rough-Face Girl bathes in the lake, all the scars disappear, her black hair grows long, and his sister dresses the girl in finest of buckskin robes and a necklace of perfect shells. Rough-Face Girl and Invisible Being are married and live happily together. Exquisite full-page paintings contain authentic details about the traditional Algonquin Indians' features, hairstyles, houses, clothing, jewelry, ceremonial celebrations, and the geographical setting of this "Cinderella" variant. They add immeasurably to the mood and tone of this story as delivered by this very competent and acclaimed storyteller. Slightly different versions of this tale are included in each of two folktale collections: "Little Burnt Face," in *The Talking Stone: An Anthology of Native American Tales and Legends,* edited by Dorothy de Wit (Greenwillow, 1979, pp. 34–38) and "The Indian Cinderella," in *World Folktales: A Scribner Resource Collection,* compiled by Atelia Clarkson and Gilbert B. Cross (Scribner, 1980, pp. 43–45).

259 Meddaugh, Susan

HOG-EYE   *5–8* YEARS

Illustrated by Susan Meddaugh. Boston: Houghton
Mifflin, 1995

This refreshing tale of comeuppance could be classified as an example of a good cautionary tale or a tall tale, or both. A young pig dreaded having to ride on the school bus each day; she thought the children who rode on it were too noisy and rowdy. One morning she dallied on her way to the bus stop and unbeknownst to her, she missed her regular bus and got on the wrong one. Not only did she not get to school that day, she caused her parents considerable worry when she failed to get home at her usual time. The explanation she offered was exciting and more than a little imaginative. Furthermore, she told her story most convincingly and the clever ink line and watercolor-wash cartoon-style pictures in this book corroborate her story perfectly. Her parents (and the young readers of this picture book) can only wonder how much of her tale of outwitting and putting the "hog-eye" on the wolf, who had grabbed her as she walked through the forest and carried her to his home to make her into a soup, was true and how much of it was a wonderfully concocted tall tale. Compare the theme and the details of this engrossing fantasy with those in Dr. Seuss's classic tale *And To Think That I Saw It on Mulberry Street* (Random House, 1937) and *John Patrick Norman McHennessy: The Boy Who Was Always Late,* written and illustrated by John Burningham (Crown, 1988).

260 Nash, Ogden

CUSTARD THE DRAGON AND THE WICKED KNIGHT   *5–9 YEARS*

Illustrated by Lynn Munsinger. Boston: Little, Brown, 1995

> Once again Ogden Nash's well-loved classic character, Custard the dragon, demonstrates solidly that he can be brave, even heroic when necessary, especially when his beloved Belinda is being threatened by Sir Garagoyle, a wicked knight. Lynn Munsinger's expressive cartoon illustrations, done in ink line and watercolor wash, cleverly and most effectively reflect and extend the personalities and action in this wonderfully humorous narrative verse. Her illustrations of Belinda's pet dog, depicted as a cairn terrier, are a delight! Compare and contrast Munsinger's illustrations interpreting this same narrative verse with those illustrated by Quentin Blake and included (along with eighty-three other poems by Nash) in *Custard and Company* (Little, Brown, 1980). Also, be certain to share one or more picture-book versions of Ogden Nash's "The Tale of Custard the Dragon" when you introduce the children to *Custard the Dragon and the Wicked Knight.* For fun-filled, unique insights into illustrative techniques used by different graphic artists, encourage the children to compare several illustrated versions of this poem. Two picture-book versions that are worthy of note are the one illustrated by "Linell," who is Ogden Nash's daughter, Linell Nash Smith (Little, Brown, 1936), and the one illustrated by Lynn Munsinger (Little, Brown, 1995). Quentin Blake's illustrated version of it is in *Custard and Company* (Little, Brown, 1980). Like the children of past generations, today's children take great delight in the wonderful wordplay Nash has created in both of these poems about Custard; no doubt they will also delight in these illustrated versions created by contemporary graphic artists.

261 Paxton, Tom

THE STORY OF THE TOOTH FAIRY   *5–9 YEARS*

Illustrated by Robert Sauber. New York: Morrow, 1996

> Full-page Victorian-like paintings done in watercolor and gouache constitute a perfect match with this old-fashioned original fairy tale about how a seven-year-old mortal child named Emily and a tiny fairy named Glynnis became fast friends and began what is now a firmly established custom of exchanging a coin for a "milk tooth."

262 Pushkin, Aleksandr

THE MAGIC GOLD FISH   *6–8 YEARS*

Translated by Louis Zelikoff. Adapted and illustrated by
Demi. New York: Holt, 1995

> An old fisherman and his wife were very poor and lived in a dilapidated hut by the shore of the ocean. One day the fisherman caught a gold fish

that could speak; the fish begged the man to put it back in the ocean and promised to give him whatever he asked. When the old man went home and told his wife about the fish, she scolded him and told him to go back to the fish and ask for a new washtub, for theirs was falling to pieces. The old man did so, and by the time he got back home they had a new tub. Repeatedly the old man's wife scolded him for not asking the fish for more and sent her husband to ask the fish for something more grand; each time her wish was granted. When she demanded to be made mistress of the sea with the magical gold fish as her servant, the fish said nothing and disappeared in the water. The old man got home to see his greedy wife in tattered clothes sitting on the doorstep of their dilapidated hut with their old washtub before her. Demi used traditional Chinese inks ("with powdered jade for good luck") and Cel-vinyl paint to create the line-and-wash full-page illustrations; a wide band of gold frames each full-color picture. The text is printed on the right-hand pages and is encircled with little sketches that are indicative of the action or the setting described in that text. The use of the circles (gold circles around pictures depicting the major aspect of the story described in the text) may well allude to the fact that because of her greed the old woman was right back where she started before her husband caught the magical fish. The circles may also reflect the cyclic view so prevalent in the Chinese tradition, especially in relation to life's rhythm of natural movement. Compare Demi's interpretation of this traditional folktale with *The Fisherman and His Wife,* retold by Jacob and Wilhelm Grimm, translated by Elizabeth Shub, and illustrated by Monika Laimgruber (Greenwillow, 1979).

263   San Souci, Robert D.

THE FAITHFUL FRIEND   *7–10* YEARS

Illustrated by Brian Pinkney. New York: Simon & Schuster, 1995

Because Pauline chose to elope with Clement, a young man her guardian, Monsieur Zabocat, did not approve of, the two young lovers were in danger of being killed by zombies and ghosts. Clement's faithful friend Hippolyte, who was accompanying the young couple to the home where they were to be married, overheard three zombies plot the young couple's demise. The said the couple would die if they (1) drank poisoned water from a brook, (2) ate the fruit of a particular mango tree beside a path, or (3) were stung by a serpent as they entered their house on their wedding night. He also heard them declare that if anyone heard their curses and repeated them, he would turn into stone. Hippolyte was able to prevent the couple from being killed when they were tempted to consume the poisoned water and the mangoes; the only way he could prevent them from being stung by the serpent was to cut it in half, but its pieces instantly disappeared. Since neither Pauline nor Clement saw the serpent, Hippolyte was forced to explain his presence in their bedroom. He gradually turned to stone from the tips of his toes to the top of his head as he identified each of the three curses the zombies had planned for them. How Hippolyte is brought back to life again and what happened to Monsieur Zabocat all fall nicely into place. The full-color scratchboard pictures add considerably to the eerie aura and the sense of evil and doom that is so prevalent throughout this tale. The story is set in Martinique, but is based on a blending of a West Indian folktale with African, European, and South American traditions and imagery. Brian Pinkney received two prestigious awards for his illustrations in *The Faithful Friend;* he received the 1996 Coretta Scott King Honor Award for the Winning Illustrator, and this book was named a 1996 Caldecott Award Honor Book.

264   Sanderson, Ruth

PAPA GATTO: AN ITALIAN FAIRY TALE   *5–9* YEARS

Illustrated by Ruth Sanderson. Boston: Little, Brown, 1995

> This Italian Cinderella-type fairy tale "takes place many years ago when cats could talk." Papa Gatto, the prince's trustworthy adviser, hired the beautiful, but lazy and selfish, Sophia to take care of his eight tiny, motherless kittens while he was away on business. But Sophia neglected the kittens, left their house in shambles, and stole a priceless diamond necklace that Papa Gatto had given to his wife the day the kittens were born. When Papa Gatto returned from his travels, he promptly dismissed the inept Sophia and retrieved the beautiful necklace before she departed. When he had to travel again, he hired Sophia's humbler stepsister Beatrice to take care of the kittens. Upon his return, he was most pleased to see Beatrice had taken good care of his kittens and house. Since she refused to take any money for her work, he gave her the priceless necklace. How Papa Gatto and the necklace brought Beatrice and the Prince together will surely delight children and will convince them that this Italian fairy tale is another variant of the "Cinderella" story. The full-page paintings, rendered in oils, are reproduced in full color. Some of the pictures, especially those of the cats and kittens and the close-up views of the stepsister, are meticulously proportioned; made with just the right amount of detail and shading, they are given a dimensional quality that adds a lifelike quality and makes them look quite like photographs. These beautiful and detailed illustrations make this romantic fairy tale most credible and are bound to be examined carefully by young readers many times.

265   Shaefer, Carole Lexa

THE SQUIGGLE   *4–7* YEARS

Illustrated by Pierr Morgan. New York: Crown, 1996

> While on a walk to the park with her teacher and classmates, a little Chinese girl picked up a long string she noticed on the sidewalk. Each time

she shook and wiggled it, squiggles of different shapes and patterns were formed. Each of these patterns and shapes evoked quite specific images. She "saw" in them such things as a big scaly dragon, the Great Wall of China, the path of a circus acrobat, popping and flashing fireworks, a stormy thundercloud, and a full moon. The simple sketches, done with black marker ink and a gouache wash, are printed on "oatmeal" colored speckle-tone paper, which looks quite like kraft wrapping paper. This easy-to-read book should motivate children to create images of their own as they wiggle and shake long pieces of string, rope, or ribbon. Compare this child's imaginings with those depicted in Crockett Johnson's classic *Harold and the Purple Crayon* (Harper, 1955.)

266 Stanley, Diane

THE GENTLEMAN AND THE KITCHEN MAID   *7–10+ YEARS*

Illustrated by Dennis Nolan. New York: Dial, 1994

What fun the author and the illustrator must have had creating this fanciful romance about the subjects of two Dutch paintings, *The Kitchen Maid* and *Portrait of a Young Gentleman,* which hung directly across from the other for many years in room twelve of the art museum! And what fun readers are certain to have reading this unique story of how the subjects of these two paintings fell in love with each other. All of the subjects of the other paintings hanging in room twelve knew the subjects of these two paintings were in love with each other, but of course no one on the museum staff was aware of it, nor were most of the museum visitors. Luckily, a young art student by the name of Dusty, who often visited the museum to study and copy some of her favorite paintings, noticed how fondly the maiden and the gentleman looked at each other. One day, as she was copying the *Portrait of a Young Gentleman* she noticed his eyes looked much sadder than before; she also noticed that the painting of *The Kitchen Maid* was gone. When she asked a guard about it he told her it had been moved to another room with Dutch paintings of a later period. Dusty quickly copied what she wanted to of the painting of the young man, then moved into the room where *The Kitchen Maid* now hung and copied the young woman in that painting onto the same canvas on which she had painted the young man. Her painting shows the two figures standing side-by-side and looking lovingly at each other; she hung it in her favorite room in her home. As the narrator of this picture book said, "And who could ask for a happier ending than that?" According to the Illustrator's Note, the illustrations throughout this picture book, which were done in watercolor, are intended to be suggestive of some of the master artists; and indeed they are. The artists he mentions are Pablo Picasso, Claude Monet, Jan Vermeer, Pieter De Hooch, Jacob van Ruisdael, Meyndert Hobbema, Jan van der Heyden, Frans Hals, Rembrandt van Rijn, Gerald Ter Borch, Jan Cornelisz Verspronck, Jan Steen, Willem van de Velde, Alvert Cuyp, Abraham Van Beyeren, Philips Wouwerman, Henri Rousseau, Amedeo Modigliani, and Marc Chagall.

Nolan modeled the frames for the paintings in this picture book after those that hang in the Yale Center for British Art. The palette Dusty used to make her paintings of the gentleman and the kitchen maid follows the arrangement of pigments suggested by the famous American painter James McNeill Whistler.

267   Trosclair (pseud. J. B. King Jr.)

CAJUN NIGHT BEFORE CHRISTMAS   *8–12+ YEARS*

Edited by Howard Jacobs. Illustrated by James Rice. Gretna,
La.: Pelican, 1976

> This very clever parody of Clement Moore's classic poem, "The Night Before Christmas" is told in a Cajun dialect that is as authentic and as close as one can get to suggesting in a written form its pronunciation and intonation. The full-page pen-and-ink, crosshatch drawings in black-and-white, alternating with pen-and-ink crosshatch with full-color watercolor paintings, depict the alligators (instead of reindeer), the Louisiana bayou people and their culture, the homes along the marshy waterways, and the swampy terrain in a thoroughly accurate but witty manner. An excellent book to read aloud. Compare and contrast the language and the illustration of this clever parody of Moore's classic poem with the picture-book versions illustrated by Tasha Tudor (Rand McNally, 1975), Arthur Rackham (Weathervane/Crown, 1976), and Tomie de Paola (Holiday House, 1980).

268   White, Linda

TOO MANY PUMPKINS   *4–8 YEARS*

Illustrated by Megan Lloyd. New York: Holiday House, 1996

> This is a refreshing tall tale! When Rebecca Estelle was a little girl, money was scarce in her home, and all she and her family had to eat for a month was pumpkins. They ate baked, stewed, boiled, steamed, mashed, and even rotten pumpkins for breakfast, lunch, and dinner. When things improved the family had money to buy other food, but even many years later when Rebecca Estelle was an adult and grew vegetables in her own garden, she decided never to grow or eat pumpkins again. One autumn day an enormous pumpkin fell off a truck and smashed into bits and pieces at the edge of her front yard. She shoveled dirt on top of the mess of pumpkin meat and seeds, and promptly forgot about it. In spring pumpkin vines began to grow, so she cut and dug them out; to her dismay new vines sprouted. She decided to ignore them by using only the back door and never looked out her front window. In fall when she went to the front yard to rake the leaves, she was shocked to see huge round pumpkins everywhere. There were too many pumpkins for her to lift and deliver to the poor people who needed them and to those who liked to eat them. She made the pumpkin meat into pies, tarts, muffins, cakes, bread, pudding,

and cookies, but she made more treats than she could deliver. To attract
people to her home to come get the pumpkin treats, she carved jack-o'-
lanterns out of the pumpkins that still remained in the garden, put lights
in them, and placed them at strategic points from the road in front of her
house to her front porch. Soon Rebecca Estelle was inundated with
people of all ages. She took great delight in sharing with them everything
that reminded her of the pumpkins she hated. She did, however, keep a
handful of seeds for herself, for she planned to plant them the next spring.
Exuberant line and watercolor wash drawings extend and highlight, most
effectively, the range of emotions Rebecca Estelle experienced in response to her accidental inundation by pumpkins.

269 Wilde, Oscar

THE HAPPY PRINCE   *9–14+ YEARS*

Illustrated by Jean Claverie. New York: Oxford, 1980

Gilded all over with thin leaves of fine gold, eyes made of bright sap-
phires, and a large red ruby on his sword-hilt, the statue of the Happy
Prince was placed on a tall column on a hill overlooking the city and
many people came to admire it for its elegance and beauty. From this
point the Prince could see all the ugliness and all the misery of the city.
Moved by what he saw, he asked a swallow to take each of the precious
stones and the leaves of gold that decorated him to specific poor people
he saw who were in need of money which they could get by selling these
precious items. Stripped of these precious and beautiful decorations the
statue looked shabby, so the city leader declared it be removed from its
pedestal and melted down; the leaders also said that the swallow, found
dead at the base of the statue, should be thrown on the dust-heap. How
the Happy Prince and the swallow were eventually rewarded for their
sacrifices makes for a moving conclusion. The full-page expressionistic
watercolor paintings add an aura of sophistication to this classic romantic fairy tale.

270 Wilde, Oscar

THE SELFISH GIANT   *6–9 YEARS*

Illustrated by Michael Foreman and Freire Wright.
New York: Methuen, 1978

This classic fairy tale, created by Oscar Wilde for his own children, was
originally published in 1888. In this picture-book edition, fantasy art,
done in clean watercolor paintings in full color, embellishes the diverse
moods of the story of a giant who forbade children to play in his garden
because he wanted it for himself. Realizing that only when children were
present could he enjoy the garden, he eventually welcomed them back.
When he saw one waif of a boy crying because he was unable to climb the

trees as the other children did, the giant picked him up and put him in the tree. Years later, the child (a Christ figure) rewarded him for his kindness with eternal happiness in Paradise.

271   Young, Ed

LITTLE PLUM   *4–8* YEARS

Illustrated by Ed Young. New York: Philomel, 1994

> This story tells how Little Plum, a boy who never grew any larger than a plum seed, not only helped his elderly father gather wood and till the fields, but ultimately outwitted the evil lord and his soldiers. The rich, full-color illustrations reveal the Tao influence. Be certain to allow the children to look at all of the pictures in this book from a distance so they can experience more thoroughly the wonderfully dramatic effects of Ed Young's sophisticated modern impressionistic pastel paintings. They enhance the nuances of an ancient small farming village at the base of a mountain in China and heighten the feelings of fear and tension felt by the villagers when the lord and his soldiers looted their homes and beat them, stole their livestock, and later returned to wage war against them. Notice also the double-spread picture of the lord created on the front and back covers of the book when it is opened wide. Compare the story line and illustrations created by Ed Young to retell the Chinese variant of this well-known folktale with other retellers' interpretations of the variants associated with other ethnic and cultural groups: Felix Hoffmann's retelling of Jacob and Wilhelm Grimm's *Tom Thumb* (Margaret McElderry/ Atheneum, 1973); Lisbeth Zwerger's retelling of Hans Christian Andersen's *Thumbelina* (Morrow, 1980); Robert B. Goodman and Robert A. Spicer's adaptation and George Sutoka's illustrations of *Issunbōshi* (Island Heritage of Japan and Australia, 1974), and Fiona French's interpretation of *Little Inchkin* (Dial, 1994).

272   Young, Ed

SEVEN BLIND MICE   *5–9* YEARS

Illustrated by Ed Young. New York: Philomel, 1992

> Ed Young inserts several ingenious aspects in retelling the witty and humorous Indian fable of "The Blind Men and the Elephant," which tells of six blind men who each get a limited understanding of what an elephant is by feeling only a part of it. The characters in Young's interpretation of this fable are seven blind mice (six males and one female) instead of six blind men. Each mouse is a different color (red, green, yellow, purple, orange, blue, and white); on each day of the week a different mouse went out to investigate the strange Something by the pond. Each mouse felt only one part of the Something and reported what he "saw" to the others, until on Sunday, the seventh day, the seventh mouse (the

white one and the only female!) ran up one side and down the other side, across the top from one end to other. She concluded the Something was an elephant. After they ran up, down, and around the entire thing, the other mice agreed that they too could now "see" that the Something was an elephant. Each illustration is placed on a solid black background and is done in large and colorful, textured paper collage. *Seven Blind Mice* was named the 1993 Caldecott Award Honor Book. Compare the story line and illustrations of Ed Young's retelling of this well-known fable with other retellers' interpretations of the variants associated with other ethnic and cultural groups: Karen Backstein's retelling of *The Blind Men and the Elephant,* illustrated by Annie Mitra (Scholastic, 1992) and Harve Zemach's retelling of *The Judge,* illustrated by Margot Zemach (Farrar, Straus & Giroux, 1968).

Suggested Resources

⚭

*T*his section lists books about visual art, artists, and book illustrators and books illustrated with well-known works of art. Most of the titles listed here are appropriate for use by children. However, I have included a small number of very special books on these aspects of art, artists, and book illustrators which, because of their depth and detail, are obviously for adult readers; I thought teachers and librarians might enjoy reading them and sharing pertinent information with their students. Also, it should be noted that some of the book illustrators listed in the section entitled "Books about Book Illustrators" are recognized visual artists in their own right, but I thought it best to list the books about them in the section on illustrators so that teachers and students interested in focusing on that aspect of the artistic talents of these persons could find these books more easily.

Books about Creating and Responding To Visual Art

Belves, Pierre, and Francois Mathey. *How Artists Work: An Introduction to Techniques of Art.* English adaptation by Alice Bush. Illustrated. New York: Lion Press, 1968. (10–18 years)

Catalanotto, Peter. *The Painter.* Illustrated by Peter Catalanotto. New York: Richard Jackson/Orchard, 1995. (4–8 years)

Clare, John D. *Italian Renaissance.* Living History Series. San Diego: Gulliver/Harcourt Brace, 1995. (9–12 years)

Cummings, Robert. *Just Imagine: Ideas in Painting.* Illustrated. New York: Scribner, 1979. (8–12 years)

Cummings, Robert. *Just Look . . . A Book about Paintings.* Illustrated. New York: Scribner, 1979. (8–12 years)

Davidson, Rosemary. *Take a Look: An Introduction to the Experience of Art.* Illustrated. New York: Viking, 1993. (10–18+ years)

Delafosse, Claude, and Gallimard Jeunesse (creators). *Animals.* A First Discovery Art Book Series. Illustrated by Tony Ross and with reproductions of works of art. New York: Scholastic, 1995. (8–12+ years)

Delafosse, Claude, and Gallimard Jeunesse (creators). *Paintings.* A First Discovery Art Book Series. Illustrated by Tony Ross and with reproductions of works of art. New York: Scholastic, 1993. (8–12+ years)

Demi. *The Artist and the Architect.* Illustrated by Demi. New York: Holt, 1991. (8–12 years)

Dunrea, Olivier. *The Painter Who Loved Chickens.* Illustrated by Olivier Dunrea. New York: Farrar, Straus & Giroux, 1995. (6–9 years)

Duvoisin, Roger. *See What I Am.* Illustrated by Roger Duvoisin. New York: Lothrop, Lee & Shepard, 1974. (5–9 years)

Florian, Douglas. *A Painter: How We Work.* Illustrated by Douglas Florian. New York: Greenwillow, 1993. (7–11 years)

Goffstein, M. B. *An Artist.* Illustrated by M. B. Goffstein. New York: HarperCollins, 1980. (6–12+ years)

Greenberg, Jan, and Sandra Jordan. *The American Eye: Eleven Artists of the Twentieth Century.* Illustrated. New York: Delacorte, 1995. (10 years–adult)

Greenberg, Jan, and Sandra Jordan. *The Painter's Eye: Learning to Look at Contemporary Art.* Illustrated. New York: Delacorte, 1991. (10 years–adult)

Heller, Ruth. *Color.* Illustrated by Ruth Heller. New York: Putnam, 1995. (6–9 years)

Hunt, Jonathan. *Illuminations.* Illustrated by Jonathan Hunt. New York: Bradbury, 1989. (8–12+ years)

Isaacson, Philip. *A Short Walk around the Pyramids and through the World of Art.* Illustrated. New York: Random House, 1993. (11–18+ years)

James, Diane. *Play with Paint.* Illustrated by Sara Lynn. Minneapolis: Carolrhoda, 1993. (5–9 years)

James, Diane. *Play with Paper.* Illustrated by Sara Lynn. Minneapolis: Carolrhoda, 1993. (5–9 years)

Johnson, Jane. *The Princess and the Painter.* Illustrated by Jane Johnson. New York: Farrar, Straus & Giroux, 1994. (5–10 years)

Kehoe, Michael. *A Book Takes Root: The Making of a Picture Book.* Illustrated with photographs. Minneapolis: Carolrhoda, 1993. (7–11 years)

Kidd, Richard. *Almost Famous Daisy!* Illustrated by Richard Kidd and with reproductions of paintings by famous artists. New York: Simon & Schuster, 1996. (6–9 years)

Levine, Arthur A. *The Boy Who Drew Cats.* Illustrated by Frederic Clement. New York: Dial, 1993 (7–11 years).

Lewis, Samella S., and Ruth G. Waddy. *Black Artists on Art.* Illustrated. Los Angeles: Contemporary Crafts. Vol. 1 (rev. ed.), 1969; vol. 2, 1971. (11–18+ years)

Littlesugar, Amy. *Josiah True and the Art Maker.* Illustrated by Barbara Garrison. New York: Simon & Schuster, 1995. (6–9 years)

Locker, Thomas. *The Young Artist.* Illustrated by Thomas Locker. New York: Dial, 1989. (8–10 years)

MacClintock, Dorcas. *Animals Observed: A Look at Animals in Art.* Illustrated. New York: Scribner, 1993. (10–18+ years)

Markun, Patricia Maloney. *The Little Painter of Sabana Grande.* Illustrated by Robert Casilla. New York: Bradbury, 1993. (6–9 years)

Moon, Nicola. *Lucy's Picture.* Illustrated by Alex Ayliffe. New York: Dial, 1995. (4–8 years)

Morrison, Taylor. *Antonio's Apprenticeship: Painting a Fresco in Renaissance Italy.* Illustrated by Taylor Morrison. New York: Holiday House, 1996. (9–12+ years)

Nunes, Lygia Bojunga. *My Friend the Painter.* Translated by Giovanni Pontiero. San Diego: Harcourt Brace Jovanovich, n.d. (9–12 years)

Paint and Painting: The Colors, The Techniques, the Surfaces: A History of Artists' Tools. Voyage of Discovery: Visual Arts Series. New York: Scholastic, 1996. (9–18 years)

Pekarik, Andrew. *Painting: Behind the Scenes.* Illustrated. New York: Hyperion, 1992. (10–15+ years)

Pekarik, Andrew. *Sculpture: Behind the Scenes.* Illustrated. New York: Hyperion, 1992 (10–15+ years)

Ringgold, Faith, Linda Freeman, and Nancy Roucher. *Talking with Faith Ringgold.* Illustrated. New York: Crown, 1996. (8–12 years)

Roalf, Peggy. *Looking at Paintings: Children.* Illustrated. New York: Hyperion, 1993. (10–18+ years)

Roalf, Peggy. *Looking at Paintings: Circus.* Illustrated. New York: Hyperion, 1993. (10–18+ years)

Roalf, Peggy. *Looking at Paintings: Dogs.* Illustrated. New York: Hyperion, 1993. (10–18+ years)

Roalf, Peggy. *Looking at Paintings: Flowers.* Illustrated. New York: Hyperion, 1993. (10–18+ years)

Roalf, Peggy. *Looking at Paintings: Landscapes.* Illustrated. New York: Hyperion, 1992. (10–18+ years)

Roalf, Peggy. *Looking at Paintings: Musicians.* Illustrated. New York: Hyperion, 1993 (10–18+ years)

Roalf, Peggy. *Looking at Paintings: Self-Portraits.* Illustrated. New York: Hyperion, 1992. (10–18+ years)

Rylant, Cynthia. *All I See.* Illustrated by Peter Catalanotto. New York: Orchard, 1988. (5–9 years)

Rylant, Cynthia. *The Dreamer.* Illustrated by Barry Moser. New York: Scholastic, 1993. (5–9 years)

Stevens, Janet. *From Pictures to Words: A Book about Making a Book.* New York: Holiday House, 1995. (7–10 years)

Taylor, Annette. *The Adventures of the Three Colors.* Illustrated by Talus Taylor. Cleveland: World, 1971. (7–10 years)

Velthuijs, Max. *Crocodile's Masterpiece.* Illustrated by Max Velthuijs. New York: Farrar, Straus & Giroux, 1991. (5–8 years)

Waters, Elizabeth, and Annie Harris. *Royal Academy of Arts Painting: A Young Artist's Guide.* Illustrated. New York: Dorling Kindersley, 1993. (8–12 years)

What the Painter Sees: Portraits, Still Lifes, Landscapes, Trick Painting, Animals, Water, and Light. Voyage of Discovery: Visual Arts Series. New York: Scholastic, 1996. (9–18 years)

Wilson, Elizabeth B. *Bibles and Bestiaries: A Guide to Illuminated Manuscripts.* New York: Farrar, Straus, & Giroux/Pierpont Morgan Library, 1994. (10–18+ years)

Wilson, Jude. *Tate Gallery Drawing: A Young Artist's Guide.* Illustrated. New York: Dorling Kindersley, 1993. (8–12 years)

Wooding, Sharon. *The Painter's Cat.* Illustrated by Sharon Wooding. New York: Putnam, 1994. (5–9 years)

Books about Visual Artists

Bonafoux, Pascal. *A Weekend with Rembrandt.* Translated. Illustrated. New York: Rizzoli, 1992. (10–18+ years)

Brust, Beth Wagner. *The Amazing Paper Cuttings by Hans Christian Andersen.* Illustrated. New York: Ticknor & Fields/ Dutton, 1994. (9–15 years)

De Mejo, Oscar. *Oscar de Mejo, The Naive Surrealist: My Life as an Artist.* "The Naive Surrealist," Essay by Robert Morgan. New York: Abrams, 1992. (Adult)

Des Jarlait, Patrick. Recorded by Neva Williams. *Patrick Des Jarlait: Conversations with a Native American Artist.* Illustrated. Minneapolis: Runestone Press, 1995. (10–15 years)

Everett, Gwen. *Li'l Sis and Uncle Willie: A Story Based on the Life and Paintings of William H. Johnson.* Illustrated with paintings by William H. Johnson. New York: Rizzoli, 1991. (7–11+ years)

Heslewood, Juliet. *Introducing Picasso.* Illustrated. Boston: Little, Brown, 1993. (9–12+ years)

Krull, Kathleen. *Lives of the Artists: Masterpieces, Messes (and What the Neighbors Thought).* Illustrated by Kathryn Hewitt. San Diego: Harcourt, Brace, 1995. (10 years–adult)

Loria, Stefano. *Picasso.* Masters of Art Series. Illustrated. New York: Bedrick, 1996. (10–14+ years)

Lyons, Mary E. *Deep Blues: Bill Taylor, Self-taught Artist.* Illustrated. New York: Scribner, 1994. (12–16+ years)

Lyons, Mary E. *Starting Home: The Story of Horace Pippin, Painter.* African-American Artists and Artisans Series. Illustrated. New York: Scribner, 1993. (12–16+ years)

Lyons, Mary E. *Stitching Stars: The Story Quilts of Harriet Powers.* Illustrated. New York: Scribner, 1993. (9–12 years).

Maril, Nadja. *Me, Molly Midnight: The Artist's Cat.* Illustrated with drawings and paintings by Herman Maril. Owings Mills, Md.: Stemmer House, 1977. (7–11+ years)

Maril, Nadja. *Runaway Molly Midnight: The Artist's Cat.* Illustrated with drawings and paintings by Herman Maril. Owings Mills, Md.: Stemmer House, 1980. (7–11+ years)

Monthan, Doris. *R. C. Gorman: A Retrospective.* Foreword by R. C. Gorman. Illustrated. Flagstaff, Ariz.: Northland, 1990. (Adult)

Mühlberger, Richard. *What Makes a Bruegel a Bruegel?* Illustrated. New York: The Metropolitan Museum of Art/Viking, 1993. (12–18+ years)

Mühlberger, Richard. *What Makes a Cassatt a Cassatt?* Illustrated. New York: The Metropolitan Museum of Art/Viking, 1993. (12–18+ years)

Mühlberger, Richard. *What Makes a Degas a Degas?* Illustrated. New York: The Metropolitan Museum of Art/Viking, 1993. (12–18+ years)

Mühlberger, Richard. *What Makes a Goya a Goya?* Illustrated. New York: The Metropolitan Museum of Art/Viking, 1994. (12–18+ years)

Mühlberger, Richard. *What Makes a Leonardo a Leonardo?* Illustrated. New York: The Metropolitan Museum of Art/ Viking, 1994. (12–18+ years)

Mühlberger, Richard. *What Makes a Monet a Monet?* Illustrated. New York: The Metropolitan Museum of Art/Viking, 1993. (12–18+ years)

Mühlberger, Richard. *What Makes a Picasso a Picasso?* Illustrated. New York: The Metropolitan Museum of Art/Viking, 1994. (12–18+ years)

Mühlberger, Richard. *What Makes a Raphael a Raphael?* Illustrated. New York: The Metropolitan Museum of Art/Viking, 1993. (12–18+ years)

Mühlberger, Richard. *What Makes a Rembrandt a Rembrandt?* Illustrated. New York: The Metropolitan Museum of Art/ Viking, 1993. (12–18+ years)

Neimark, Anne E. *Diego Rivera: Artist of the People.* Illustrated. New York: HarperCollins, 1992. (10–14 years)

Nugent, Frances Robert. *George Bellows: American Painter.* Illustrated. New York: Rand McNally, 1963. (9–14 years)

Pippin, Horace. *I Tell My Heart: The Art of Horace Pippin.* (Print portfolio.) New York: Universe/Pennsylvania Academy of the Fine Arts, 1994. (All ages)

Powell, Richard J. *Homecoming: The Art and Life of William H. Johnson.* Introduction by Martin Puryear. New York: Rizzoli/National Museum of American Art, Smithsonian Institution, 1991. (Adult)

Raboff, Ernest. *Pablo Picasso.* Art for Children Series. Illustrated. New York: Doubleday, 1968. (9–12 years)

Richmond, Robin. *Introducing Michelangelo.* Illustrated. Boston: Little, Brown, 1992. (10–14 years)

Rockwell, Anne. *Paintbrush and Peacepipe.* Illustrated with adaptations in sinopia pencil of portraits and sketches by George Catlin. New York: Atheneum, 1971. (9–14 years)

Rodari, Florian. *A Weekend with Picasso.* Translated. Illustrated. New York: Rizzoli, 1991. (10–18+ years)

Rodari, Florian. *A Weekend with Velazquez.* Translated by Ann Keay Beneduce. Illustrated. New York: Rizzoli, 1993. (10–18+ years)

Rodman, Selden, and Carole Cleaver. *Horace Pippin: The Artist as a Black American.* Illustrated. New York: Doubleday, 1972. (9–12 years)

Shilling, Arthur. *The Ojibway Dream.* Illustrated with paintings by Arthur Shilling. Plattsburgh, N.Y.: Tundra, 1986. (10 years–adult)

Sills, Leslie. *Inspirations: Stories about Women Artists.* Illustrated. Niles, Ill.: Albert Whitman, 1991. (10–18+ years)

Sills, Leslie. *Visions: Stories about Women Artists.* Illustrated. Morton Grove, Ill.: Albert Whitman, 1993. (10–18+ years)

Skira-Venturi, Rosabianca. *A Weekend with Degas.* Translated. Illustrated. New York: Rizzoli, 1992. (10–18+ years)

Skira-Venturi, Rosabianca. *A Weekend with Leonardo da Vinci.* Translated by Ann Keay Beneduce. Illustrated. New York: Rizzoli, 1992. (10–18+ years)

Skira-Venturi, Rosabianca. *A Weekend with Renoir.* Translated. Illustrated. New York: Rizzoli, 1990. (10–18+ years)

Stein, Judith E. *I Tell My Heart: The Art of Horace Pippin.* New York: Universe/Pennsylvania Academy of Fine Arts, 1993. (Adult)

Sturgis, Alexander. *Introducing Rembrandt.* Illustrated. Boston: Little, Brown, 1993. (9–16 years)

Turner, Robyn Montana. *Dorothea Lange.* Illustrated. Boston: Little, Brown, 1994. (9–12+ years)

Turner, Robyn Montana. *Frida Kahlo.* Portraits of Women Artists for Children Series. Illustrated. Boston: Little, Brown, 1993. (9–12+ years)

Turner, Robyn Montana. *Georgia O'Keefe.* Portraits of Women Artists for Children Series. Illustrated. Boston: Little, Brown, 1991. (9–12+ years)

Turner, Robyn Montana. *Mary Cassatt.* Portraits of Women Artists for Children Series. Illustrated. Boston: Little, Brown, 1992. (9–12+ years)

Walker, Lou Ann. *Roy Lichtenstein: The Artist at Work.* Photographs by Michael Abramson. New York: Lodestar/Dutton, 1994. (9–14 years)

Wilson, Ellen. *American Painter in Paris: A Life of Mary Cassatt.* Illustrated. New York: Farrar, Straus & Giroux, 1971. (12–18+ years)

Zhang, Song Nan. *A Little Tiger in the Chinese Night: An Autobiography in Art.* Illustrated. Plattsburgh, N.Y.: Tundra, 1991. (9–12+ years)

Zhensun, Zheng, and Alice Low. *A Young Painter: The Life and Paintings of Wang Yani—China's Extraordinary Young Artist.* Introduction by Jan Stuart. Illustrated with photographs by Zheng Zhensun. New York: Scholastic, 1991. (10–18 years)

Books about Book Illustrators

Alderson, Brian. *Ezra Jack Keats: Artist and Picture Book Maker.* Gretna, La.: Pelican, 1994. (Adult)

Carle, Eric. *The Art of Eric Carle.* Introduction by Leonard S. Marcus. Illustrated. New York: Philomel, 1966. (11–18+ years)

Cech, John. *Angels and Wild Things: The Archetypal Poetics of Maurice Sendak.* Illustrated. University Park: The Pennsylvania State University Press, 1995. (Adult)

Cummings, Pat (compiler and editor). *Talking with Artists.* New York: Bradbury, 1992. (8 years–adult)

Cummings, Pat (compiler and editor). *Talking with Artists,* Vol. 2. New York: Simon & Schuster, 1995. (8 years–adult)

Enhen, Rodney K. *Randolph Caldecott: "Lord of the Nursery."* London: Bloomsbury, 1976. (12 years–adult)

Faunce, Sarah. *Carl Larsson.* Illustrated. New York: Holt, Rinehart & Winston, 1982. (12 years–adult)

Frasconi, Antonio. *Frasconi against the Grain: The Woodcuts of Antonio Frasconi.* Introduction by Nat Hentoff. Appreciation by Charles Parkhurst. Illustrated. New York: Macmillan, 1974. (Adult)

Hall, Patricia. *Johnny Gruelle: Creator of Raggedy Ann and Andy.* Gretna, La.: Pelican, 1993. (Adult)

Hamilton, James. *Arthur Rackham: A Biography.* Illustrated. New York: Arcade, 1990. (Adult)

Hobbs, Anne Stevenson. *Beatrix Potter's Art.* New York: Frederick Warne, 1989. (12 years–adult)

Jagusch, Sybille A. (editor). *Antonio Frasconi.* A lecture presented by Antonio Frasconi on May 8, 1989, for International Children's Book Day. Washington, D.C.: Library of Congress, 1993. (Adult)

Jones, Helen L. *Robert Lawson, Illustrator: A Selection of His Characteristic Illustrations.* Boston: Little, Brown, 1972. (8–14 years)

Knox, Rawle (editor). *The Work of E. H. Shepard.* London: Methuen, 1979. (10–15 years)

Larkin, David. *The Art of Nancy Ekholm Burkert.* New York: Peacock/Bantam, 1977. (12 years–adult)

Marcus, Leonard S. *75 Years of Children's Book Week Posters: Celebrating Great Illustrators of American Children's Books.* Sponsored by the Children's Book Council. New York: Borzoi/Knopf, 1994. (10 years–adult)

Martin, Douglas. *Charles Keeping, An Illustrator's Life.* London: Julia MacRae, 1993. (Adult)

Martin, Douglas. *The Telling Line: Essays on Fifteen Contemporary Book Illustrators.* New York: Delacorte, 1990. (Adult)

O'Kelley, Mattie. *From the Hills of Georgia: An Autobiography in Paintings.* Illustrated with paintings by Mattie Lou O'Kelley. Boston: Atlantic/Little, Brown, 1983. (8–12 years)

Preiss, Byron (editor). *Art of Leo and Diane Dillon.* Illustrated. New York: Ballantine, 1981. (12–18+ years)

Shepard, Ernest H. *Drawn from Life.* Illustrated by Ernest H. Shepard. New York: Dutton, 1962. (10–15 years)

Shepard, Ernest H. *Drawn from Memory.* Illustrated by Ernest H. Shepard. Philadelphia: Lippincott, 1957. (10–15 years)

Shepard, Ernest H. *Pooh: His Art Gallery: Anthology of Drawings.* Illustrated by Ernest H. Shepard. New York: Dutton, 1962. (12 years–adult)

Sibley, Brian (editor). *The Pooh Sketchbook.* London: Methuen, 1984; New York: Dutton, 1984. (12 years–adult)

Society of Illustrators (compiler). *The Very Best of Children's Book Illustration.* Cincinnati: North Light Books, 1993. (10 years–adult)

Thompson, Susan Ruth (compiler). *Kate Greenaway.* A Catalogue of the Kate Greenaway Collection, Rare Book Collection Room, Detroit Public Library. Detroit: Wayne State University Press, 1977. (Adult)

Turner, Robyn Montana. *Faith Ringgold.* Illustrated. Boston: Little, Brown, 1993. (8–12+ years)

Wheat, Ellen Harkins. *Jacob Lawrence: American Painter.* Seattle: University of Washington Press/Seattle Art Museum, 1986. (Adult)

Books Illustrated with Well-Known Works of Visual Art

Auch, Mary Jane. *Eggs Mark the Spot.* Illustrated by Mary Jane Auch. New York: Holiday House, 1995. (5–9 years)

Bible (New Testament). *The First Christmas.* Illustrated with reproductions of paintings from The National Gallery, London. New York: Simon & Schuster: 1992. (All ages)

Bolton, Linda. *Hidden Pictures.* Illustrated. New York: Dial, 1993. (9–14+ years)

Bouchard, Dave. *The Elders Are Watching.* Illustrated by Roy Henry Vickers. Tofino, B.C.: Eagle Dancers Enterprises, 1990. (10–18+ years)

De Mejo, Oscar. *Oscar de Mejo's ABC.* New York: Laura Geringer/HarperCollins, 1992. (8–12+ years)

Hamanaka, Sheila. *The Journey: Japanese Americans, Racism, and Renewal.* Book design by Steve Frederick, Illustrated by Sheila Hamanaka. New York: Richard Jackson/Orchard, 1990. (9–18+ years)

Mayers, Florence Cassen. *The Folk Art Counting Book.* Developed by Amy Watson and the staff of the Abby Aldrich Rockefeller Folk Art Center. Illustrated. New York: Abrams/The Colonial Williamsburg Foundation, Williamsburg, Va., 1992. (6–10 years)

Micklethwait, Lucy (compiler). *A Child's Book of Art: Great Pictures, First Words.* Illustrated. New York: Dorling Kindersley, 1993. (4–8 years)

Micklethwait, Lucy (compiler). *I Spy: An Alphabet in Art.* Illustrated. New York: Greenwillow, 1992. (8–12 years)

Micklethwait, Lucy (compiler). *I Spy Two Eyes: Numbers in Art.* Illustrated. New York: Greenwillow, 1993. (8–12 years)

Panzer, Nora. *Celebrate America in Poetry and Art.* New York: Hyperion/National Museum of American Art, Smithsonian Institution, 1994. (9–15+ years).

Sky-Peck, Kathryn (editor). *Who Has Seen The Wind? An Illustrated Collection of Poetry for Young People.* Illustrated. New York: Rizzoli/Museum of Fine Arts, Boston, 1991. (6–12 years)

Sullivan, Charles. *Alphabet Animals.* Illustrated. New York: Rizzoli, 1991. (7–10 years)

Sullivan, Charles (editor). *Children of Promise: African American Literature and Art for Young People.* New York: Abrams, 1991. (7–10 years)

Sullivan, Charles. *Circus.* Illustrated. New York: Rizzoli, 1992. (7–10 years)

Index

༄

This is an index to titles as well as illustrators and writers (authors, editors, compilers, translators, etc.) named in the alphabetical lists in each section as well as in the annotations and in the introduction. Numbers in **boldface** type are entry numbers; those in regular type are page numbers.

Patricia Jean Cianciolo is Professor Emeritus at Michigan State University in East Lansing, Michigan, where she taught courses in the critical reading and reviewing of literature for children, adolescent literature, and illustrations in children's books. She holds a doctoral degree from The Ohio State University and a master's degree from the University of Wisconsin, Milwaukee. She has done extensive research in children's response to literature and to book illustrations as well as in the study of teaching and learning of literature in the elementary grades. Cianciolo has published numerous professional books and articles on aspects of literature for children and adolescents, has presented papers and led workshops and institutes at the state, national, and international levels, and has served as a visiting professor at universities and as a literacy consultant to school systems nationally and internationally. She has also served on several children's literature award committees.